BLUES GUITAR TECHNIQUE

MICHAEL WILLIAMS

To access audio visit:
www.halleonard.com/mylibrary

Enter Code
3021-0095-3921-2252

IN THE STYLE OF
B.B. KING
ALBERT COLLINS
T-BONE WALKER
AND OTHER BLUES GUITAR MASTERS

Berklee Press

Editor in Chief: Jonathan Feist
Vice President of Online Learning and Continuing Education: Debbie Cavalier
Assistant Vice President of Operations for Berklee Media: Robert F. Green
Assistant Vice President of Marketing and Recruitment for Berklee Media: Mike King
Dean of Continuing Education: Carin Nuernberg
Editorial Assistants: Matthew Dunkle, Reilly Garrett, Amy Kaminski, Zoë Lustri, Sarah Walk, José Rodrigo Vazquez
Cover Design: Ranya Karifilly, Small Mammoth Design
Cover Photo: Wolfie, www.coronium.co.uk

ISBN 978-0-87639-114-3

1140 Boylston Street
Boston, MA 02215-3693 USA
(617) 747-2146

Visit Berklee Press Online at
www.berkleepress.com

DISTRIBUTED BY

HAL•LEONARD®
CORPORATION
7777 W. BLUEMOUND RD. P.O. BOX 13819
MILWAUKEE, WISCONSIN 53213

Visit Hal Leonard Online at
www.halleonard.com

Berklee Press, a publishing activity of Berklee College of Music, is a not-for-profit educational publisher.
Available proceeds from the sales of our products are contributed to the scholarship funds of the college.

CONTENTS

AUDIO TRACKS v

ACKNOWLEDGMENTS vii

PREFACE viii

CHAPTER 1. RHYTHM PARTS IN THE JIMMY REED STYLE: "MARCH IN E" 1
- Performance Tips 1
- "March in E" 2
- Bass Variations 3
- Rakes between Chords 4
- Low-End Variation for "March in E" 5
- Another Low-End Variation for the "March in E" 6
- "March in E" Four Choruses with Rhythm Section 7
- Performance Tips 7

CHAPTER 2. MORE RHYTHM PARTS IN THE JIMMY REED STYLE: "MARCH IN A" 13
- "March in A" Variation 1 14
- "March in A" Variation 2 16
- "March in A" with Rhythm Section 17
- Performance Tips 17

CHAPTER 3. CLASSIC CHICAGO STYLE: DOWNTOWN AND UPTOWN SHUFFLES 22
- Downtown Shuffle in F 22
- Uptown Shuffle in G 24
- Sliding Ninths Rhythm Parts 25
- G9 (Assumed Root 6) 27
- C9 (Root 5) 27
- "Downtown Shuffle in F" Five Choruses 28
- "Downtown Shuffle in F" Solo 32
- Performance Tips 33

CHAPTER 4. FUNKY BLUES IN D: "FUNKY ALBERT" 40
- Performance Tips 40
- Funky Eighth-Note Feel: Mixing Scratches and Chords 44
- Funky Sixteenth-Note Feel: Mixing Scratches and Chords 46
- "Funky Albert" Solo 48
- Performance Tips 48

CHAPTER 5. FAST SHUFFLE IN E: "LIKE A ROCKET" 53
- Performance Tips 53
- "Like a Rocket" Rhythm Part 2 54
- Performance Tips 55
- "Like a Rocket" Solo 63
- Performance Tips 63

CHAPTER 6. **T-BONE SWING STYLE: "JUMPIN' BONES" 72**
Flat-Tire Rhythm Parts 72
"Jumpin' Bones" Solo 74
Performance Tips 74

CHAPTER 7. **SLOW BLUES, T-BONE STYLE: "SLOW BONE" 83**
"Slow Bone" 85
Performance Tips 85

CHAPTER 8. **TWO RHYTHM PARTS IN THE STYLE OF ROBERT LOCKWOOD JR.: "SHUFFLE IN A" 90**
Fills and Turnarounds in "Shuffle in A" 90
Performance Tips 90
Walking Tenths on "Takin' a Stroll" 96
Performance Tips 96

CHAPTER 9. **QUICK TAKES ON TWO RHYTHM PARTS: "SLOW BLUES IN E" 101**
"Slow Blues in E" 101
Performance Tips 102
Rhythmic Hits over a "Shuffle in F" 108
Performance Tips 108

CHAPTER 10. **RHYTHM AND SOLO WORKOUT OVER A SHUFFLE IN G: "DOGGIN' IT" 112**
Performance Tips 112

CHAPTER 11. **LOCKING IN WITH THE BACKBEAT 118**
Feeling the Backbeat 118
Practicing with the Backbeat 119
Walking Bass/Comp Part: Jazz/Blues in B♭ with Backbeat 120
Performance Tips 120

CHAPTER 12. **PENTATONIC AND BLUES SCALE FINGERINGS 123**
Suggestions about Tone and Sound 125
Stop Those Open/Ringing String Noises! 125
Exercise 1. A Minor Pentatonic in Five Positions 126
Understanding Relative Major and Relative Minor Scales 127
Exercise 2. C Major and Pentatonic with A Natural Minor and A Minor Pentatonic Fingerings 127
Exercise 3. Fingering Position Diagrams 130
Exercise 4. A Blues Scale in Five Positions 132
Exercise 5. A Blues Scales: Shifting through Five Positions 133
Exercise 6. Mixing A Blues with A Pentatonic in Five Positions 134
a. A Pentatonic and A Blues: Positions 4 and 5 134
b. Mixing A Pentatonic and A Blues: Position 2 136
c. Mixing A Pentatonic and A Blues: Positions 6 and 7 137
d. Mixing A Pentatonic and A Blues: Positions 9 and 10 138
e. Mixing A Pentatonic and A Blues: Positions 11 and 12 139
Exercise 7. Phrases that Mix A Pentatonic and A Blues, in Five Positions 141

CLOSING 143

APPENDIX. BLUES GUITAR GLOSSARY AND ARTICULATION KEY . 144

ABOUT THE AUTHOR 147

AUDIO TRACKS

1. Tuning Notes: Open Strings
2. "March in E" Basic Rhythm Part
3. "March in E" Variation 1
4. "March in E" Variation 2
5. "March in E" Rhythm Part
6. "March in E" No Guitar
7. "March in A" Basic Rhythm Part
8. "March in A" Variation 1
9. "March in A" Variation 2
10. "March in A" Rhythm Part
11. "March in A" No Guitar
12. "Downtown Shuffle in F" Basic Rhythm Part
13. "Uptown Shuffle in G" Basic Rhythm Part
14. "Uptown Shuffle in G" with Sliding Ninth Chords
15. Sliding Ninths Chords Explained
16. "Downtown Shuffle in F" Rhythm Part with Sliding Ninths
17. "Downtown Shuffle in F" No Guitar
18. "Downtown Shuffle in F" Full Band
19. "Funky Albert" Rhythm Part
20. "Funky Albert" No Guitar
21. Funky Eighth-Note Feel Exercise
22. Funky Sixteenth-Note Feel Exercise
23. "Funky Albert" Full Band
24. "Like a Rocket" Rhythm Parts
25. "Like a Rocket" No Guitar
26. "Like a Rocket" Full Band
27. "Shuffle in Bb" Flat-Tire Rhythm Part
28. "Jumpin' Bones" Full Band
29. "Jumpin' Bones" No Guitar
30. "Slow Bone" Basic Rhythm Part
31. "Slow Bone" Full Band
32. "Slow Bone" Rhythm Part, No Guitar on Intro
33. "Shuffle in A 'Lockwood-Style'" Rhythm Part
34. "Shuffle in A 'Lockwood-Style'" No Guitar
35. "Takin' a Stroll" Rhythm Part

36. "Takin' a Stroll" No Guitar
37. "Slow Blues in E" Full Band
38. "Slow Blues in E" No Guitar
39. "Shuffle in F" Rhythmic Hits, Rhythm Part
40. "Shuffle in F" Rhythmic Hits Extended, No Guitar
41. "Doggin' It" Full Band
42. "Doggin' It" No Guitar
43. Locking In with the Backbeat, Basic Rhythm Exercise
44. "March in E" with Backbeat Only
45. "Like a Rocket" with Backbeat Only
46. "Funky Albert" with Backbeat Only
47. "B♭ Blues with Walking Bass" with Backbeat Only, 50 bpm
48. "B♭ Blues with Walking Bass" with Backbeat Only, 100 bpm
49. Chapter 12 Opening Phrase
50. A Minor Pentatonic Scale: Positions 2 and 5
51. A Minor and C Pentatonic Scales: Positions 2 and 5
52. C Major and Pentatonic Scales: Positions 2 and 5
53. A Blues Scale: Positions 5 and 12
54. A Blues Scale Shifting Positions: 2nd to 5th
55. A Blues Scale Shifting Positions: 2nd to 5th
56. A Blues Scale Shifting Positions: 5th to 7th
57. A Blues Scale Shifting Positions: 7th to 9th
58. A Blues Scale Shifting Positions: 10th to 12th
59. A Blues Scale Shifting Positions: 15th to 13th
60. A Pentatonic and Blues Scales: Positions 4 and 5
61. A Pentatonic and Blues Scales: Position 2
62. A Pentatonic and Blues Scales: Positions 6 and 7
63. A Pentatonic and Blues Scales: Positions 9 and 10
64. A Pentatonic and Blues Scales: Positions 11 and 12
65. Mixing A Pentatonic and Blues: Positions 4 and 5
66. Mixing A Pentatonic and Blues: Positions 5 and 7
67. Mixing A Pentatonic and Blues: Position 2
68. Mixing A Pentatonic and Blues: Position 14
69. Mixing A Pentatonic and Blues: Positions 11 and 12

THE BAND

Mike Williams	Guitar
Bruce Bears	Keyboards
Jesse Williams	Bass
Mark Teixeira	Drums

Recorded and mastered by Craig Hlady at Tower Productions

ACKNOWLEDGMENTS

Thanks to my wife Anna and son Calvin, for their continued support and patience with my (at times, crazy) work/gigs schedule.

Thanks to Larry Baione and Rick Peckham, chair and assistant chair of the Berklee Guitar Department, for leading by example, and for their enthusiasm and support for projects such as this.

Thanks also to Debbie Cavalier, Carin Nuernburg, and Boriana Alexiev, from Berklee's Online Learning and Continuing Education Department. And a shout-out to Mike King and the fantastic marketing team at Berklee Online, for getting the message out about Berklee's lessons and music!

I'd also like to thank Jonathan Feist, editor in chief of Berklee Press, for his editing skills, guidance, and never-ending patience along the way.

All guitar parts on the accompanying audio were recorded with AmpliTube Fender software, so thanks to IK Multimedia for their killer Fender amp sounds.

Thanks also to Hugh Gilmartin and D'Addario and Company, for their excellent sounding/playing electric and acoustic strings.

Once again, thanks to Bruce Bears (keyboards), Jesse Williams (bass), and Mark Teixeira (drums), for their soulful and oh-so greasy grooves on the rhythm section tracks. Thanks also to Craig Hlady at Tower Productions in Dedham, MA for his great work in recording, engineering, and mastering this project.

—Mike Williams

PREFACE

Thanks for picking up *Blues Guitar Technique*. The rhythm and soloing examples and exercises presented here are intended as a companion to my other book, *Berklee Blues Guitar Songbook* (Berklee Press, 2010). My hope is that they both help you learn to adapt and reuse techniques and concepts from the greats, such as T-Bone Walker, B.B. King, Freddie King, Magic Sam, Robert Lockwood, Jr., and others, to expand your own playing skills.

If you've poked around your local music shop lately, you may have noticed that there's an abundance of books on how to solo over the blues. However, in order for our solos to sound their best, all rhythm parts need to be grooving, supportive, and locked in "like a junkyard dog" with the drums, bass, and the rest of the rhythm section. So, since the planning stages of this book, one of my goals has been to devote equal time and emphasis toward strengthening rhythm-guitar skills. Roughly half of it is geared toward rhythm guitar techniques; the other half covers soloing concepts and techniques.

Chapters 1 to 10 cover various classic/popular styles and tempos of blues, such as downtown and uptown shuffles, jump/swing, funky blues, and/or slow blues progressions, etc. Chapter 11 demonstrates methods for practicing along with the all-important backbeat. Chapter 12 wraps up the book with technical material, such as how pentatonic and blues scales connect/intersect along the fretboard, and how they're combined as part of the foundation of our soloing vocabulary.

In the early stages of this project, my intention was to include as many styles, variations, and exercises as possible, given page-count limitations, etc. As my work got underway, one blues style and variation led to another… and another… and so on. As a result, this project began to grow—and grow—in size, and it started to take on a life of its own… *("It's alive!")* Thankfully, just as it was about to break free and devour unsuspecting neighborhoods around the Metro West suburbs of Boston, we managed to reign it back in. So, while it was not possible to include every style or artist in the chapters that follow, I hope that you'll agree that the music that's presented represents a varied and comprehensive mix of styles, grooves, and tempos.

This book is maxed out with 69 audio tracks for you to hear and practice these techniques. To access this audio, go to www.halleonard.com/mylibrary and enter the code found on the first page of this book. This will grant you instant access to every example. The examples that include audio are marked with an audio icon throughout the book. If possible, I strongly recommend using digital technology that's available, such as the Amazing Slow Downer or Transcribe, to loop and extend the backing tracks, and to slow down rhythm parts and solos when necessary.

The truth is, we're never going to learn everything about the blues from just one book. So, get out, when you can, to your local blues clubs, jams, and open mics, to watch, interact, and learn from other players, and from the greats, whenever possible. There's no quicker way to learn than taking it directly into the musical trenches!

Thanks, and best wishes with your music.

CHAPTER 1

Rhythm Parts in the Jimmy Reed Style: "March in E"

To get inside the feel for Jimmy Reed's style of shuffle, listen extensively and practice along with his classic recordings, such as "Take Out Some Insurance," "Baby What You Want Me to Do," and "Bright Lights, Big City." Eddie Taylor (1923 to 1985) was the primary guitarist on Jimmy Reed's recordings, and he provided much of the "heavy lifting" by playing the signature (and influential) intros, fills, and rhythm parts on Reed's hits. Eddie Taylor recorded many sides as a leader as well, with classics such as "Bad Boy" and "Big Town Playboy," which are also essential listening for this style.

Performance Tips

Pick all of the low-end notes (downbeats and upbeats) as downstrokes. Dig in, with an aggressive and rock-solid picking attack, to play this rhythm part with as much intensity as possible. Accent all upbeats ("and" of each beat) at least as much as the downbeats, and really lean into the heavy triplet feel throughout.

This Jimmy Reed shuffle style is often referred to on the bandstand as a "march," and so the exercises that follow feature variations on the "March in E." This *lazy* shuffle is also commonly referred to as a "dump-ty, dump," and that's an accurate description of the rhythmic feel. So if you're having difficulty capturing the feel for this part, try saying or "verbalizing" beats 1 and 2 and 3 and 4 and as "dump-ty, dump-ty, dump-ty, dump-ty," etc. This may sound a little strange, but it works! Listen closely as you practice along with the rhythm section tracks. Really zero in on the triplet pattern (the "dump-ty dump" feel) in the drums, to lock in "like a junkyard dog" with that feel, as you play this shuffle.

"MARCH IN E"

Example 1.1, the "March in E," features one chorus of a basic low-end rhythm part, with a bass line that's derived from a typical boogie-woogie piano pattern. Note that the low root anchors the bottom end of the I7, IV7, and V7 chords throughout the 12-bar form. This chorus features a classic turnaround in bars 11–12, which starts on beat 2, on top of the E7 chord in the open position. To play it, keep that E7 chord from beat 1, and then pick chord tones B G♯ B (the 5, 3, and 5 of E7) as triplets that alternate between the 5th, 3rd, and 5th strings. Next, that same triplet motif/fingering ascends chromatically for beats 3–4 of bar 11, and finally resolves into chord tones ♭7 and 5 of the E7 (I7) chord on beat 1 of bar 12.

Listen to the "March in E," and when you're ready, practice it along with the audio. This audio track fades after one chorus. I recommend practicing the part repeatedly, though, so repeat symbols are included in the notation here and throughout this book, even when the audio doesn't repeat.

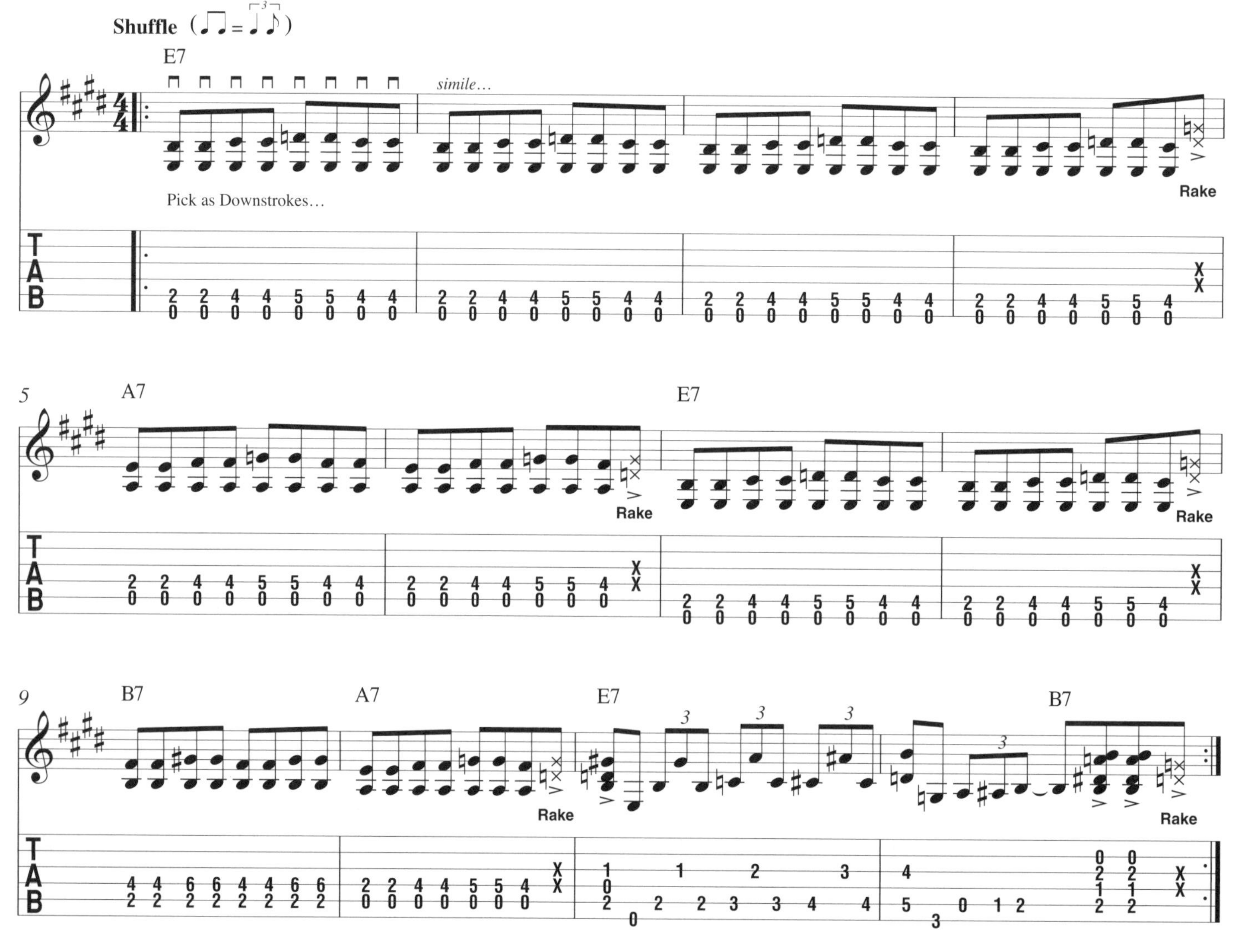

FIG. 1.1. March in E

This basic low-end bass pattern, along with the variations that follow, is derived from a boogie-woogie piano part. As you'll notice in the bass pattern analysis (figure 1.2), the lowest note stays on the root (1) of the chord, and the upper note begins on the 5 of the chord. If you're new to rhythm parts such as this, it may be helpful to first look at how the bass motion is constructed, and to practice the bass pattern over the I7, IV7, and V7 chords individually before working through the "March in E" progression.

Bass Variations

In example 1.2, the bass patterns for the I7 and IV7 (E7 and A7) chords sit directly on top of open position E and A chords. The bass pattern for the V7 (B7) chord sits on top of a B barre chord on the 2nd fret.

Example 1.2 features two typical variations for the bass pattern over the B7 (V7) chord. Note that the first version in bar 3 includes what, for many, is a tough fourth (pinky) finger stretch to the ♭7: the A on the D string, 7th fret. This variation can sound great. However, depending on the size of your hand and level of playing experience, the fourth finger stretch (7th fret on the D string) may be painful or even impossible to play. If that's the case for you, try playing the second variation (in bar 4) for the B7 chord, instead. That eliminates the potentially painful stretch to the ♭7 and sounds fine also.

To familiarize yourself with the basic chord forms and the bass pattern for the "March in E," listen and practice along with example 1.1 on track 2. Also practice the bass patterns for each chord individually, in example 1.2. Repeat each bar until you're comfortable with the sound, feel, and fingering for each chord.

To reach the ♭7 (D) on beat 3 of the E7 chord and the ♭7 (G) on beat 3 of the A7, I like to slide my third (ring finger) up to the 5th fret, instead of using my fourth finger, but feel free to fret that ♭7 with your fourth finger instead—whatever works for you. Remember to play this with a heavy triplet ("dump-ty dump") feel; pick all of the notes as downstrokes, and accent/emphasize all upbeats at least as much as the downbeats.

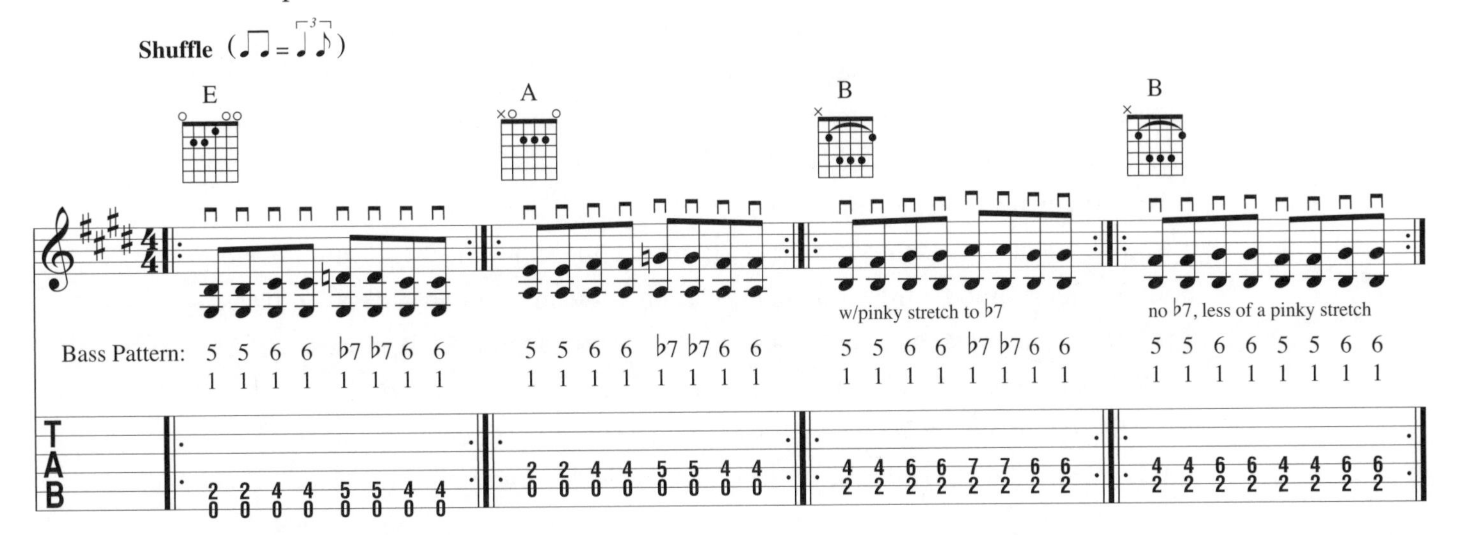

FIG. 1.2. Jimmy Reed Bass Pattern on I IV V

Rakes between Chords

A *rake* can be defined as an aggressive upstroke or downstroke picking attack or strum through open or muted strings. A few well-placed rakes can create extra momentum and "attitude" for the part, making it a little easier to play, by allowing the fretting hand an extra instant to get to the next chord or bass pattern. Rakes can produce a wide range of sounds and effects for your rhythm parts. When played as more staccato "choked off" strums, they can sound much like explosive snare drum hits. To make the rakes "pop" like a snare, strum top to bottom through the strings with an aggressive right-hand attack, while immediately choking off the strings with the fingers (and thumb) of your left hand. Rakes also sound great when played with a less percussive attack. To produce that effect, choke the strings off more gradually with your left hand (and thumb) to let as much of the chord or strings sound through (sustain) as you choose.

In example 1.1, note the upstroke rakes right before the chord change, such as in:

- bar 4, on beat "& of 4," just before the A7 (IV7) chord
- right at the end of bar 6, before the E7 (I7) chord
- at the end of bar 8, right before the V7 chord

On the subject of rakes and other nuances of this rhythm style, there are a couple of influential contemporary players worth noting. Jimmie Vaughan is known for his mastery of rhythm guitar, including this Jimmy Reed style. To hear his command of rakes, turnarounds, passing chords, and other powerful techniques over a shuffle in E, listen to his lean-and-mean rhythm part on "She's Tough," recorded in 1979 by the Fabulous Thunderbirds.

Powerhouse rakes, strums, and rhythm parts were also essential elements of Jimmie's younger brother, Stevie Ray Vaughan, in his performances. On songs such as "Cold Shot" and "Pride and Joy," Stevie Ray literally bashed the strings with huge right-hand strumming patterns and an explosive picking attack. His rhythmic feel on tracks such as "Rude Mood" was massive enough to shake the ground around your feet. To tap the explosive sound from his right-hand picking/strumming attack, Stevie Ray's left-hand thumb was often wrapped over the top of the neck, while his fingers were clenched around the neck and resting on the strings. That allowed him to mute/choke off the notes, when he chose to, for those huge rakes and strums, and to stop any unintended noises from straying into his rhythm parts or solos.

Experiment with using a similar left-hand muting technique, with your thumb and fingers wrapped around the neck, so that you can dampen notes/chords as you choose, and to stop those (annoying) extraneous ringing string noises.

Rakes between the chords are optional, so they don't have to be played at exactly the same place in every chorus. When the situation calls for it, you can improvise by adding a rake here or there as you feel it. Again, rhythmic nuances such as rakes can create extra rhythmic kick and energy for the part. However, they're most effective when used occasionally. With techniques such as this, less is more, so don't overdo it by playing rakes at the end of every bar.

LOW-END VARIATION FOR "MARCH IN E"

The "March in E" Variation 1 (figure 1.3) features a classic variation on the low-end bass motion for the IV7 and V7 chords. Note that the open A string anchors the bottom of the bass pattern throughout the B7 chord in bar 9. That ♭7 in the bass over the V7 (B7/A) chord creates a fat, dark, and greasy sound and feel that's easily recognizable as a "signature" of Jimmy Reed's style. To play this bass/chord pattern for the V7 chord (B7/A), simply shift your left hand up two frets while playing the same fingering and pattern that you played for the IV7 (A7) chord. This is easy to play, plus it sounds huge. Those are two big reasons for getting it under your fingers!

In the place of the upstroke rakes between chords at the end of bars 4, 6, 8, and 12, this variation of the "March in E" features a low G (the ♭3) played on the 6th string, 3rd fret. As noted earlier, Jimmy Vaughan is one of the very best at playing a shuffle in the Jimmy Reed style, so if you've checked out his rhythm parts on shuffles such as this, you may have noticed that he often "smacks" the low ♭3 at various places between the chords. So, try smackin' that low G to create a little extra kick for the part!

Listen to example 1.3, "March in E" Variation 1. When you're ready, practice it along with the audio.

3

March in E
Variation 1

Mike Williams

Shuffle ♩ = 91

E7 A7 E7 B7 A7 E7 B7

FIG. 1.3. "March in E" Variation 1

ANOTHER LOW-END VARIATION FOR THE "MARCH IN E"

This variation of the "March in E" features another popular bass pattern over the IV and V chords in bars 9 and 10. Like Variation 1, the low note in the bass pattern for the B7 (V7) sits on the open A string, creating B7/A with the classic Jimmy Reed ♭7 sound in the bottom. Analyzed against a B7 chord, the upper note in the pattern outlines 5 5, ♭3 3, 5 5, 6 6. The same pattern continues in bar 10, played two frets lower over the A7 (IV7) chord, with the open A string/root anchoring the bottom.

This variation also features a mix of upstroke rakes, and low G (♭3) in several places throughout the progression. The turnaround is the same as in figure 1.3.

Listen to the "March in E" Variation 2. When you're ready, practice it along with the audio.

4

March in E
Variation 2

Mike Williams

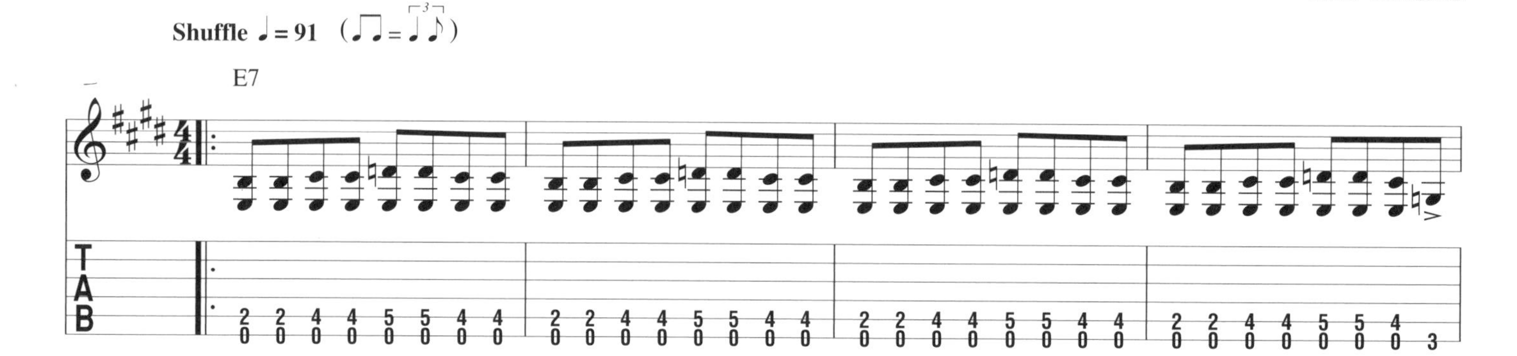

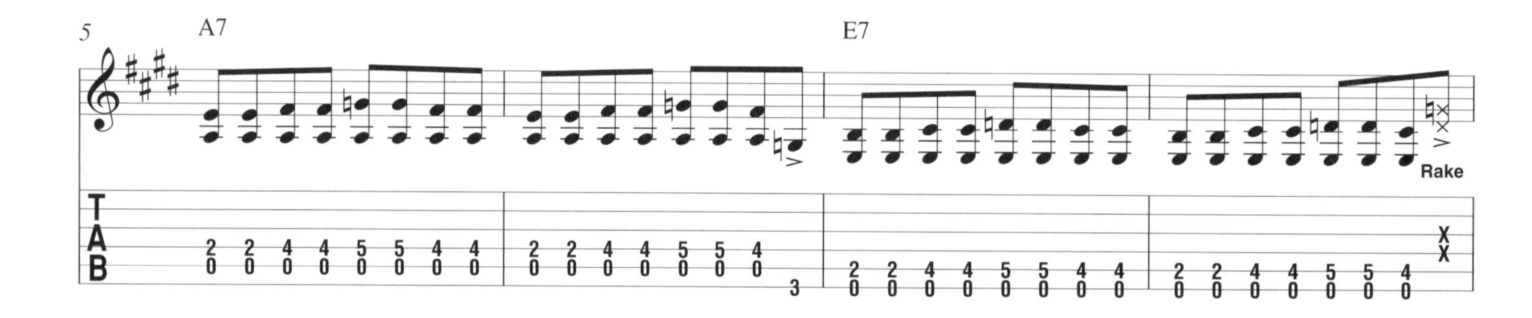

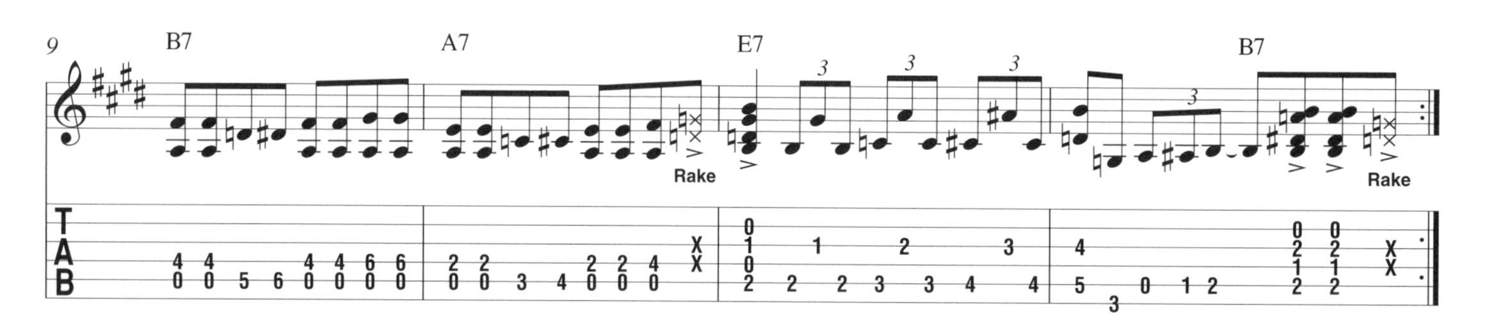

FIG. 1.4. "March in E" Variation 2

"MARCH IN E" FOUR CHORUSES WITH RHYTHM SECTION

Now it's time to put the progressions to work in a longer performance setting. Example 1.5 features four varied choruses of the "March in E," along with intro and ending fills that are based on the open-position E blues scale.

Performance Tips

Choruses 1 and 2

Choruses 1 and 2 have bass/chord patterns and turnarounds that are similar to what we've already covered. Note that the descending triplets in bar 15 of chorus 1, which start in position 4, again alternate between strings 5 and 3. The triplet phrase resolves on beat 1 of bar 16 into the E7 chord tones B and G♯.

Note that the B7 (V7) chord(s) at the end of choruses 1–3 feature the low F♯ (5) in the bass. That second inversion B7 chord (B7/F♯) creates extra gravity and depth for the turnaround, and it can be heard in hundreds of recordings by the greats, including Robert Lockwood Jr., Jimmy Rodgers, and T-Bone Walker.

Choruses 3 and 4

Choruses 3 and 4 introduce a few more challenging fills and rhythm techniques, so they're going to take a little more time to learn. Bars 29 and 35 feature an A *passing chord* on beat 4, which quickly moves/ "passes" back to E7 on "and" of 4. (That's a first-inversion A triad, with notes C♯ E A C♯, on strings 5-4-3-2.) In bar 30, the note F♯ is added to the top of the (same) A triad, creating an A6 passing chord. Both the A and A6 passing chords create a powerful forward push back to E7, and together, they're another easily recognizable component of the Jimmy Reed sound and style.

Note the slide-influenced fill that starts in beat 4 of bar 31 and continues through most of bar 32, to create a strong pull into the A7 (IV7) chord in bar 33. To play it, slide fingers 1 and 2 repeatedly (as triplets) into chord tones B and D, the 5 and ♭7 of E7.

The turnaround starts on beat 2 of bar 39 with hammer-ons into E (triplets). From there, it descends and then ascends back up the open position E blues scale, eventually landing on open position B7 (V7).

Chorus 4 introduces another triplet-based fill that starts on beat 4 of bar 43, which continues through bar 44. This 3-note fingering, with notes D, E, and B (♭7, root, and 5), forms an incomplete E7 chord. The G♯ (3) can also be added on the fourth string, 6th fret, to play this voicing as a 4-note chord, but it also sounds great as a 3-note voicing. Try transposing this voicing/fill to position 10 for A7 (IV7) and to position 12 for the B7 (V7) chords—because it also sounds right at home over the I7, IV, or V7 chords!

Bars 41, 42, and 46 include more passing chords, and beats 3 and 4 of bar 47 work in a brief open-position E blues fill that leads back to an open E7 chord on beats 1 to 3 of bar 48. Bar 49 introduces another variation in the bass pattern, with the ♭7 in the bass.

Several classic rhythm techniques are packed into these four choruses, so good luck with this track!

Listen and then play along with the audio for example 1.5, first with the full band, and then with the backing track.

March in E
Mike Williams
5
Rhythm Part
6
No Guitar
Shuffle ♩ = 91
NC
A7
E7
Chorus 1
B7
Rake
TAB

Chorus 2

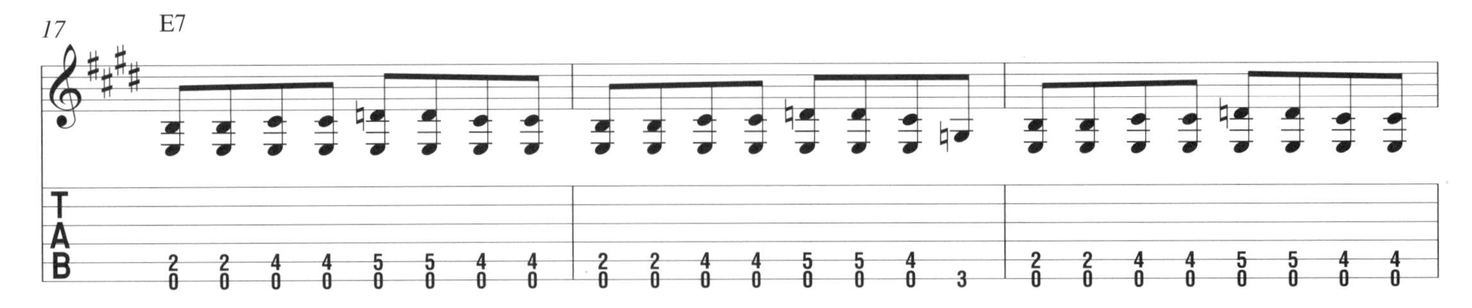

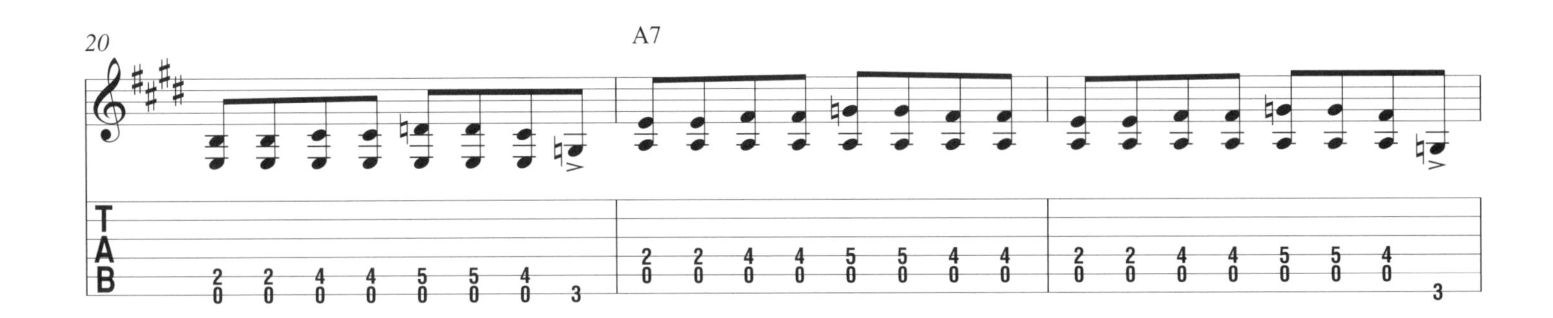

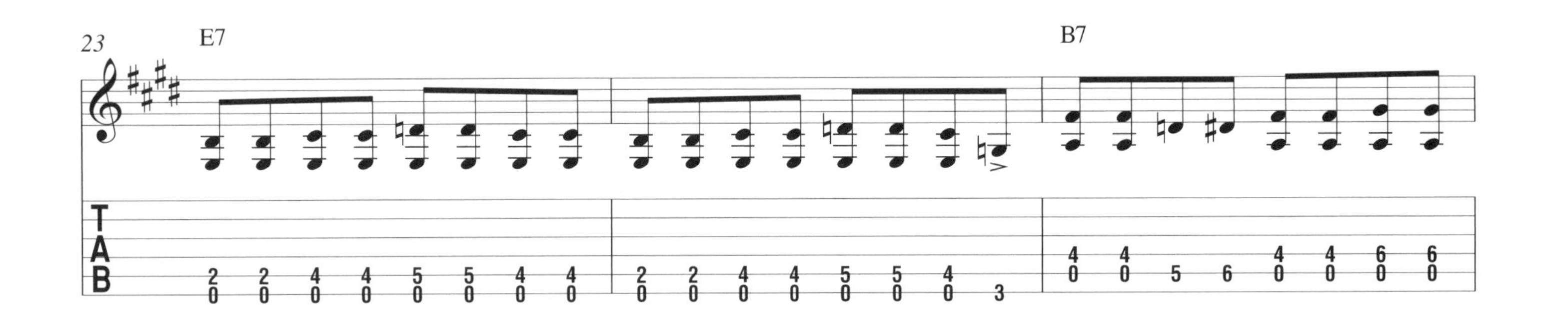

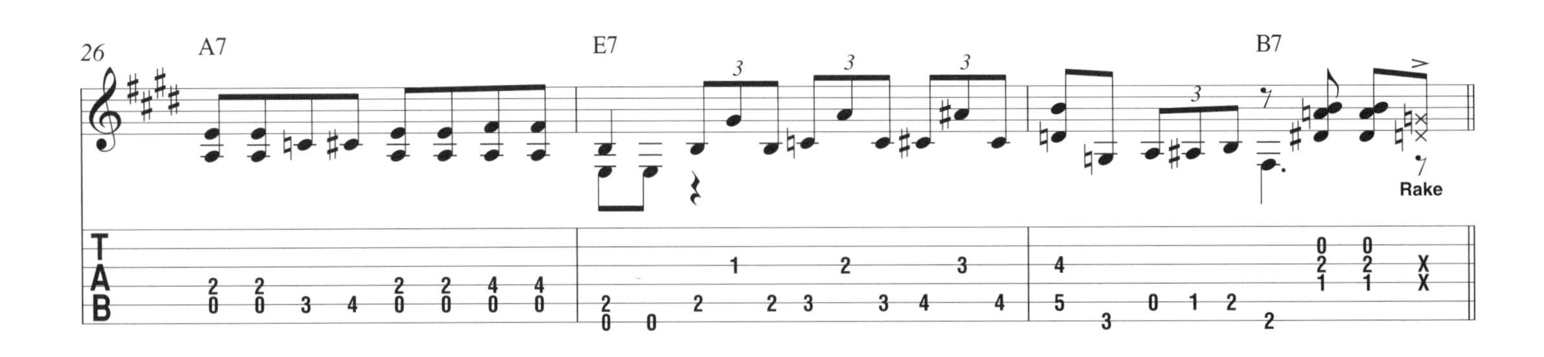

Chorus 3

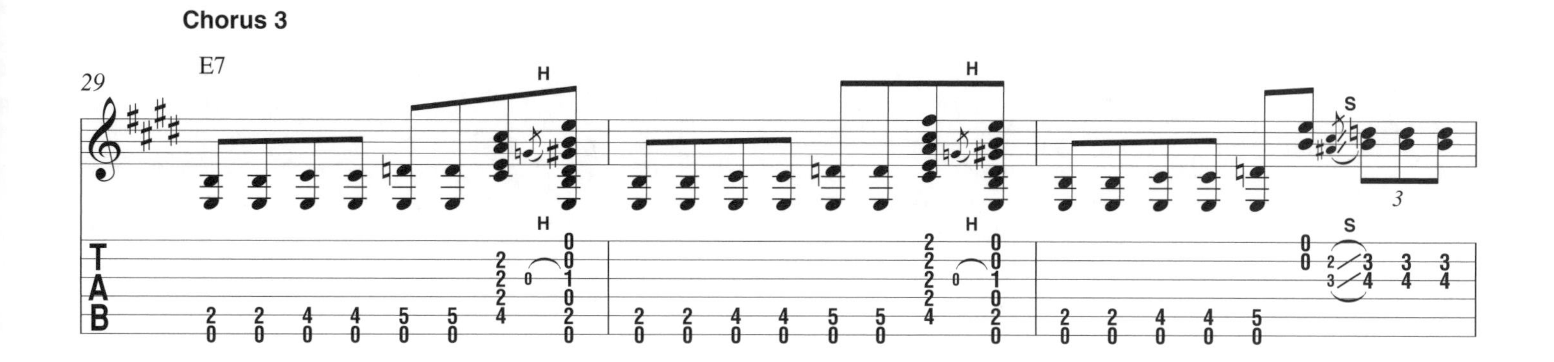

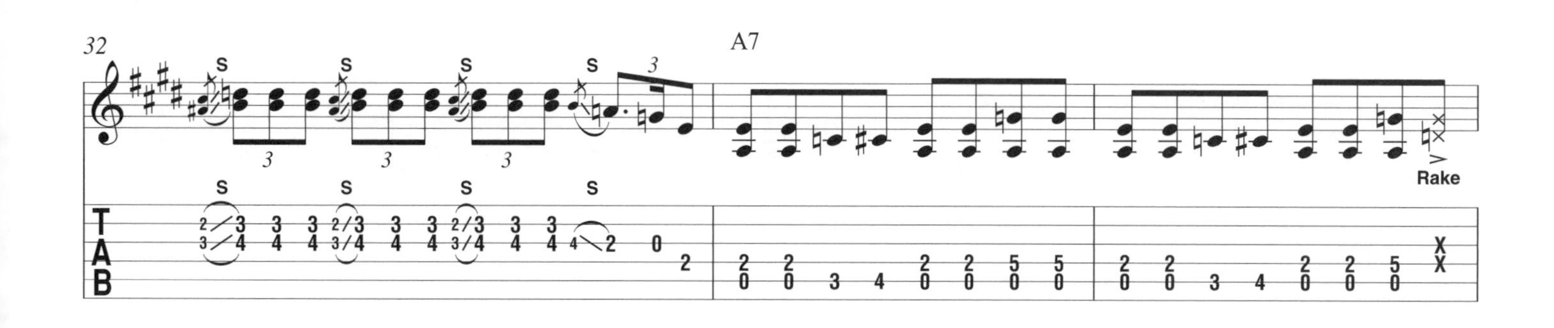

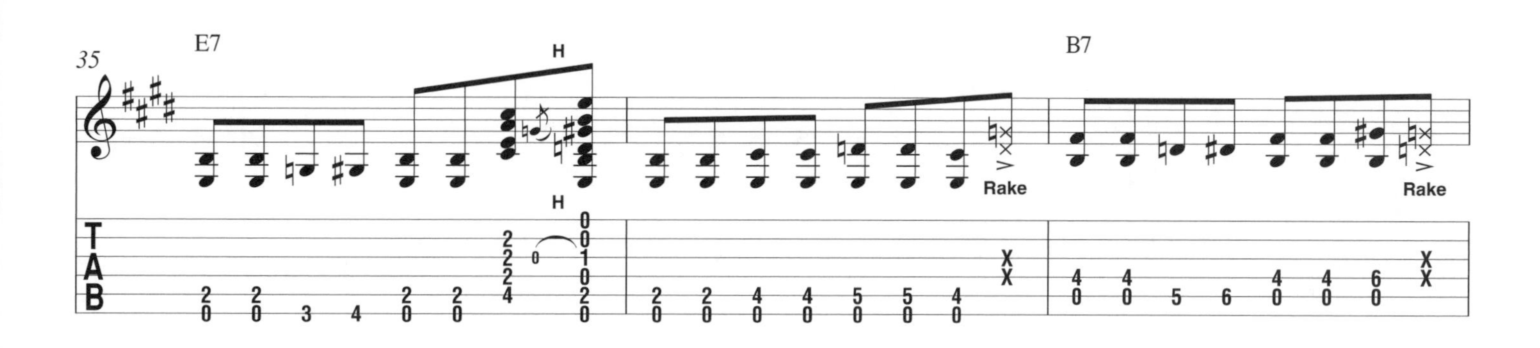

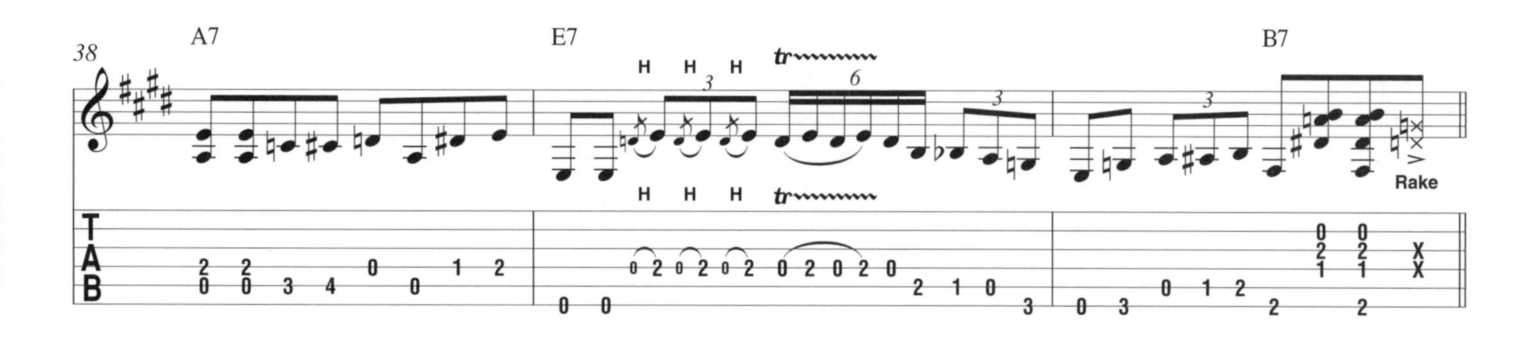

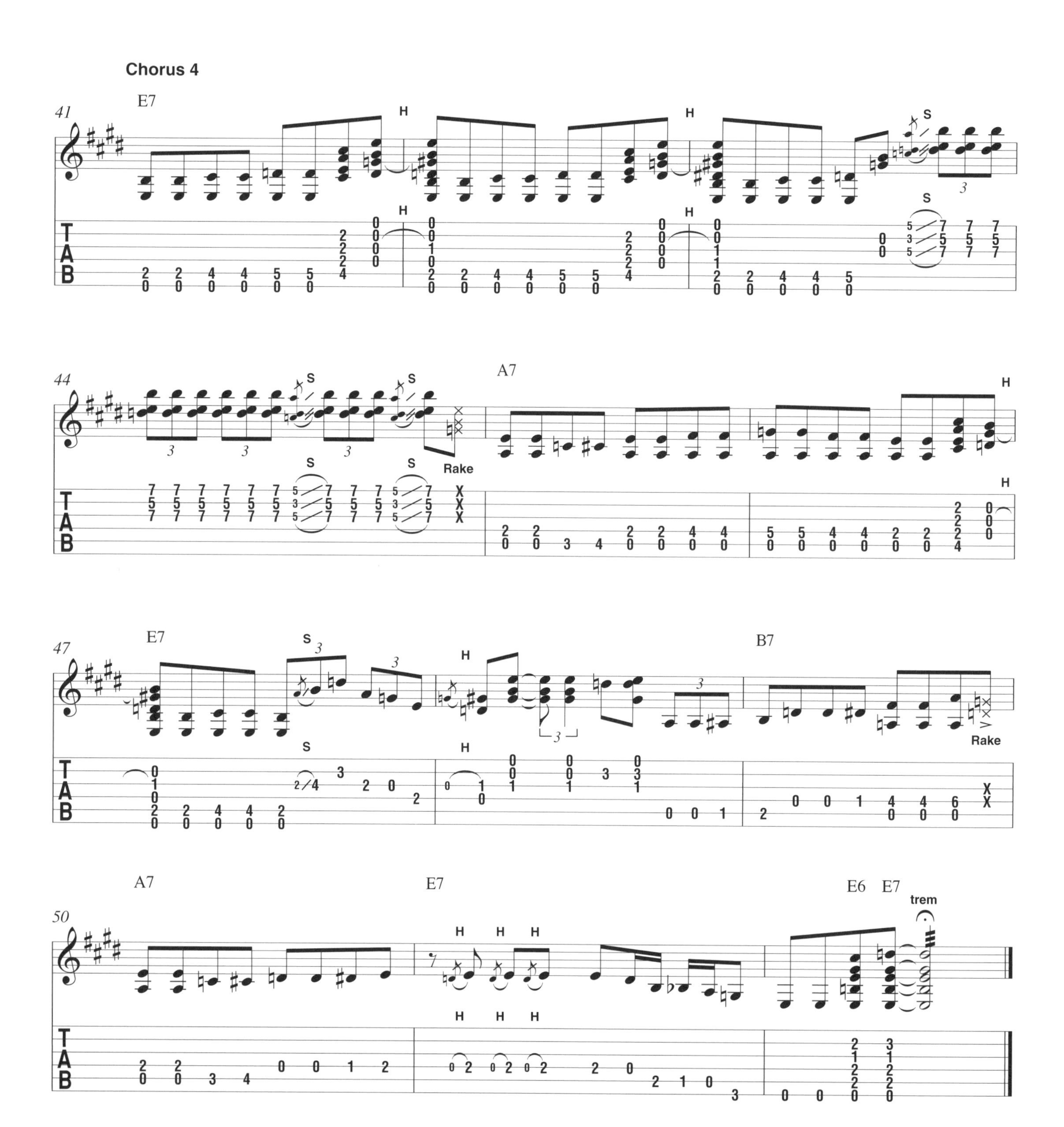

FIG. 1.5. "March in E" Four Choruses

CHAPTER 2

More Rhythm Parts in the Jimmy Reed Style: "March in A"

The key of A is another essential key for blues guitar. Example 2.1, the "March in A," features a bass pattern fingering that sits right on top of the I7, IV7, and V7 (A7, D7, and E7) chords. The bass pattern for each chord is anchored by its respective low open string: I7 (A), IV7 (D), V7 (E). The fingerings of the A7 (I7) and E7 (V7) chords and bass pattern are the same as played in the basic "March in E" (see example 1.1), and the D7 chord is fingered similarly—again, with the open D string anchoring the bottom. This progression also features rakes that are similar to the "March in E."

The turnaround starts on the "and" of beat 1 in bar 11, with notes G, E, A (the ♭7, 5, and root) on strings 4-2-1. The two lower notes (G and E) descend chromatically through beats 3 and 4, and eventually resolve (on beat 1 of bar 12) to E and C♯, which are chord tones 5 and 3 of A7. Notice that the A note/root (1st string, 5th fret) is picked repeatedly, while the lower notes (strings 4 and 2) descend throughout bar 11, which taps into influences from earlier blues guitarists, such as Robert Johnson.

Listen and practice along with example 2.1, the "March in A."

March in A

Mike Williams

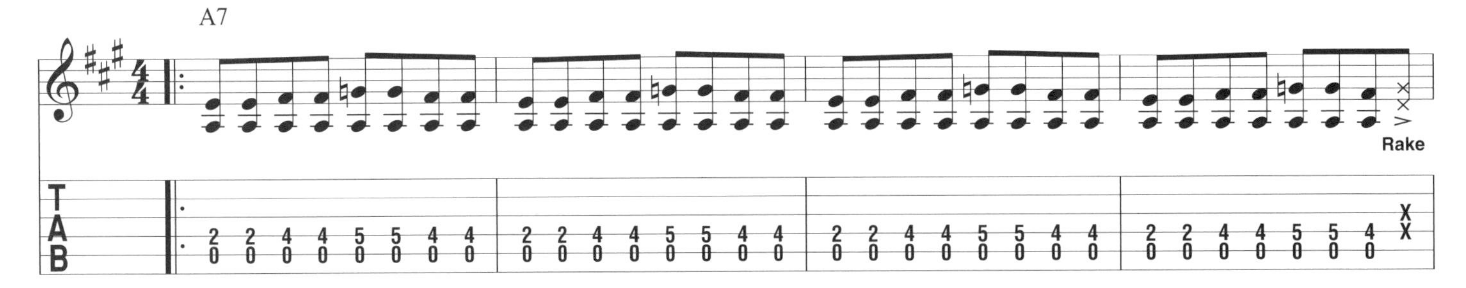

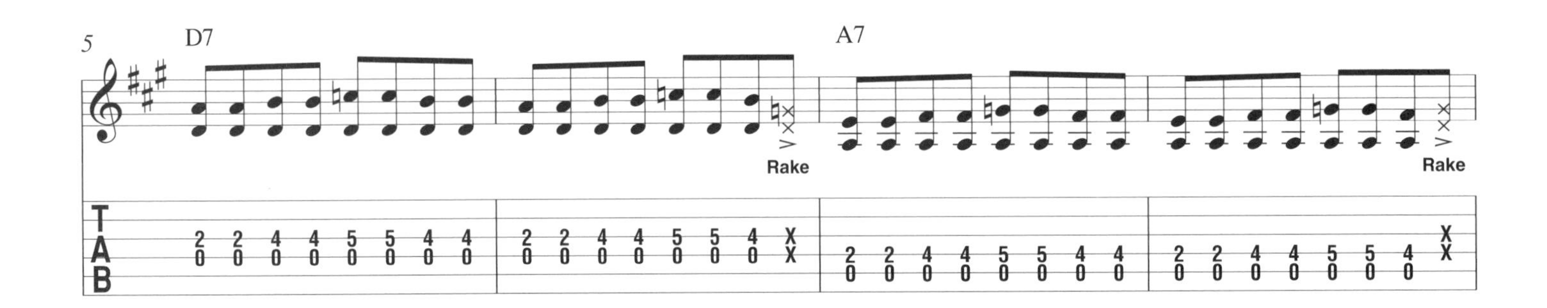

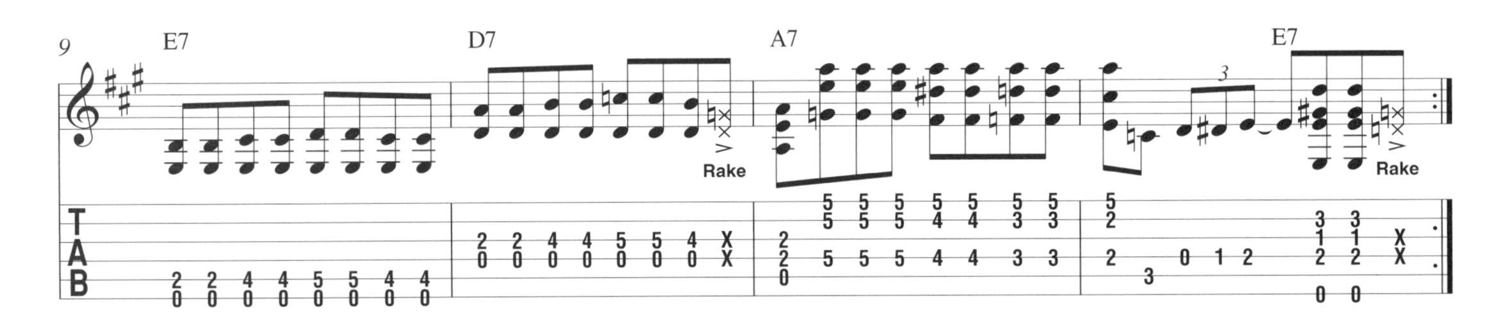

FIG. 2.1. March in A

"MARCH IN A" VARIATION 1

Like example 2.1, the progression in example 2.2 features low, open-string root notes to anchor the bottom of A7 and D7 (I7 and IV7).

E7 is anchored by the open D/4th string, creating an E7/D for bar 9. Once again, that's easily recognizable as part of Jimmy Reed's style.

Note the low C (♭3) notes (5th string, 3rd fret) played in the place of rakes at the end of bars 4, 6, 8, and 10.

The turnaround in bars 11–12 taps heavily into Eddie Taylor's phrasing and influences. It's based on the A blues scale in position 2/3 and then shifts down to a partial open A chord (root, 5, root on strings 5-4-3) on beat 1 of bar 11. That's followed immediately by an open E7 (V7) to complete the chorus.

Listen and play along with example 2.2, the "March in A" Variation 1.

8

March in A
Variation 1

Mike Williams

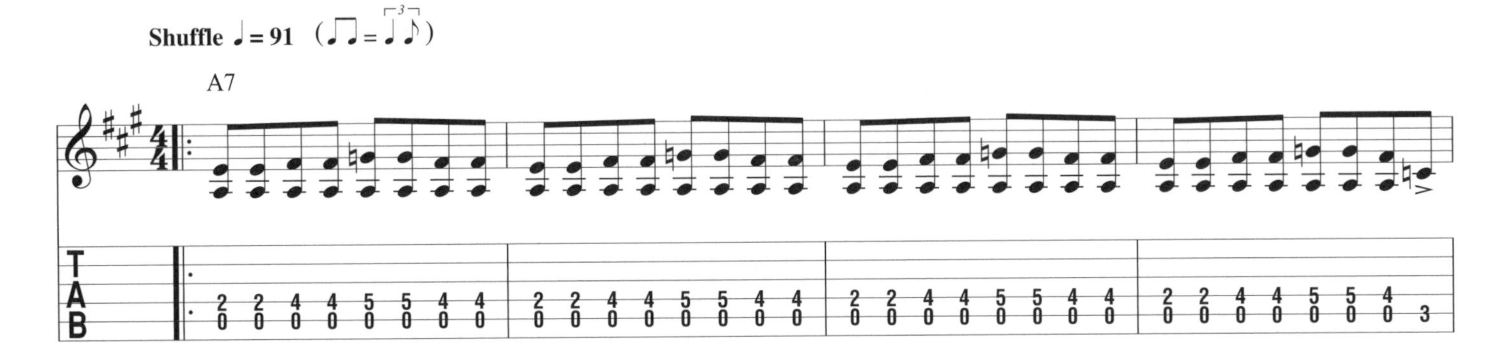

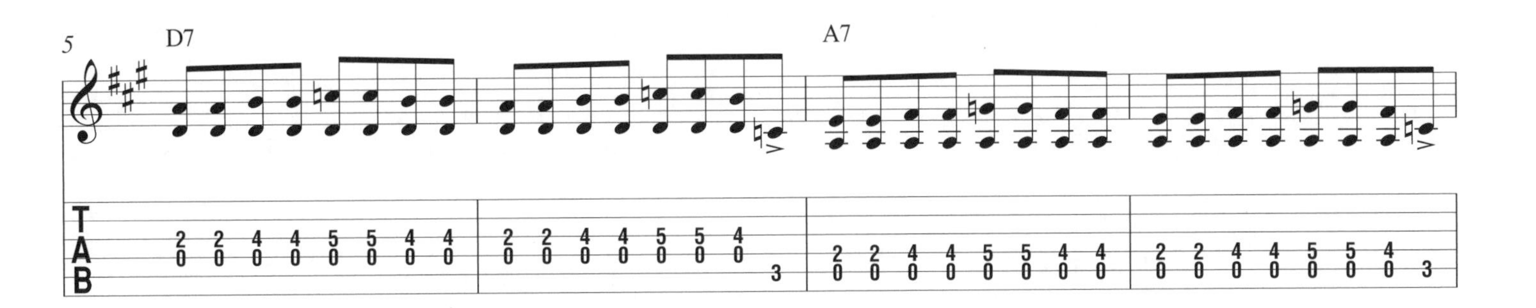

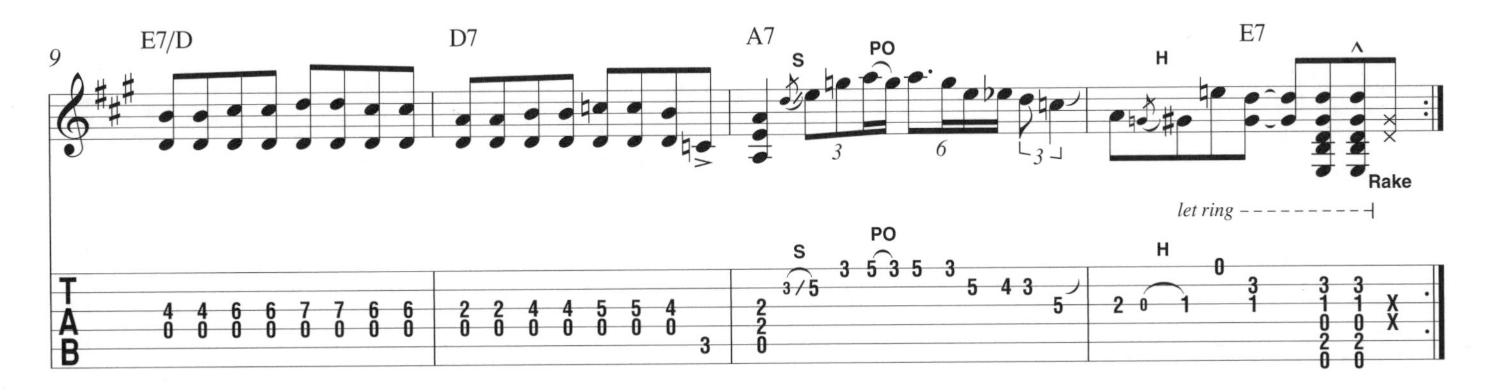

FIG. 2.2. "March in A" Variation 1

"MARCH IN A" VARIATION 2

This chorus introduces passing chords (as we saw in chapter 1), which are classic components of Jimmy Reed's style. Like rakes, these passing chords create extra momentum into the next chord change.

Bars 2 and 6 feature a passing D (IV) triad on beat 4, which immediately passes on "and" of 4, back to the A triad (I chord). Bar 4 features a similar D6 passing chord on beat 4, and also note the A triad on beat 4 of bar 8, which creates extra pull into the E7 (V7) chord.

Play along with example 2.3, the "March in A" Variation 2 on the audio.

March in A
Variation 2

Mike Williams

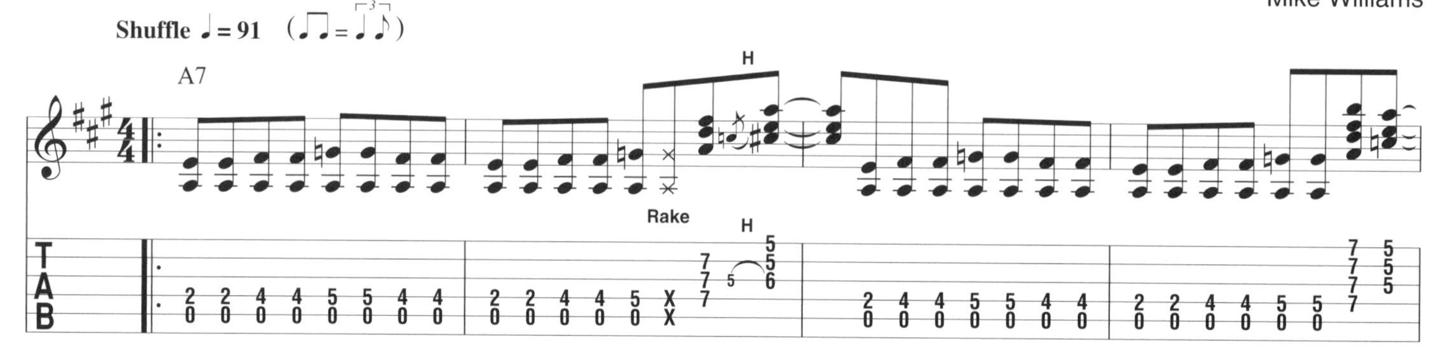

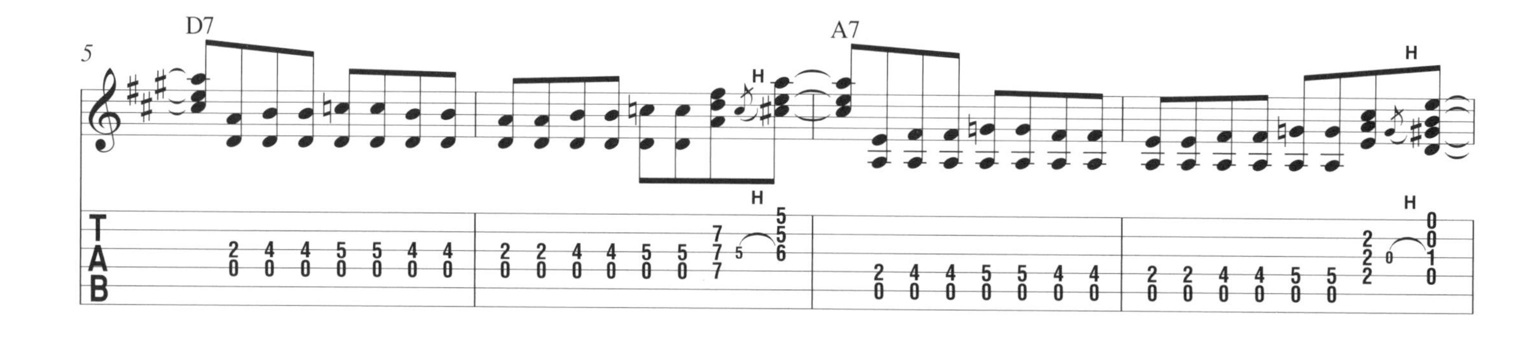

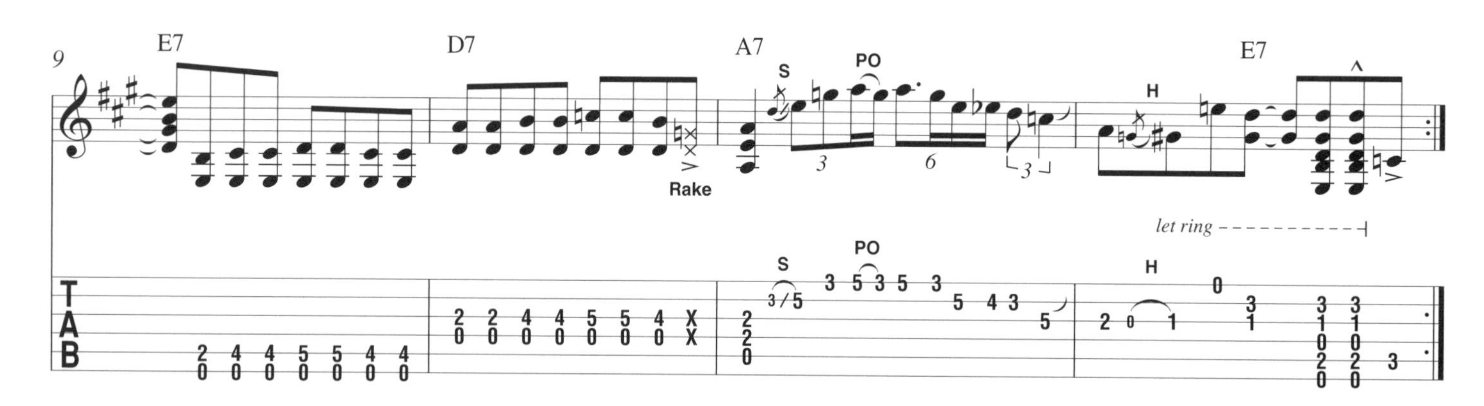

FIG. 2.3. "March in A" Variation 2

"MARCH IN A" WITH RHYTHM SECTION

Example 2.4. features five varied choruses of the "March in A" with intro and ending fills that are based around the open position A blues scale. Choruses 1 and 2 are a little more basic. Choruses 3 and 4 feature a few more challenging fills and techniques, so they should take a little longer to get under your fingers.

Performance Tips

Choruses 1 and 2

The intro fill is a big tip of the hat to Eddie Taylor's playing style, since his rhythm parts and solos are full of greasy fills that are great for expanding our soloing vocabulary. Both choruses feature a bass pattern that's similar to example 2.1. Each chord is anchored by its respective open (low) string: I7 (A), IV7 (D), V7 (E).

Chorus 3

Beat 4 of bars 2, 6, and 7 feature a D passing chord on beat 4, which quickly passes back (resolves) to the A chord on "and" of 4. Also note the slide-influenced 2-note fill throughout bar 4, played as triplets into chord tones E and G (5 and ♭7) of A7, which creates extra gravitational pull into the D7 (IV7) chord in bar 5.

The IV7 (D7/F♯) chord in bar 10 features F♯ (3) in the bass, that's played with the thumb. That's another technique and sound with roots all the way back to Robert Johnson and the earliest country blues players.

Chorus 4

In bar 5, note the powerful 3-note voicing, with notes C, D, and A (♭7, root, 5) on strings 3-2-1. This forms an incomplete D7 chord; it's missing the 3 (F♯), which can be added (4th string, 4th fret) to play this as a complete seventh chord. This sounds great as a 3-note voicing, though, whether it's over the I7, IV7, or I7 chord in rhythm parts such as this. So, transpose this voicing to position 10 for A7 (I7) and to position 5 for the E7 (V7), because it sounds right at home over those chords, also.

Chorus 5

Chorus 5 features a more dense mix of bass/chord patterns and fills from previous choruses, so it should keep your hands busy. The final turnaround in bar 11 is a descending one-octave A blues scale that's played in the open position. That phrase is also easy to finger in position 5, so feel free to play it there, as well. The ending chords in bar 12 begin with B9, which descends chromatically to B♭9, and finally resolves "home" to A9. That's a popular blues ending for a multitude of progressions, styles, and tempos, so it's well worth having under your fingers!

Listen and then play along with the audio for example 2.4, first with the full band, and then with the backing track.

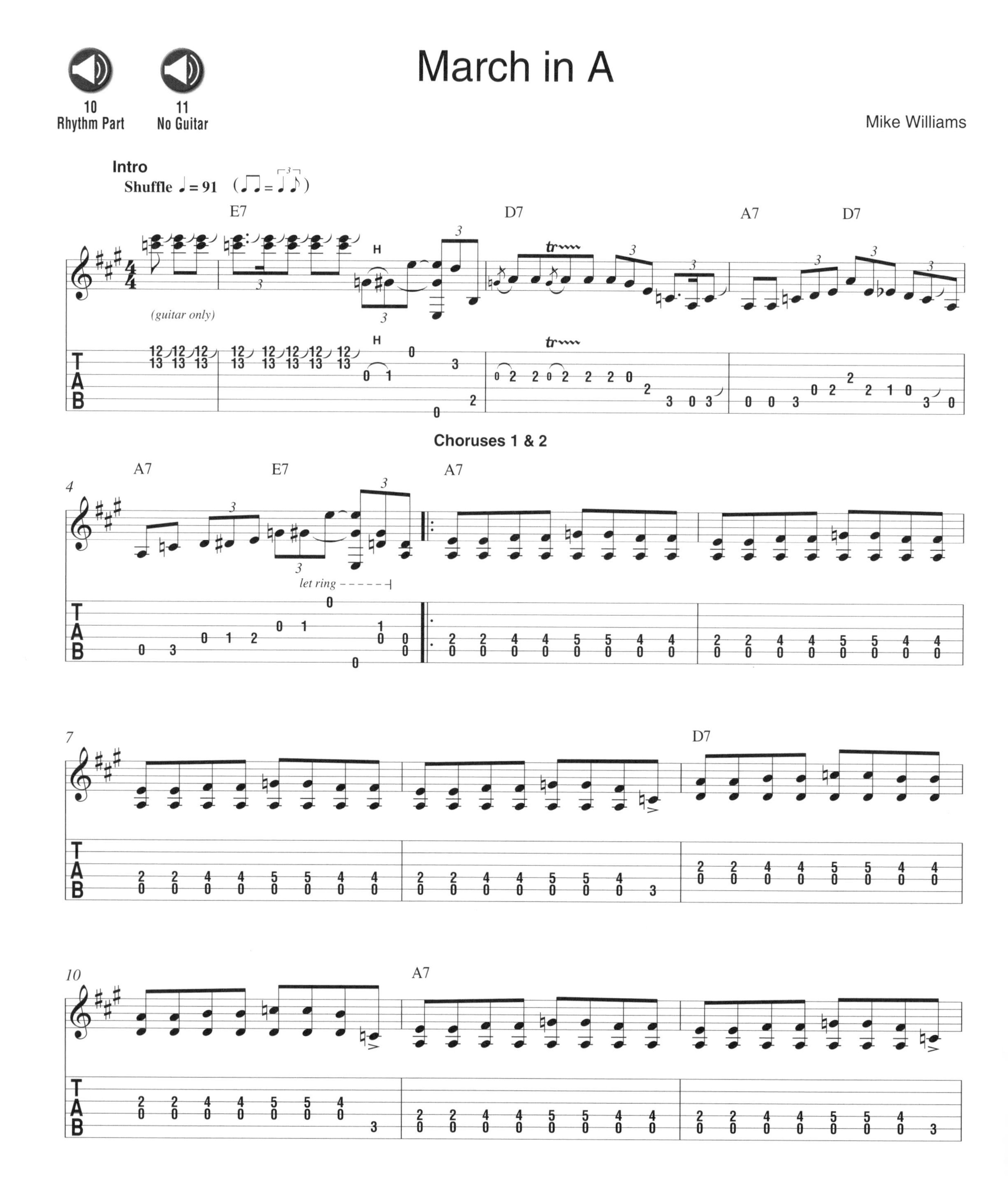

E7
D7
A7
let ring
1.
2.
E7
H
Chorus 3
A7
H
S
Rake
D7
A7
E7
let ring
TAB

D7
A7
E7
H
PO
let ring
Chorus 4
S
6
Rake

Chorus 5

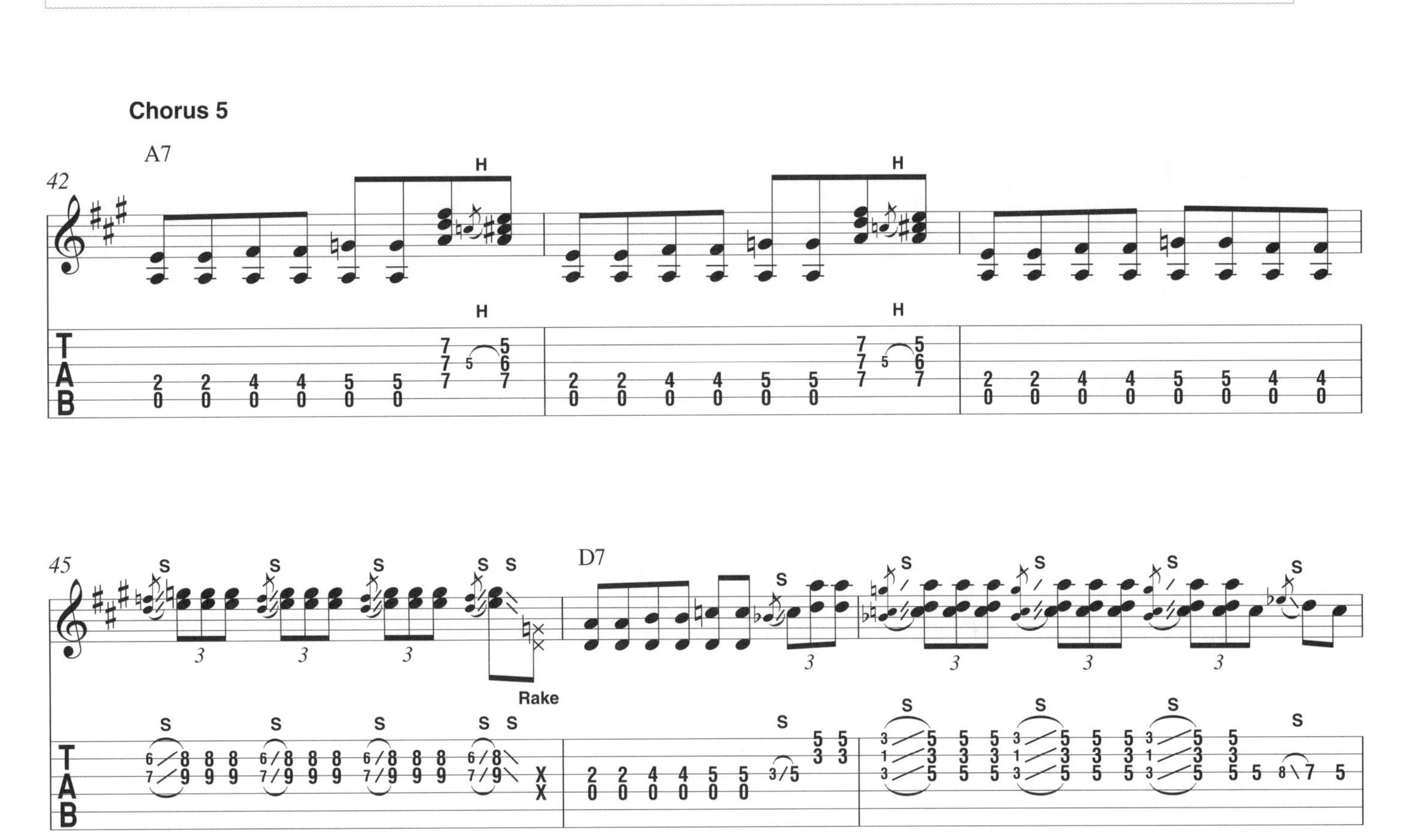

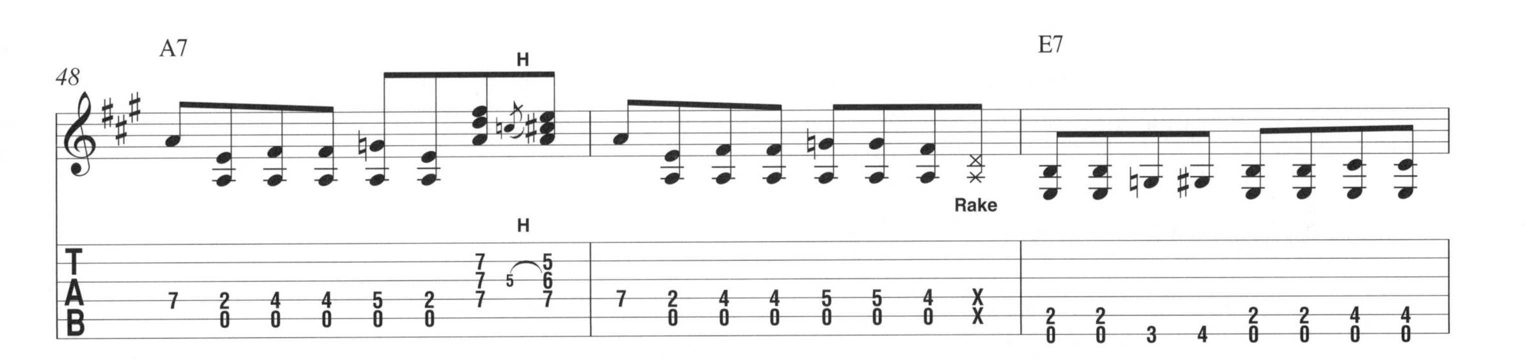

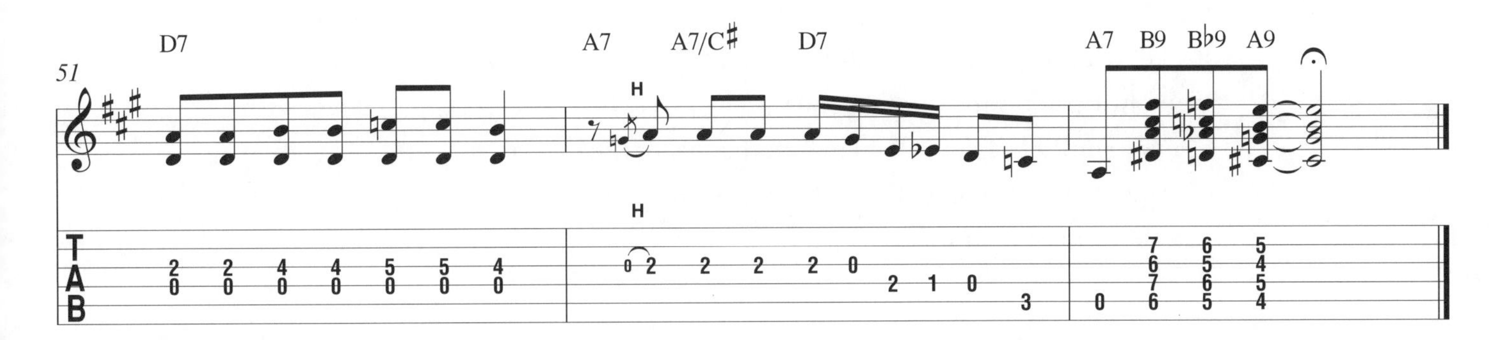

FIG. 2.4. “March in A” with Rhythm Section

CHAPTER 3

Classic Chicago Style: Downtown and Uptown Shuffles

In this chapter, you'll learn a couple of rhythm parts in the classic Chicago style. Downtown and uptown shuffles have been featured on hundreds of blues recordings over the last several decades, so they're great rhythm parts to have under your fingers.

DOWNTOWN SHUFFLE IN F

Both the downtown and uptown parts are single-note bass patterns, often played together in unison, between the bass and guitar. The downtown part on the next page is based on a 1-bar bass line/pattern (1, 1, octave 1, octave 1, ♭7, ♭7, 5, 5) that repeats through the 12-bar form. Pick each note as a downstroke, with a very punchy, staccato, and consistent attack, to create as much momentum and "attitude" for the part as possible. Play all of the upbeats with a heavy shuffle/triplet feel, to match the feel of the drums. As in the "March in E" in chapter 1, you may find it helpful to verbalize the feel for the downtown line as "dump-ty, dump..."

Listen to example 3.1, and practice the part. When you're ready, play along with the audio.

12

Downtown Shuffle in F

Mike Williams

Shuffle ♩ = 122

FIG. 3.1. "Downtown Shuffle in F"

Classic Recordings of the Downtown Shuffle

Examples of the downtown shuffle include Freddy King's classic "Tore Down," and his instrumental "Side Tracked," which was also covered in a more recent live recording by guitarist Anson Funderburgh. Funderburgh has recorded several other downtown shuffles, including "Empty Arms" and "Everything's Gonna Be Alright." "Country Girl," by Junior Wells and Buddy Guy, is a classic variation on the downtown pattern. Other examples of the downtown shuffle include "Wait on Time," by the Fabulous Thunderbirds (with Jimmy Vaughan), and "So Excited," by Stevie Ray Vaughan.

UPTOWN SHUFFLE IN G

The *uptown* shuffle is another popular single-note pattern. This part is referred to as the "uptown" shuffle because the bass line moves *up* from the root (G) to the 5 (D), then to the ♭7 (F), and ends on the root (G, one octave higher than the first note of the pattern).

Like the downtown part, each note is played twice (counted 1 and 2 and 3 and 4 and). That pattern continues through the IV and V chords of the 12-bar form. Again, play each note as a downstroke, with a very punchy and staccato picking attack.

Listen to the "Uptown Shuffle in G." Practice the part, and when you're ready, play along with the audio.

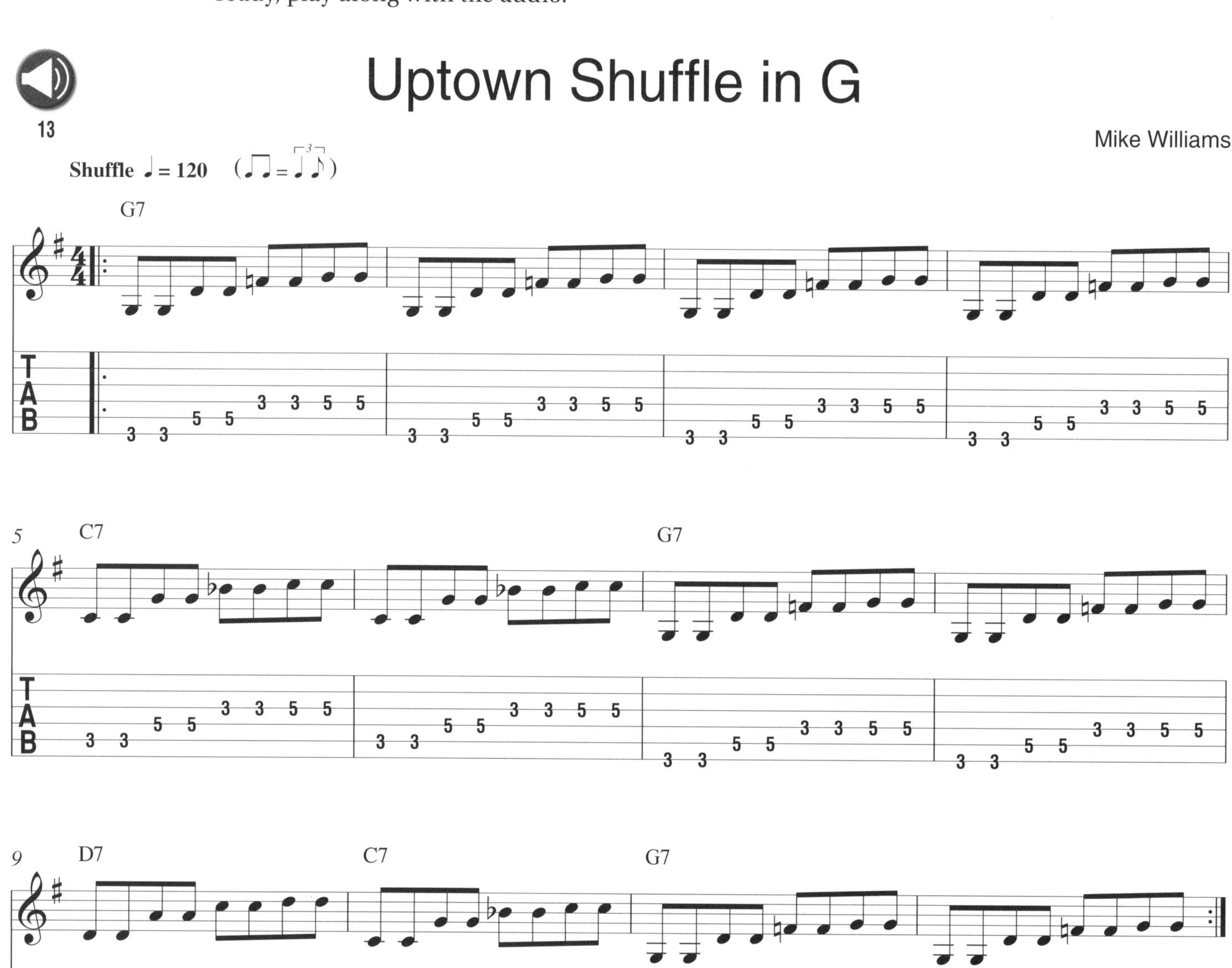

FIG. 3.2. "Uptown Shuffle in G"

Classic Recordings of the Uptown Shuffle

Like the downtown part, there are many recorded versions and variations of the uptown shuffle. At times, it's been recorded exactly as written in figure 3.2. There are also several variations, where one or more notes and/or rhythms are changed, such as "The Things I Do for You" and "Little By Little I'm Losing You," by Junior Wells (covered more recently by Susan Tedeschi). Otis Rush's track, "I Miss You So" is also based on an uptown shuffle.

SLIDING NINTHS RHYTHM PARTS

Sliding-ninth chords can produce a huge variety of sounds for rhythm parts and solos in blues, jazz, funk, and other styles, so they're very useful parts to have under your fingers.

When there's just one guitar in the band, it can either double the bass on the downtown or uptown pattern, or it can move onto another rhythm part, such as the sliding ninths, while the bass player holds down the bottom end.

When two or more guitarists are playing rhythm together, it can be tricky to stay out of each other's way. With parts such as the uptown/downtown and sliding ninths, it's very possible to accompany vocal parts and solos, and stay out of each other's sonic "air space" at the same time. It sounds great when one guitarist plays the lower (downtown or uptown) part, while the other plays fills or chords in a contrasting higher range. Each part has its own clearly defined range and rhythmic "pocket," so when the two parts are combined, they complement each other perfectly.

Notation Note: G9 vs. G7(9)

In this book, we will use the common shorthand of notating diatonic 9 and 13 tensions, where we use just a 9 or 13 to indicate 7(9) or 7(13) chords. So, a G9 chord can include G, B, D, F, and A. G9 is a shorthand for G7(9), and it means exactly the same thing. However, *altered* 9 and 13 will be written in their full form: G7(♭9), to clarify that the alteration refers to the tension and not the chord root. So, G♭9 is a G♭ dominant seventh chord with a T9. G7(♭9) will always be written in the long form.

Listen and practice the sliding ninths part along with the "Uptown Shuffle in G" in example 3.3. (Exercise 3.4 will illustrate how the sliding ninth chords sound great against the G9, C9, and D9 chords in figure 3.3.)

Uptown Shuffle in G
with Sliding Ninth Chords

Mike Williams

FIG. 3.3. "Uptown Shuffle in G" with Sliding Ninth Chords

G9 (Assumed Root 6)

Let's look at the structure of the G9 (I), C9 (IV), and D9 (V) chords that the sliding ninths are derived from. The G9 chord on the top line of figure 3.4 consists of four notes, played on the inside four strings. Note that this G9 voicing has no root. The notes in the voicing are (bottom to top): B F A D, to form the 3 ♭7 9 5 of the chord. To move (i.e., transpose) the chord up and down along the neck, you'll need to need to "visualize" the root; it would be on the 6th string, 3rd fret, in the same fret as your front fingers (3rd and 4th). That's why this type of chord voicing is referred to as *assumed root 6*. This classic fingering sounds great even without the root, and that leaves more room for the bass player to provide the low end.

The top three notes of this G9 chord (F A D, on strings 4-3-2) form a D minor triad, which functions as the ♭7 9 5 of G7. If you slide the D minor triad up two frets to notes G B E, it produces an E minor triad, which functions as 1 3 6 (or 13) of the chord, to produce a G6 or G13 sound. Combining the notes/sounds of the D minor triad (♭7 9 5) and E minor triad (1 3 6) against the G7 chord creates a jazzy (G13) color/texture that's versatile for many rhythm parts and solos.

C9 (Root 5)

The C9 (IV chord) uses a different fingering, known as a root-5 chord, which means that the root (C) is on the 5th string. Unlike the G9 fingering, this voicing has the root in it. From the bottom up, the notes in this voicing are C E B♭ D G, which are respectively, the 1 3 ♭7 9 5 of the chord. Like on the G9 chord, you can slide the top three notes between G minor and A minor triads to create a C7/13 sound.

Sliding G9

Practice fingering for the 4-note G9 chord along with the 3-note sliding chords. First, slide the chords up and back down using fingers 2-3-4. Also try sliding with fingers 1-2-3. Both fingerings work well.

Play these fingerings for the full C9 and D9 chords, then practice sliding up and down the top three strings using a half barre with your third (ring) finger, since it's part of the fingering. Also try sliding with your first finger, since either finger works well for the slides on the top three strings. Notice that the slides over the D9 chord are the same as the slides over C9; simply play them two frets higher on the neck.

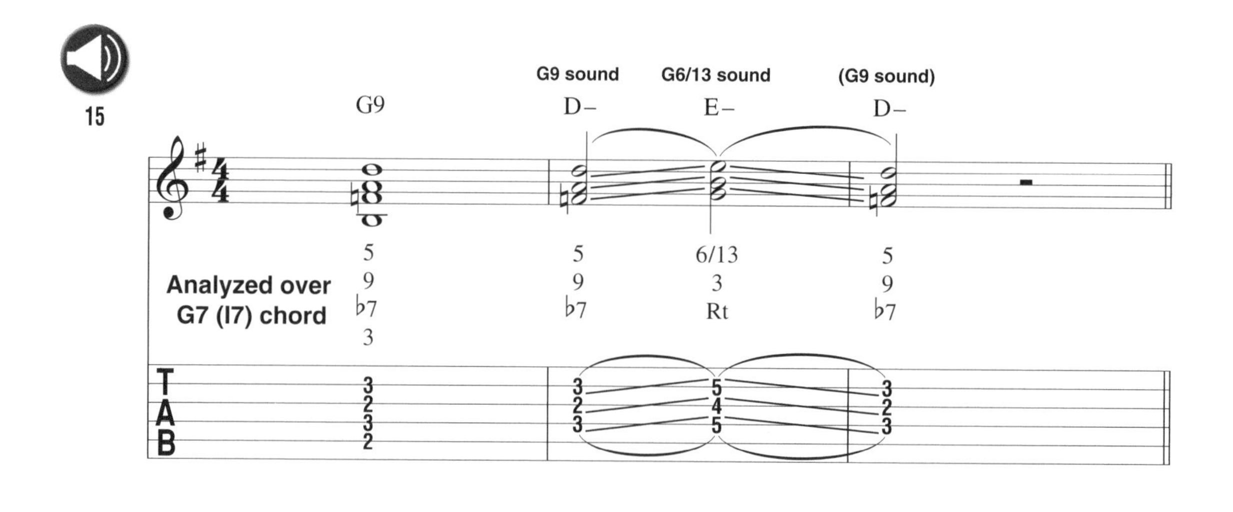

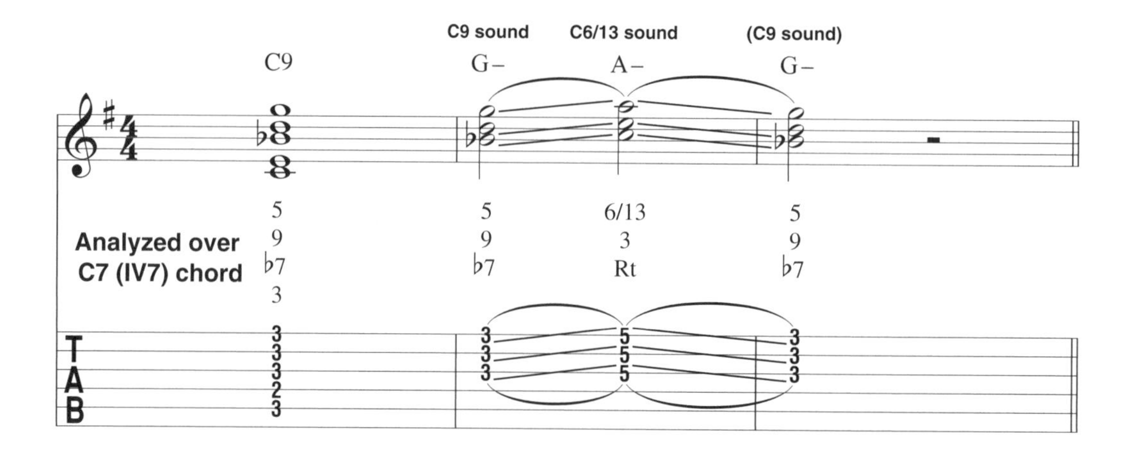

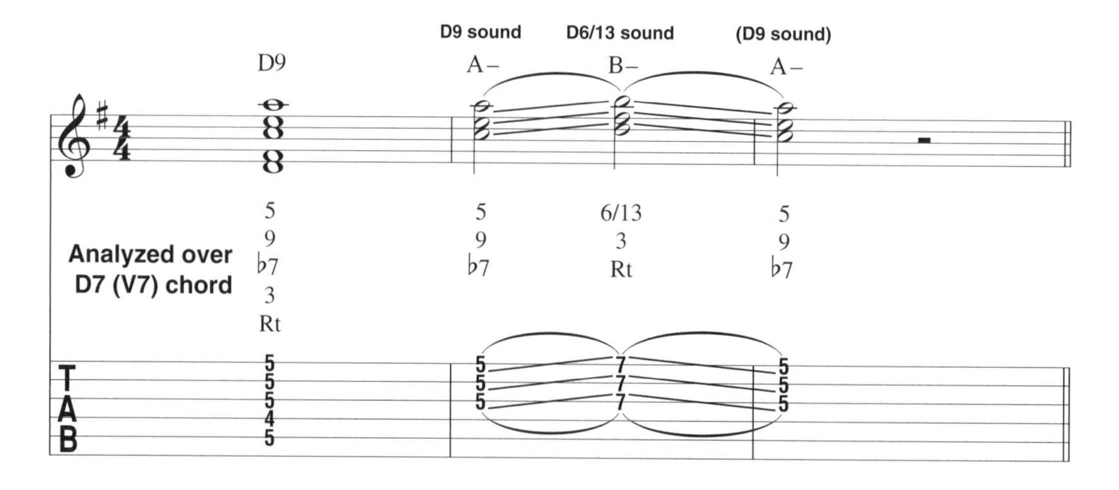

FIG. 3.4. Sliding Ninths Exercise

"DOWNTOWN SHUFFLE IN F" FIVE CHORUSES

Next, let's put all three rhythm parts to work in a five-chorus performance. In figure 3.5, we'll revisit the "Downtown Shuffle in F." This track features two different turnaround phrases in bar 12, which are written as alternating endings 1 to 5. It also sounds fine to continue the downtown pattern through bar 12 (with the same notes as bar 11), so feel free to play it that way also.

16
Rhythm Part with Sliding Ninths

17
No Guitar

Downtown Shuffle in F

Mike Williams

FIG. 3.5. "Downtown Shuffle in F"

Example 3.6 introduces a few variations of the sliding ninths, played as a second part along with the "Downtown Shuffle in F." This part features a mix of single-note and chord-based turnarounds in bars 11–12 of each chorus. Also note that the rhythm of the sliding ninths varies in several places in later choruses. Varying the rhythms for the sliding ninths opens up a wider range of sounds and textures, and that can help create energy and momentum as you interact with the soloist and other instruments on the bandstand.

Keep in mind that while laying down rhythm parts such as this, it's essential to stay in the pocket, and it always sounds best not to overplay. So, when in doubt, keep it simple. Play less, to leave plenty of room for the soloist and other instruments!

Listen to the "Downtown Shuffle in F" with the sliding ninths chords. Practice both parts. When you're ready, play along with the audio tracks. The arrangement is five choruses in length.

Downtown Shuffle in F
with Sliding Ninths

Mike Williams

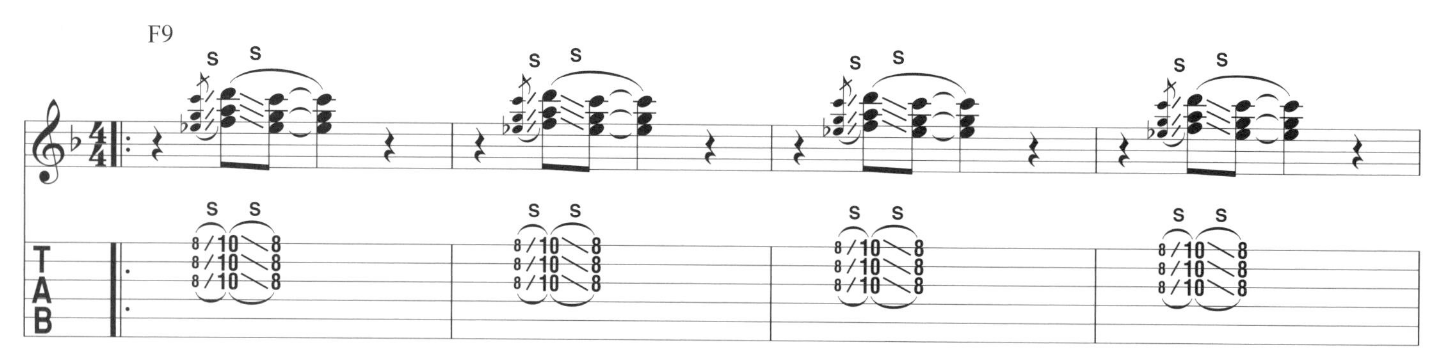

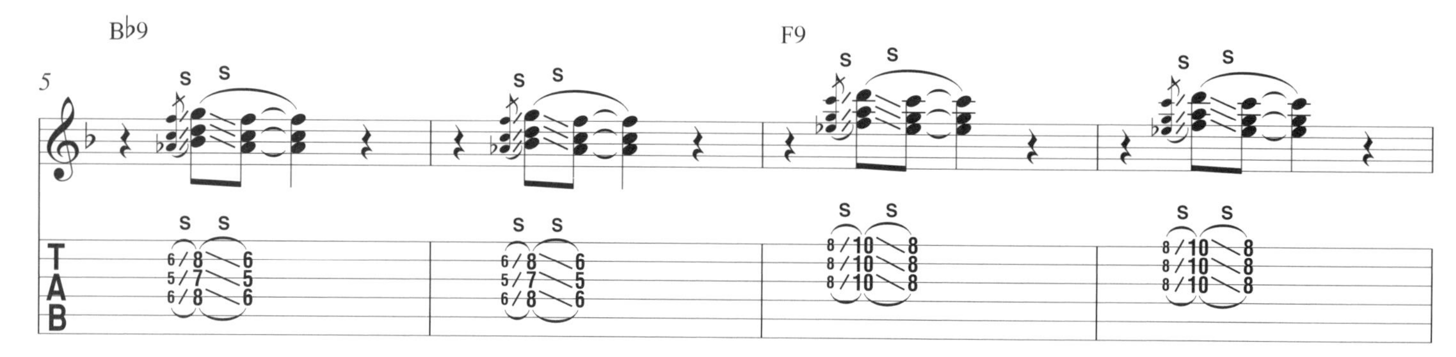

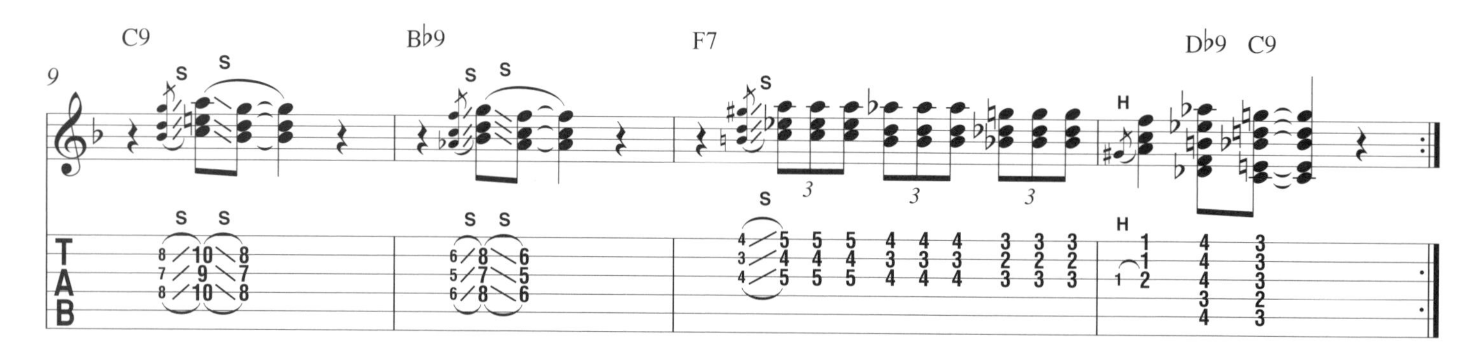

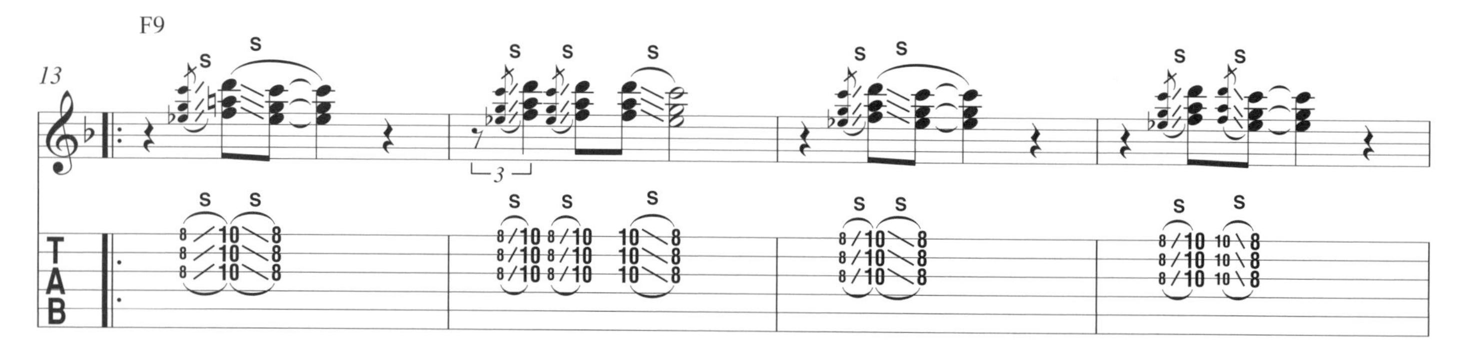

FIG. 3.6. "Downtown Shuffle in F" with Sliding Ninths. Five Choruses with Rhythm Section.

"DOWNTOWN SHUFFLE IN F" SOLO

Call and response is a powerful technique for solos, since it can help tie your phrases together like a lyric, or conversation through the 12-bar blues form. So, one goal for this solo was to play phrases that connect with each other by using call and response throughout all five choruses.

Having a loose mental "road map" for pacing and soloing activity can be helpful, as you begin a solo. Then, as the solo progresses, it's fine to take an alternative route—if that's where the creative process, or "muse," takes you. *Soloing activity* is essentially what, where, when, and how much takes place in the solo. Let's take a look at a few of the important factors and choices that come into play while soloing.

Range is a powerful technique to command, since it plays a huge role in shaping the intensity level and pacing of the solo. Phrases in the lowest range, or the deep/low speaking low voice, can create a sense of drama that makes the listener take notice. As a contrast to that, playing in the high range can generate extra intensity for the solo. Listen to some of your favorite blues and/or soul tracks; you'll notice that many of the great soloists and vocalists use range by gradually working their way up toward the top end of their instrument, to climax a solo.

One of my objectives for this solo over the "Downtown Shuffle in F" was to raise the intensity level as the track progressed, so I started the first chorus in the lower range and gradually worked my way into the higher register for the later choruses.

Here are a few other factors and options that shape the pacing and intensity level for solos:

sparse vs. crowded: Sparse phrases (few notes) can set up a relaxed or a very low-down blues feel. For a contrast to that, playing dense, crowded phrases tends to create an intense, on-edge feel.

sustained vs. short notes: Other choices for varying activity include playing sustained, long tones, or instead, spittin' out shorter, faster bursts or flurries of notes.

long vs. short phrases: Like sentences in a story or conversation, phrases can vary in length—from short to long, or anywhere in between.

breaths between phrases: The length and frequency of breaths/pauses between the phrases can also shape the feel and intensity level of a solo. A few well-timed pauses... can make the rhythmic pulse of the conversation a little less predictable. That can help your phrases project more, to have maximum impact on the listener. So as you solo, keep in mind that the silences between your phrases can have as much impact as the phrases themselves!

Mixing up the conversation with varied soloing activity can make for much more interesting phrasing, so experiment with that as you solo. Mix sparse phrases with faster-paced ideas. Mix long tones with quick bursts of notes. Vary the range of your solos; start low, and then work your way into the higher range, or vise versa. Relax your feel and phrases in places. Then, when you're feelin' it, take the intensity level through the roof.

Performance Tips

Chorus 1

As noted earlier, call and response plays an important roll in my phrasing on this solo, so listen for that throughout the track. Similar to a blues lyric over the 12-bar song form, the opening phrase (or call) is roughly four bars in length. Likewise, the reply (or response) starts just before bar 5 and continues through most of bar 8. To cap off the first chorus, the last phrase (or answer) starts just before bar 9 and continues through beat 2 of bar 12.

All five choruses of this solo are based on notes/phrases from the F blues scale (F A♭ B♭ B C E♭), combined with the 2/9, 3, and 6/13 (G A D) from the F pentatonic scale. The F blues and F pentatonic scales are notated in positions 13 and 12 in figure 3.7.

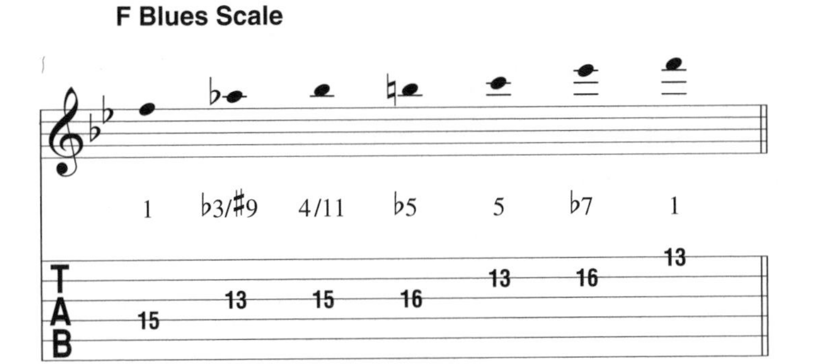

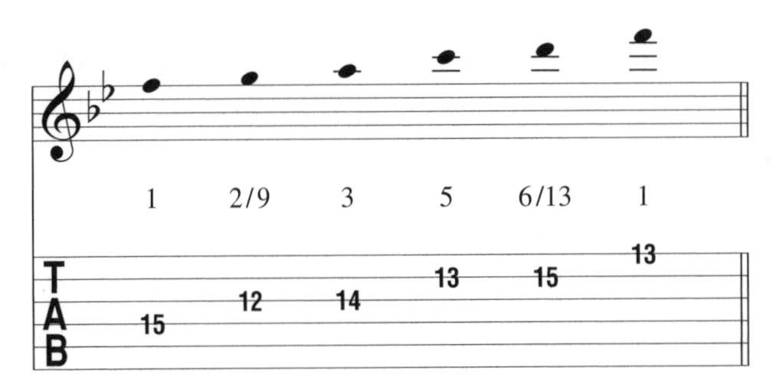

FIG. 3.7. F Blues and F Pentatonic Scale

NOTE: If you're not clear on the fingerings for the F blues and F pentatonic scales all along the fretboard, I recommend working through the scale exercises in chapter 12.

Bars 1 and 2, through beat 1 of bar 3, sit inside the F minor pentatonic scale fingering ("home base" box) in position 1. The rest of bar 3 (into beat 1 of bar 4) leans toward the brighter F pentatonic sound (from position 2), with a five-note phrase (notes C D F D F, analyzed as 5 6/13 root 6/13 root). Albert Collins leaned hard and often into the 6/13 with powerful results, and his influences made their way into that phrase.

Bars 5–7 tap into the F blues tonality, with repeated string bends from B♭ (4/11) into B (♭5). Moving into bar 8, the F pentatonic sound returns as a six-note phrase (notes C D F G D F) for a variation on the previous five-note phrase. Bars

9–10 return to mostly F blues, with a quick succession of string bends between notes B♭ and B (4/11 and ♭5). Note that the major pentatonic sound returns, with hammer-ons from A♭ (the ♭3) to A (the 3) on beat 4 of bar 10 and on beat 2 of bar 12.

Chorus 2

Again, the intention was to tie the three statements together like a blues lyric over the 12-bar form, so this chorus begins with more call and response over 4-bar phrases. Note that the opening statement begins before the "top" of the chorus. So, this chorus, along with choruses 3 to 5, all begin with phrases that play across the barline. That's common practice for blues, jazz, and rock solos, since it can help the phrases sound less compartmentalized within the song form. Playing across the barline can create forward momentum and make the phrases feel more natural, like the flow of a conversation, or lyric. Listen for it in solos by B.B. King, Freddy King, and others, and experiment with it for your own solos.

Bars 13 through 17 lie in the F blues scale in position 3, which is the next box up from the home base/position 1 fingering for the F blues scale. On beat 1 of bar 18, note the quick slide down the B string that lands back to the home position. To play it, fret the F (B string, 6th fret) with your third finger, then pull off to E♭ (first finger, 4th fret), and then immediately slide your first finger down to C (1st fret). That's a great-sounding technique for shifting down from one position to the other, and it's one of many B.B. King phrases that have been adopted throughout world of blues guitar. So, hats off to Mr. King for that!

Bar 20 revisits a very bluesy 3-note voicing, with notes B♭, C, and F that was first introduced in chorus 1, in beat 4 of bar 2. In both instances, it's played over F7 (I7). To finger it, play an F minor triad with a first-finger barre across the top three strings (in the 1st fret), and then hammer the A♭ note (G string, first fret) up two frets, into B♭. This chord also sounds great over the B♭7 (IV7) and C7 (V7) chords, so experiment with it!

Bars 21 and 22 feature a classic triplet-based riff that sets up a very cool "3-against-4" feel. I first learned this phrase from blues/jazz great Billy Butler's landmark guitar part on "Honky Tonk," one of his many hits with Bill Doggett. It lays in position 1, and to play it, fret the F (D string, 3rd fret) with the third finger, then alternate that (F) between dyads (2-note chords) A♭ and C, and then B♭ and D. Adding the note F to both dyads creates alternating F minor and B♭ major triad sounds. The pattern repeats every four notes, and it's played with a strong triplet feel; that's what creates the strong 3-against-4 push/pull feel. This vintage lick has been assimilated into today's blues vocabulary by greats such as Jimmy Vaughan, Stevie Ray Vaughan, Robert Cray, Duke Robillard, and others. If you're not familiar with Billy Butler, you should be—so listen and learn from his innovative parts on Bill Doggett's tracks such as "Honky Tonk" and "Big Boy."

While on the subject of influences, the very next phrase in bar 22 (into beat 1 of bar 23) taps into another major influence over the years, Freddy King. Similar phrases can be heard in King's turnarounds and fills on tracks such as "Tore Down," "Hide Away," and "Side Tracked."

Chorus 3

The first four bars of this chorus were played with mostly tremolo picking, which is essentially playing the same note repeatedly with alternate, down/up/down/up picking at a high rate of speed. The phrase in bars 27 and 28 climbs up the first string with tremolo picking up chord tones C, E♭, and F (5, ♭7, and root). Tremolo picking can generate intensity for your solos, and it's not too difficult to get a handle on.... Those are two good reasons to work it into your playing.

Another technique that can add color, stylistic continuity, and, at times, humor to a solo is to reference or restate part of a well-known melody or solo. That's referred to as a "quote," and in bar 29, I quoted the classic "Blues in the Night," by playing the song's opening melody (with lyrics), "My mamma done tol' me...."

Freddy King's influences reappear throughout the rest of the third chorus, such as in bar 32 with the repeated bends, pre-bends, and release-bends on the B string, between notes E♭ and F, and E and F. This bend/release/bend is one of Freddy King's many unique and "should-have-been patented" licks. To play it, bend up a whole step (e.g., from E♭ to F), then release ("drop") the bend a half step from F to E, and then bend it back up to F. The release into the major 7 (E) creates tension against the F7 chord, so it really catches your ear. On some solos, King played this bend/release/bend lick repeatedly, and he killed it every time by playing it with tons of intensity and conviction—like everything that he played. Keep Freddy King in mind as an inspiration, when you're bending strings. Play them with as much accuracy and conviction as you can tap into!

Choruses 4 and 5

Chorus 4 begins with more call/response. In addition to featuring three 4-bar phrases over the 12-bar form, it's played here in smaller subdivisions also. Listen again to the first four bars, and notice the smaller subset of call/response. Bar 37 is a statement (call), bar 38 is a response, and then bars 39 and 40 answer that.

Bars 37 through 41 sit in the 15th position F blues scale. That's the same fingering as chorus 2, but twelve frets (one octave) higher. Lots o' string bends here (once again), from the B♭ (4) to B (♭5) and C (5). Also note the first finger bend from A♭ (♭3) to A (3) on beat 3 of bar 38.

In bars 44 and 45, Billy Butler's powerful 3-against-4 phrase returns. This time, it's played one octave (twelve frets) higher. The momentum from that phrase continues for the rest of the chorus (bars 45–48), with repeated slides into notes C and E♭. Both notes are chord tones (5 and ♭7) of F7, but they sound great over the B♭7 in bar 46 also. This is another of those licks that fits like a glove over the I7, IV, or V7, so work it into your solos over the blues!

Chorus 5 starts on the home-base fingering for F blues in position 13, with an opening “call” on the triplet right before bar 49. The “response” in bar 50 continues into bar 52, with a combination of quarter- and eighth-note triplets. Note the repeated high F minor triad (notes A♭, F, C) played on the first and second strings, which creates an F7(♯9) sound. Beat 3 of bar 52 shifts back up to position 15, with more tremolo picking and repeated slides in the high F (B string, 18th fret). That’s followed by more repeated whole-step bends from B♭ to C, mixed with other notes from F blues. Finally, for the last four bars, I returned to the position 13 (home base) fingering, to close out the solo.

Phrasing is a lifelong study for each of us, so listen actively to solos by your favorite players. Really pay attention to their phrasing. Note their range and activity. Note the length and frequency of breaths between their phrases. Note the rise and fall of the intensity level, and the reasons for it. Then take those concepts into the practice room for months and beyond, to adapt and apply them to your own solos.

Listen and practice along with the solo over the “Downtown Shuffle in F” in figure 3.8. When you’re ready, play along with the audio.

18
Full Band

16
Rhythm Part with Sliding Ninths

Downtown Shuffle in F

Solo

Mike Williams

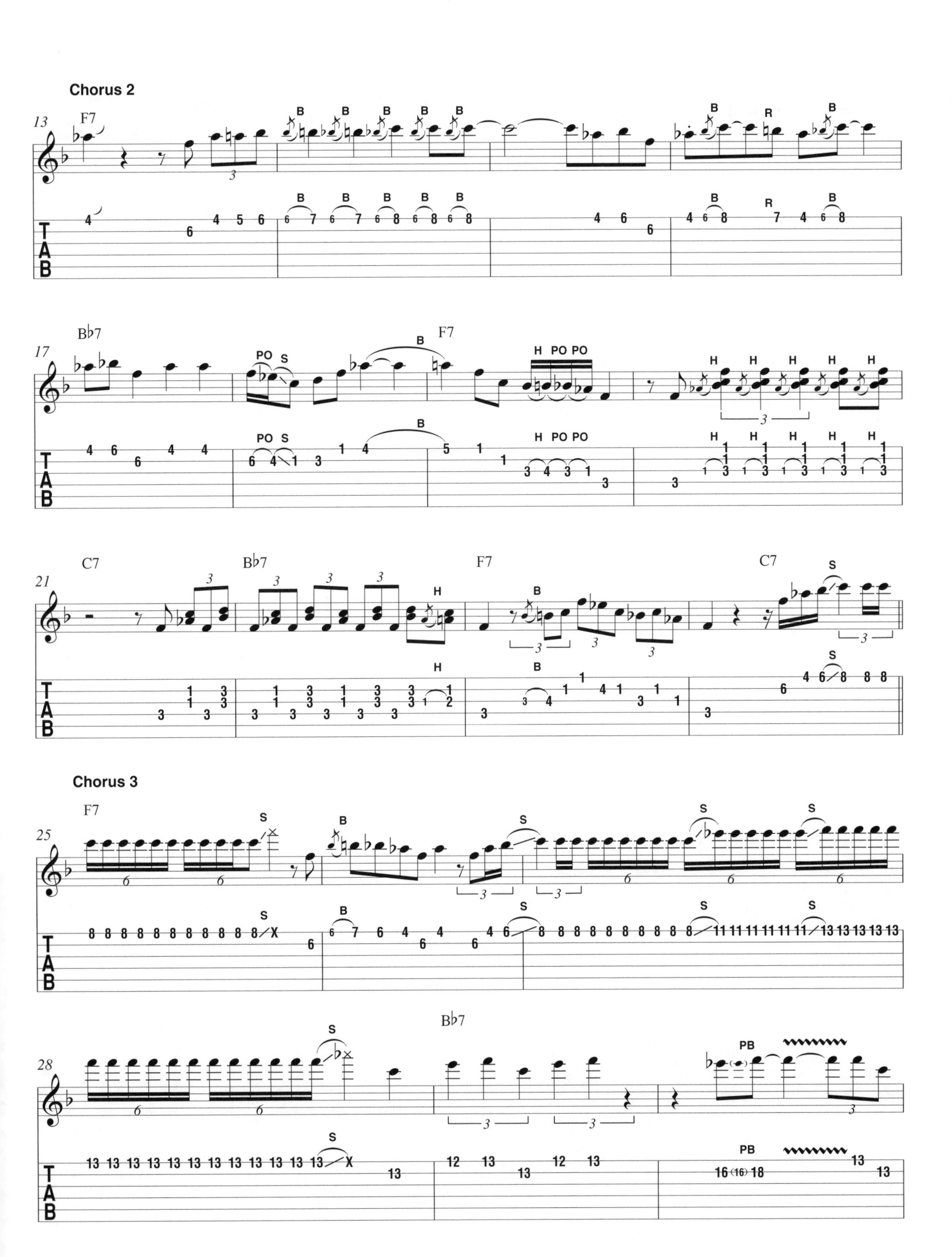
Chorus 2
F7
Bb7
F7
C7
Bb7
F7
C7
Chorus 3
F7
Bb7

F7
C7
Bb7
F7
C7
Chorus 4
F7
8va
(8va)
Bb7
loco
F7
C7

FIG. 3.8. "Downtown Shuffle in F" Solo

CHAPTER 4

Funky Blues in D: "Funky Albert"

In this chapter, we'll work through a few rhythm techniques over a funky blues in D. "Funky Albert" (example 4.1) combines straight-eighth (i.e., even-eighth) strums with muted strums (or "scratches"), along with a couple of variations of the sliding ninth chords, from chapter 3.

Two often-imitated players that have had a monumental impact on funk/soul guitar over the past several decades are Jimmy Nolen and Steve Cropper. Nolen was James Brown's longtime guitarist and played on his landmark tracks, such as "Cold Sweat," "I've Got You (I Feel Good)," and "Papa's Got a Brand New Bag." Steve Cropper created a multitude of classic guitar parts and hooks, and he produced hit after hit as a member of Stax Records' house band, Booker T. & the M.G.'s. Cropper has enjoyed a long and productive career of more than fifty years.

Robert Cray has also recorded dozens of creative and inspiring tracks in the soul/blues style over the past few decades. So, the rhythm guitar part for "Funky Albert" was inspired and influenced (directly or indirectly) by Jimmy Nolen, Steve Cropper, and Robert Cray.

Performance Tips

All five choruses of "Funky Albert" are based on a 2-bar rhythmic figure that's first presented in bars 1 and 2. That figure repeats throughout the progression, until the turnaround in bar 11. The strumming pattern is mostly based on eighth-note rhythms that alternate as down/up/down/up (etc.) strums. Note that down-strums are played on downbeats, and up-strums are played on the upbeats. That pattern continues throughout all five choruses.

Bar 1 of each 4-bar phrase begins with a rest or a muted/percussive strum on beat 1, since for funk styles such as this, the "pocket" on beat 1 is generally played/owned by the bass. (We'll let the bass have beat 1, and the groove will sound better because of that!) Beat 2 is another story, though; that typically belongs to the guitar and drums—and possibly, other instruments, such as keyboards or horns. The D7 chord is played as a dotted-eighth/sixteenth rhythm, with chords on 2 and on the last sixteenth of beat 2—again, strummed as a downstroke followed by an upstroke. Note that the D7 chord on beat 2 intentionally locks in with the backbeats. Guitar parts frequently accent and reinforce the backbeats with powerful chord hits and/or percussive strums, since beats 2 and 4 are essential rhythmic elements for styles such as blues, funk, and jazz. Backbeats will be discussed in much greater detail in chapter 11.

Instead of playing more standard V7 IV I7 harmony in bars 8 to 12, this progression instead uses B♭9 (analyzed as ♯V7 or ♭VI7) and C9 (♭VII7) to resolve home to D9.

The punchy top-four-strings fingering for the B♭9, C9, and D9 chords throughout the track is the same as Freddy King's powerful E9 break (stop) chord, from the fifth chorus of his instrumental hit, "Hide Away." That's essential listening and repertoire for every electric blues guitarist, so take a listen to it, and witness more of the power and punch of that ninth-chord voicing!

Listen and practice along with "Funky Albert." When you're ready, play along with the audio.

19
Rhythm Part

20
No Guitar

Funky Albert

Mike Williams

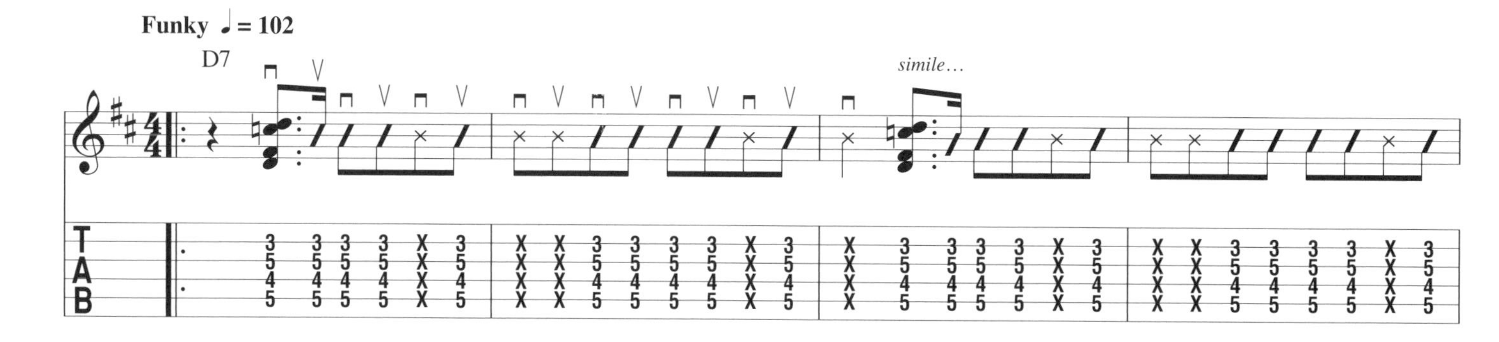

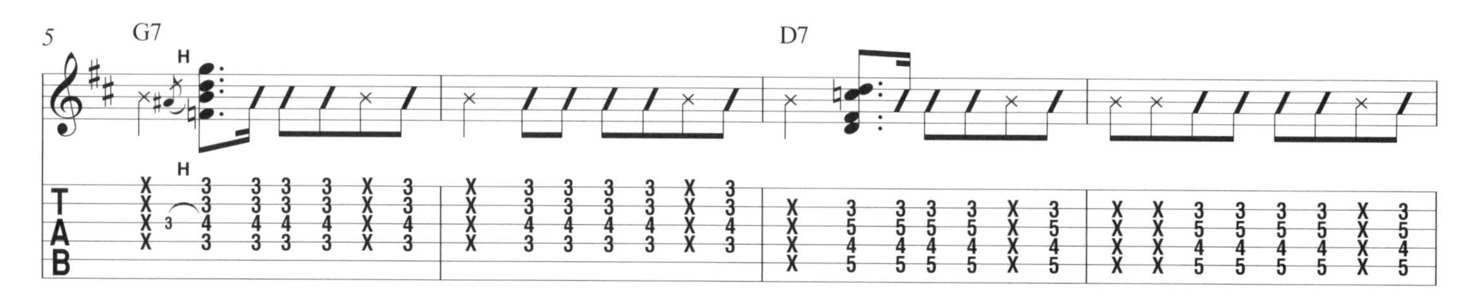

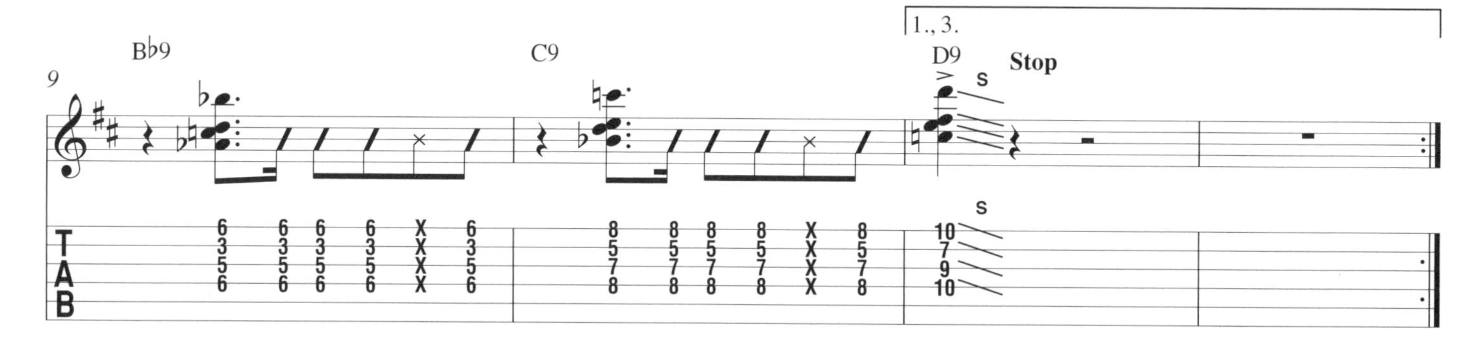

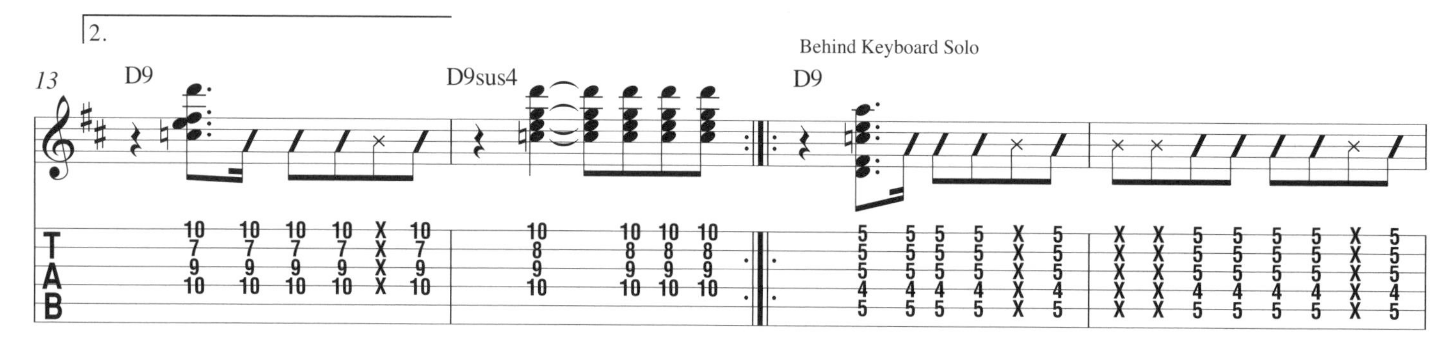

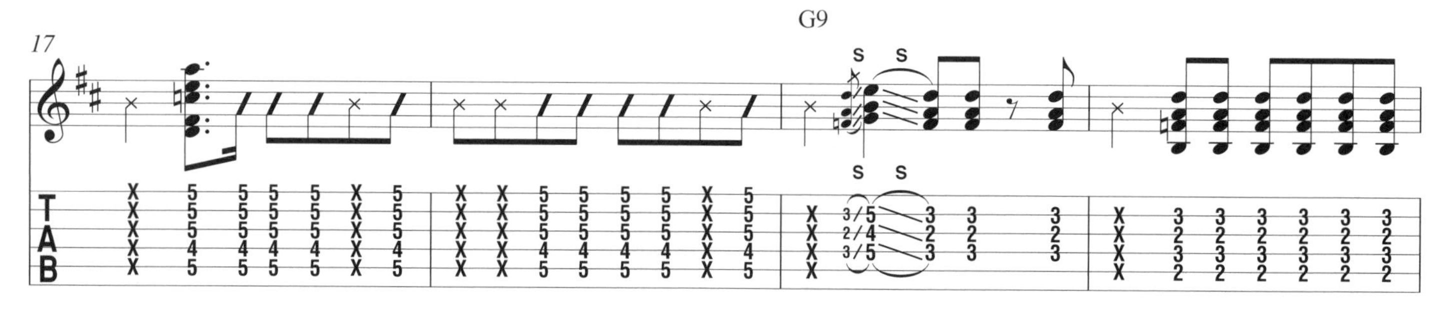

FIG. 4.1. "Funky Albert"

FUNKY EIGHTH-NOTE FEEL: MIXING SCRATCHES AND CHORDS

The following exercises will help you to fine-tune your feel and skills for mixing even-eighth strums with funky/muted strums.

In figure 4.2, play the pattern in each measure four times. Play through the entire page with a strict, alternating down/up/down/up... strumming pattern. Down-strums are played on downbeats, and up-strums are played on upbeats. The constant eighth note subdivisions and beats in each bar are counted: 1 and 2 and 3 and 4 and. The entire exercise is demonstrated/performed along with a backbeat click on 2 and 4. Focus on locking in with the backbeats as you practice this exercise!

Strive to produce a consistent and even volume, attack, and feel from every chord, and/or muted strum (or "scratch") in this exercise. Focus on matching the sound and feel of the recording.

Pattern 1: Begin with a D7 chord, strummed as even eighth notes.

Pattern 2: Scratch across the muted strings. Play this with a very relaxed arm and wrist. (Again, use strict alternating down/up/down/up eighth-note strums throughout the entire exercise.)

Pattern 3: Accent beat 1 (only) by releasing the mute, to let the D7 chord sound through, and continue constant eighth note scratches for the remainder of the bar.

Pattern 4: Accent "&" of 1 only by releasing the mute. Continue constant eighth note scratches for the remainder of the bar.

Patterns 5 to 10: Each displaces the D7 chord back further by an eighth note.

If left-hand muting is new to you, this exercise may be a challenge, but keep working at it until you're comfortable with it. This can help you play with a funky and consistent eighth-note feel, mixing chords and scratches, and accenting various subdivisions within each beat. So, mess with it!

Listen and practice along with the "Funky Eighth-Note Exercise" below. When you're ready, play along with the audio.

Funky Eighth-Note Feel Exercise

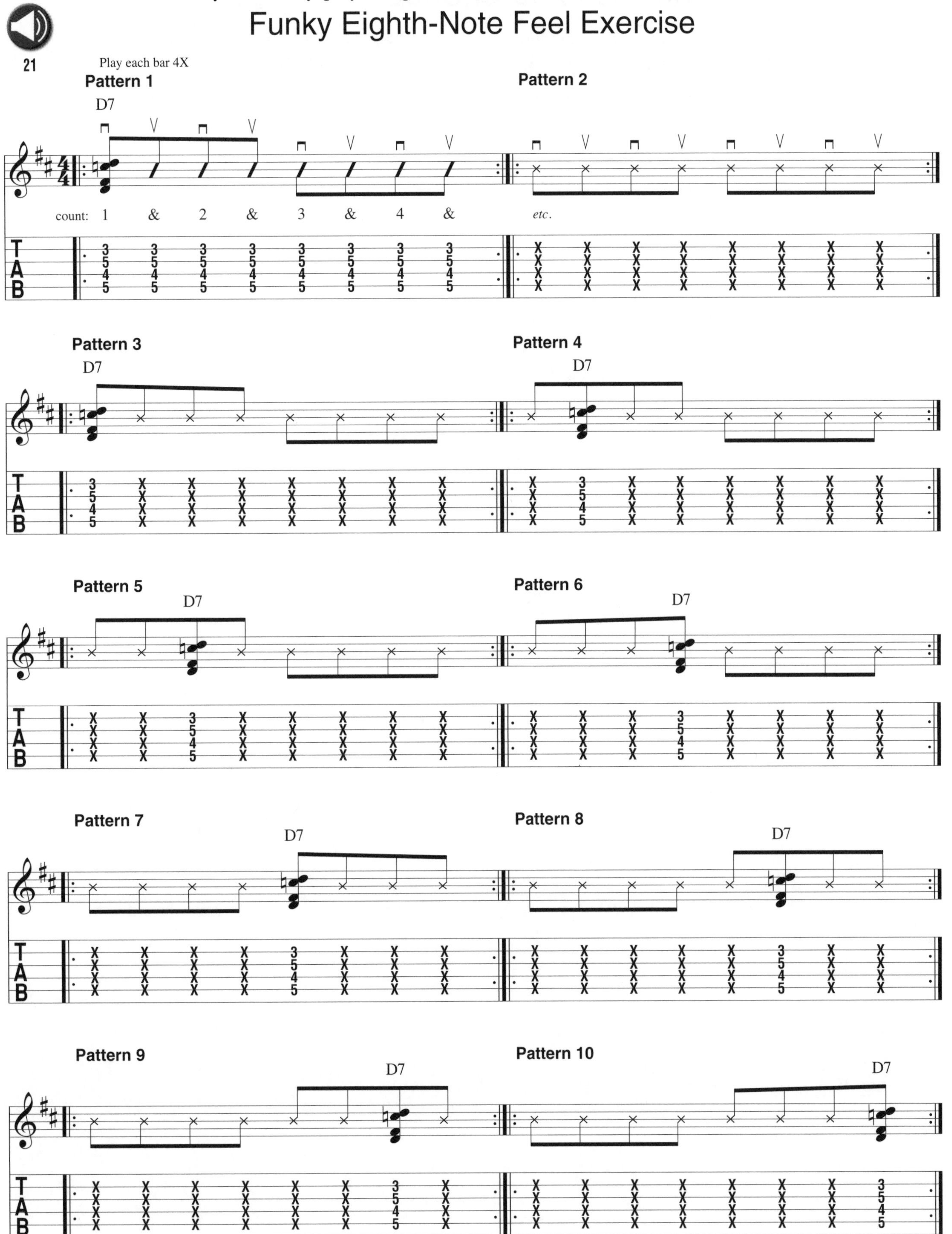

FIG. 4.2. Funky Eighth-Note Exercise

FUNKY SIXTEENTH-NOTE FEEL: MIXING SCRATCHES AND CHORDS

This next exercise is great for loosening up your right (picking) hand and locking way down in the pocket with the funky sixteenth-note feel of the drums. That's essential for rhythm parts such as "Funky Albert." This study is similar to the previous one, only it's based on sixteenth- instead of eighth-note patterns.

To make this funky style groove as much as possible, keep your right hand totally relaxed as you strum through the chords and/or muted scratches. Play the entire exercise with alternating down/up/down/up... sixteenth-note strums. The constant sixteenth-note subdivisions and beats in each bar are counted like this: 1e&a 2e&a 3e&a 4e&a ("ee and a").

Play each pattern four times. Once again, focus on locking in with the back-beats on 2 and 4 as you practice with the recording.

Pattern 1: Begins with a D9 chord, strummed as even sixteenth notes.

Pattern 2: Scratch across the muted strings with constant sixteenth notes. Remember to keep your strumming arm and wrist totally relaxed.

Pattern 3: Accent downbeats 1, 2, 3, 4 only, by releasing the mute to let the D9 chord sound through. Continue constant sixteenth-note scratches for the remainder of the bar.

Pattern 4: Accent "e" of each beat only, by releasing the mute. Continue constant sixteenth note scratches...

Patterns 5 to 6: Both displace the D7 chord back further by one sixteenth note.

This exercise teaches you how to keep those funky sixteenth note chords and scratches going nonstop, while you accent various subdivisions (1, e, &, a) within each beat.

Listen and practice along with the "Funky Sixteenth-Note Exercise." When you're ready, play along with the audio.

22

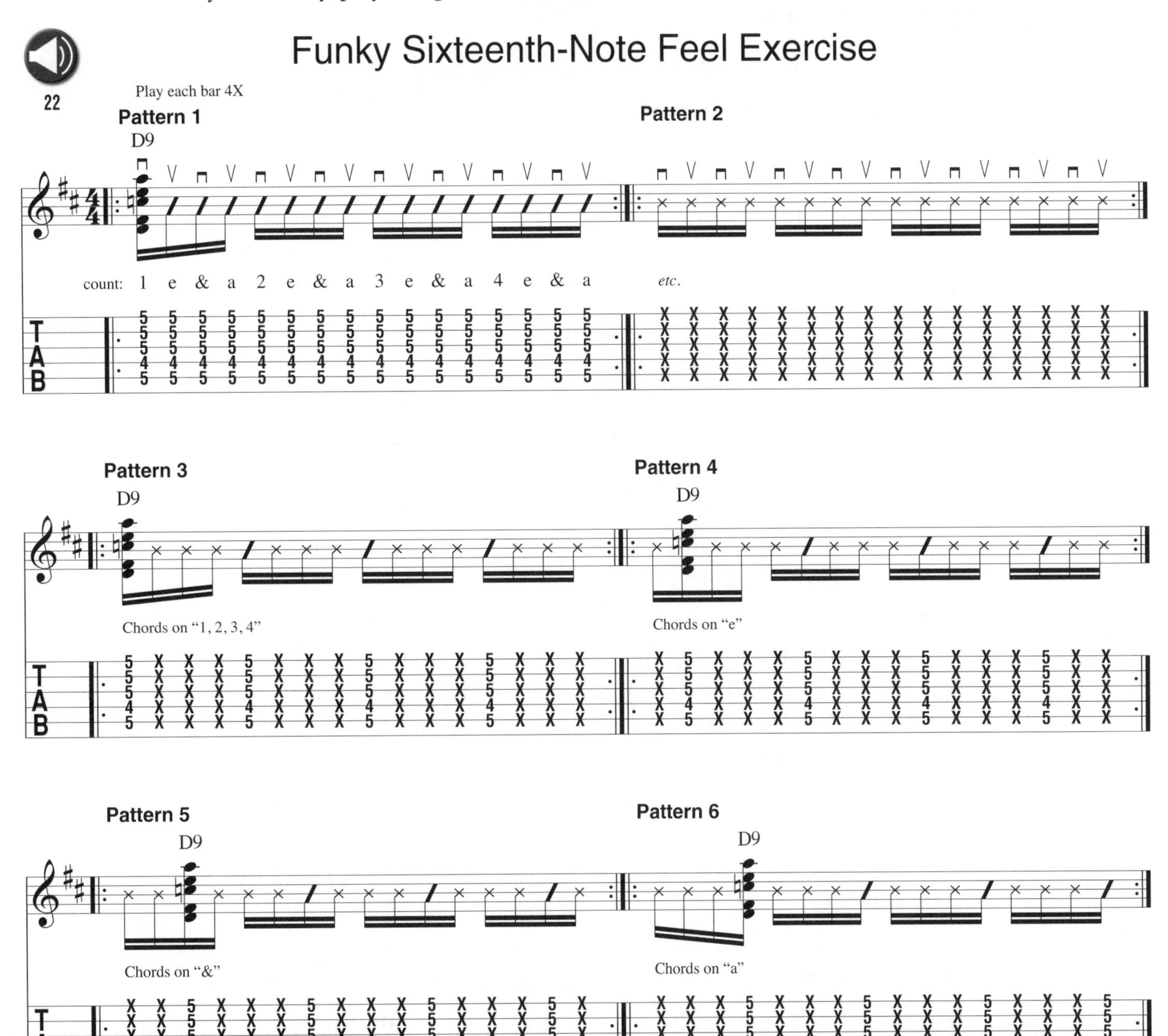

FIG. 4.3. Funky Sixteenth-Note Exercise

"FUNKY ALBERT" SOLO

Performance Tips

Albert Collins' unique soloing style has inspired me for decades, so one of my objectives for this project was to tap into at least a portion of his intensity, vocabulary, and influences, to mix with my own approach over this progression. Collins, a.k.a. "the Master of the Telecaster" and "the Iceman," was also known for tearing into shuffles, funk grooves, and slow blues solos with equal abandon. So, to mix things up a bit, "Funky Albert" was written and performed in the funk style, as the name implies. As mentioned earlier, instead of the standard V7 IV7 I7 chords for bars 9–12, this progression plays ♭VI7 (B♭9) in bar 9 and ♭VII7 (C9) in bar 10, which leads "home" to the I7 (D9) for bars 11 and 12.

"Funky Albert" is in D, the same key as Collins's classic instrumental "Frosty," since my intention was to adapt and reuse his phrasing concepts and vocabulary in my own way. Collins's solo on "Frosty" is chock full of funky licks, with a stinging mix of phrases based in the D blues and D pentatonic scales, so if you're not familiar with it already, "Frosty" is highly recommended listening. ("Frosty" is transcribed and analyzed in detail in my book, *Berklee Blues Guitar Songbook*).

Albert Collins's phrasing and feel is uniquely original, and that's due (at least, in part) to the fact that he played a nonstandard, open F minor chord. His open strings sounded, bottom to top, as notes F C F A♭ C F. Collins also played with a capo, which he moved up and down the neck, accordingly. His capo was parked at the 9th fret for "Frosty," so his open strings sounded as an open D minor chord. Many of "the Iceman's" signature licks from "Frosty" lean *hard* into the note B (6/13 of D pentatonic), combined with notes/phrases from the D blues scale.

The D blues and D pentatonic scales are notated in positions 9 and 10 in figure 4.4. **NOTE:** If you're unclear on how to combine notes from both fingerings up and down the fretboard, I recommend working through the exercises in chapter 12.

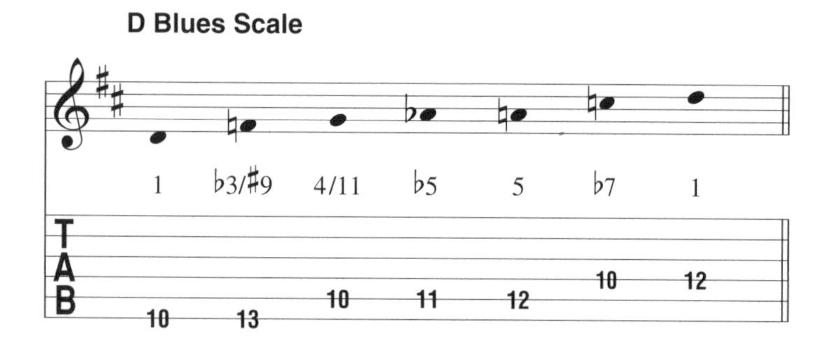

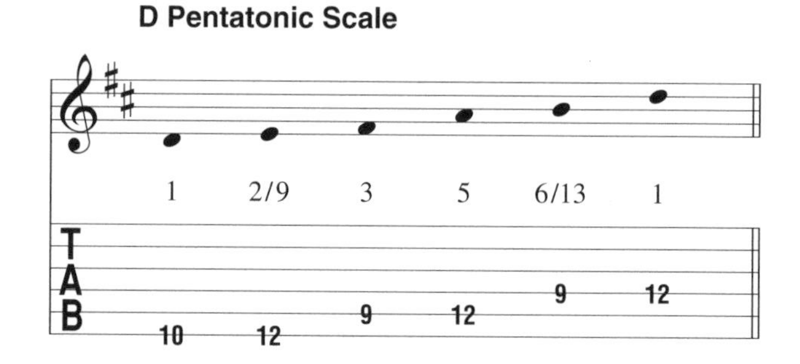

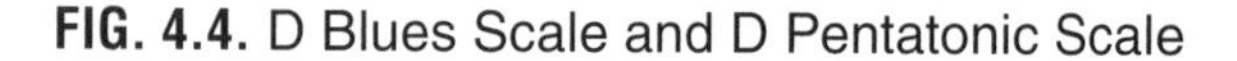

FIG. 4.4. D Blues Scale and D Pentatonic Scale

About the Solo

The opening phrase (or "call") in bars 1–3 of chorus 1 sits right on top of the D blues scale in position 10. I often refer to this popular blues box as the "world's favorite fingering," or "home base." Like much of the solo that follows, this phrase mixes sixteenth notes with other rhythms.

Bar 4 answers the opening call with a phrase that combines D pentatonic and D blues (as noted above). It begins in position 7 and taps into Collins's classic vocabulary and influences, with sixteenth notes that alternate between D (the root) and B (6/13) from D pentatonic. Note the shift to D blues on the "and" of beat 4, as the first finger slides up from the note D (G string, 7th fret) to F (G string, 10th fret). Bar 5 clearly outlines the IV7 with chord tones B and F (the 3 and ♭7 of G7). Immediately following that are sixteenth-note triplets on beat 2 that scurry down the D blues scale, to land on the note F, on beat 3. After a quick breath, bar 6 is approached with sixteenth notes A B D B, again leaning into the brighter D pentatonic sound. Beats 3 and 4 of bar 6 create G7 (IV7) chord sound, and continue the D pentatonic sound at the same time, with notes B and D, which are played together on the top two strings. Beat 1 of bar 7 starts with the same notes (B and D) now played over D7, followed by a faster/more crowded D blues lick that's played as *quintuplets* (groups of five) on beats 2 and 3, with sixteenth-note triplets on beat 4, again scurrying down the D blues scale. This phrase lands/resolves on note F♯ (the 3) from D pentatonic.

Bars 8 through 10 lie in position 13, the next box up the neck from the 10th position blues scale. This fingering for the D blues scale is another region on the neck that Collins frequented with powerful results during his solo on "Frosty."

The high D notes in bars 8 and 9 are played with the third finger on the B string, 15th fret, and the slightly bent (or "tweaked") F note in bar 9 is played with the first finger on the high E string (13th fret). Bar 10 is fingered as whole-step bends from G (third finger, 15th fret) to A (17th fret). The band stops on beat 1 of bar 11 and stays out for the last two bars, so this first chorus features a guitar fill through bars 11 and 12. With the exception of the second note, B (the 6/13), this fill is comprised entirely of notes from the D blues scale in position 10. This first chorus sets the tone for choruses 2 and 3, with a big mix of D blues and D pentatonic, played with as much intensity as possible.

Albert Collins' dead-on string bends, vibrato, and phrasing consistently broke through the ice with maximum intensity, so remember to take on that attitude when playing in his style. I took my best shot at steppin' out onto the Iceman's frozen tundra for this solo, so I hope you enjoy playing it. (And don't forget your earmuffs and gloves when you leave the practice room... 'cause it's *cold* out there!)

Listen and practice along with solo to "Funky Albert." When you're ready, play along with the audio. **Note:** Both versions feature an organ solo in choruses 4 and 5. The full band version ends with one more chorus of guitar solo that's not written out here.

23 Full Band
19 Rhythm Part

Funky Albert

Solo

Mike Williams

Chorus 2
D7
G7

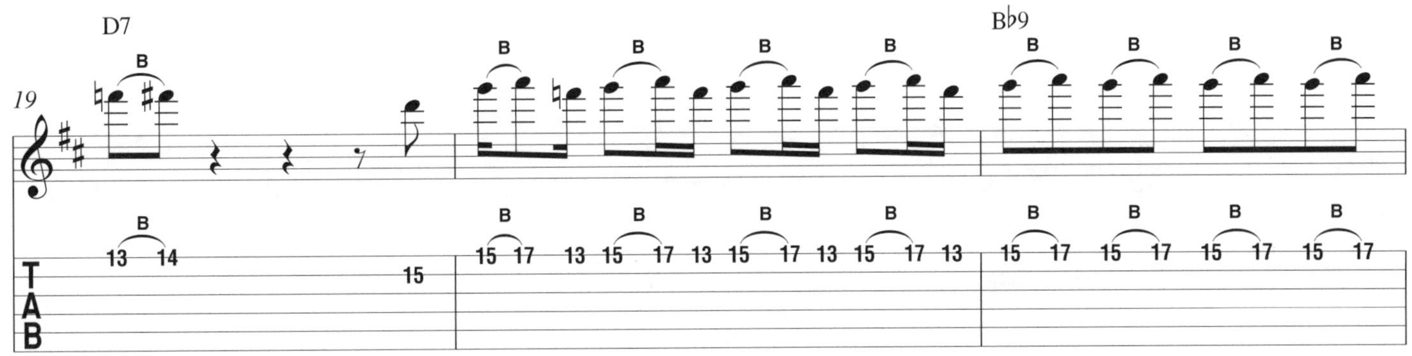
D7
B♭9

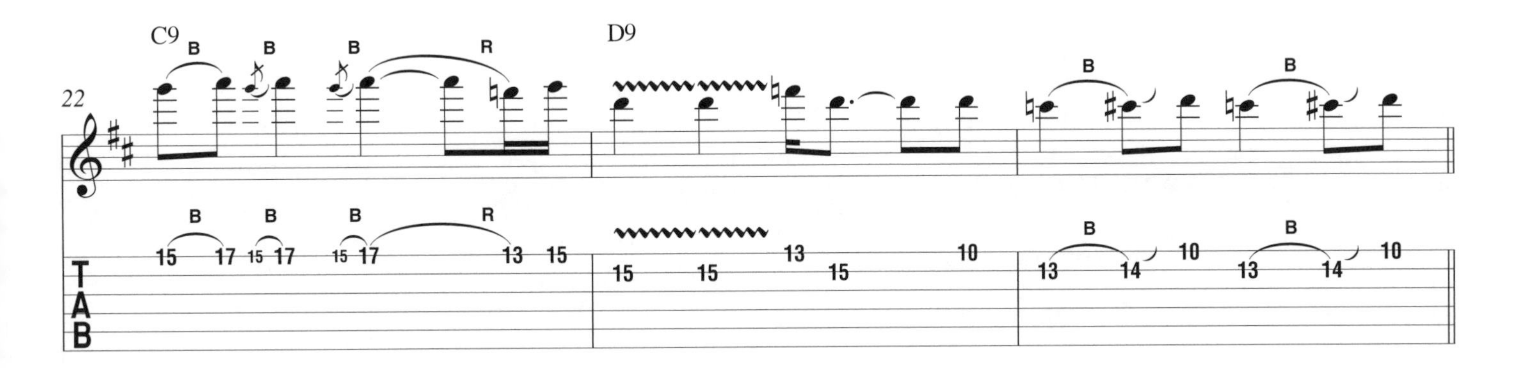
C9
D9

Chorus 3

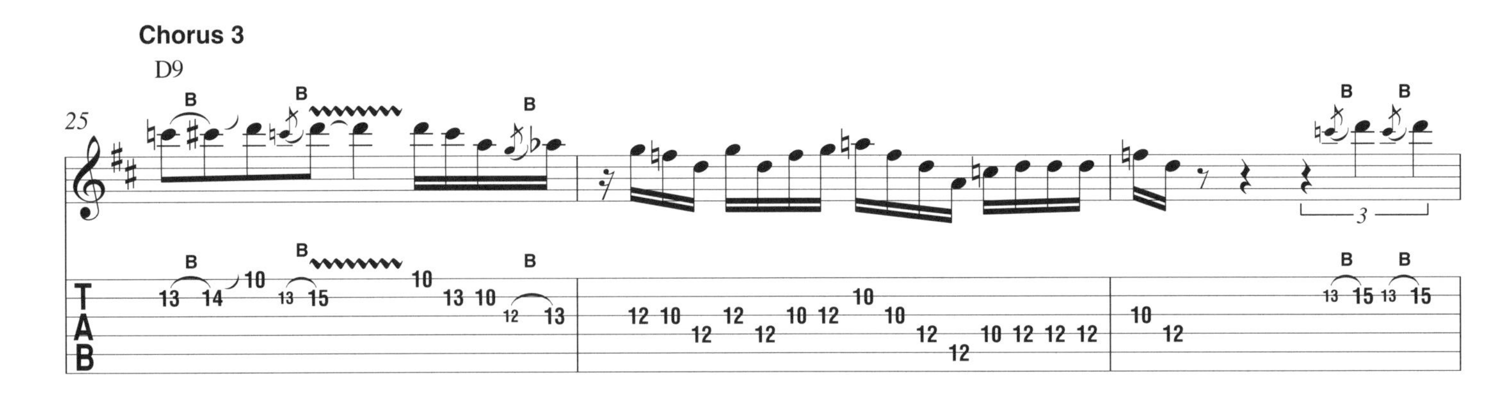
D9
25
B
B
B
B
B
3
T
A
B

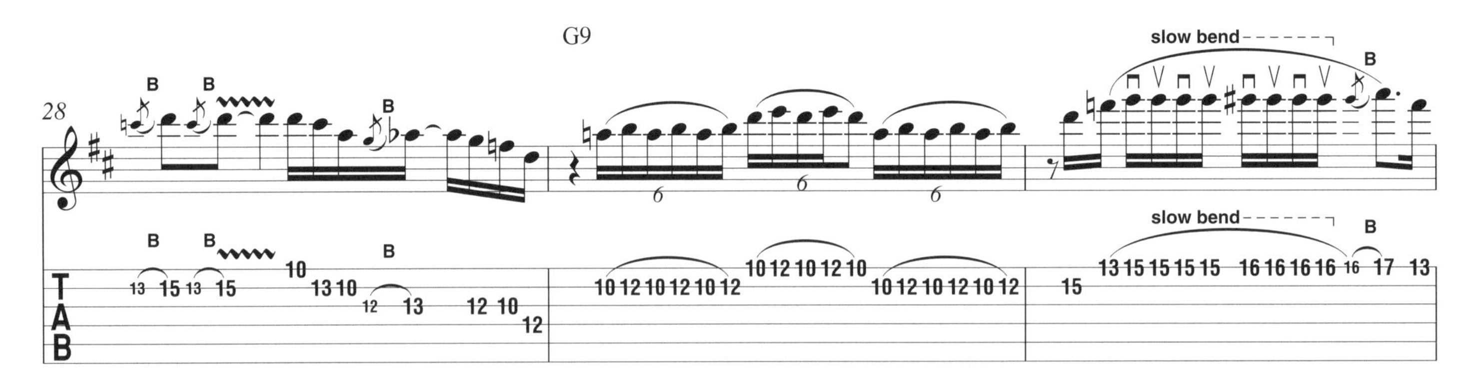
G9
slow bend
28
B
B
B
6
6
6
T
A
B

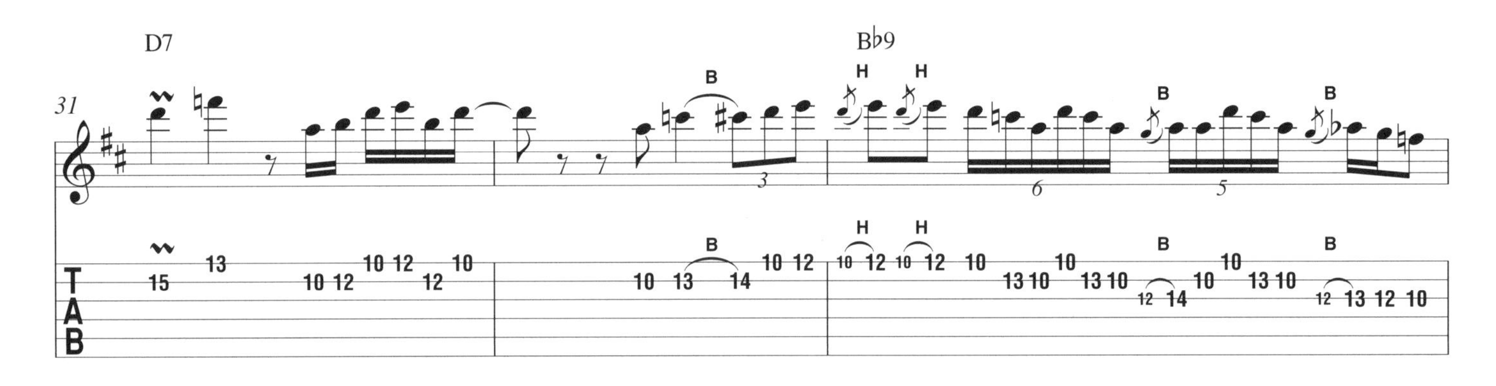
D7
B♭9
31
H
H
B
B
B
3
6
5
T
A
B

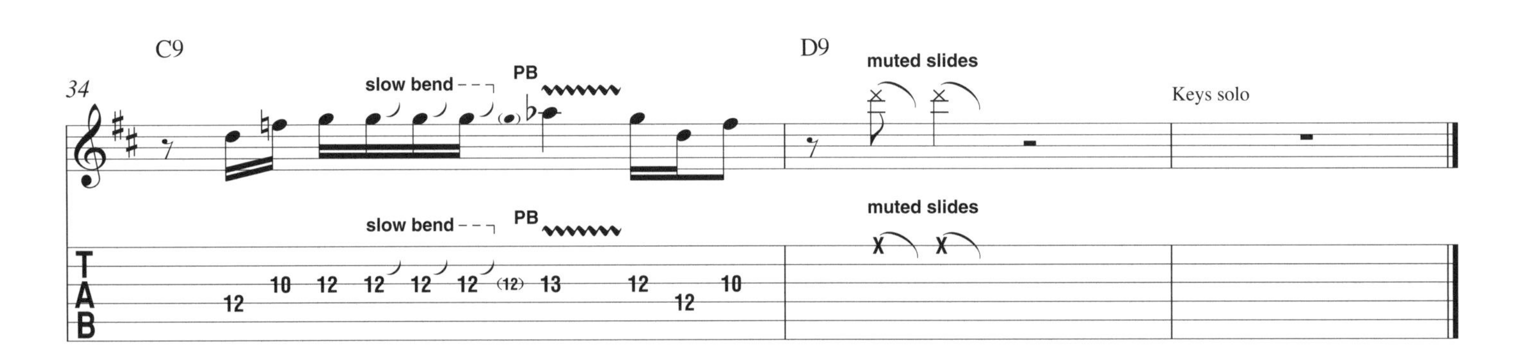
C9
D9
34
slow bend
PB
muted slides
Keys solo
T
A
B

CHAPTER 5

Fast Shuffle in E: "Like a Rocket"

In this chapter, you'll lay down a low-end single-note part, along with a second chord-based rhythm part over a rockin' shuffle in E. "Like a Rocket" is created in the style of Jackie Brenston's "Rocket 88." His original track cruised along at a medium tempo, but it sounds great at faster/higher–octane tempos also; that's how it's been recorded and performed for years by the great harp player, James Cotton.

Performance Tips

The low-end part for "Like a Rocket" (figure 5.1) is played as nonstop eighth notes, and position 2 is a great place to finger the entire 12-bar line. Most of the notes are double picked in a 1-bar pattern (root root, ♭3 3, 5 5, 6 5) that repeats through the I7 and IV7 chords in bars 1 through 8. For the E7 chord, the notes are E E, G G♯, B B C♯ B on strings 6 and 5, and for the A7 chord, the pattern is transposed, played with the same fingering on strings 5 and 4. Bars 9–12 of Brenston's "Rocket 88" featured a V7 IV7 I7 turnaround, but "Like a Rocket" has a II–7 V7 I7 (F♯–7 B7 E7) turnaround instead. Note that the A's on bar 9, beat 3 and bar 10, beat 2 can also be fingered on the fifth fret of the low E string.

Play this part with an aggressive, punchy, and rock-solid picking attack, and emphasize all upbeats as much as the downbeats. Practice this line slower at first, to really get inside the feel for accenting all of the downbeats *and* upbeats with as much intensity and "attitude" as possible. Listen and practice along with the low-end part for "Like a Rocket."

When you're ready, play along with the audio.

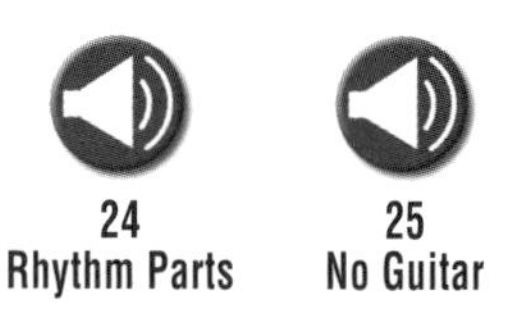

Like a Rocket

Mike Williams

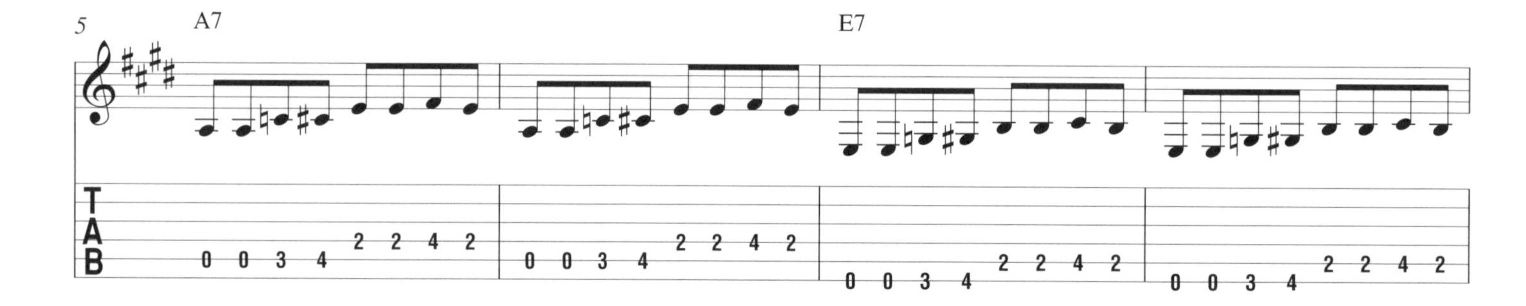

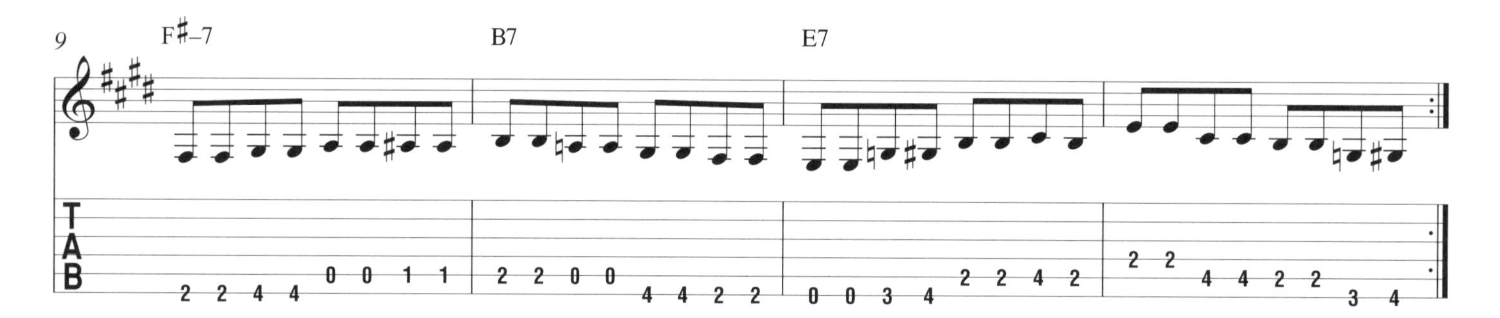

FIG. 5.1. "Like a Rocket"

"LIKE A ROCKET" RHYTHM PART 2

Here are a few techniques for playing the chord changes, for a second rhythm part to "Like a Rocket."

For rhythm parts in this style and tempo, the goal is to provide support and momentum behind the vocal parts and solos, and stay out of the way of the other instruments at the same time. Riff-based comp rhythms are perfect for this faster tempo, so all nine choruses of this rhythm part were played in that style.

A *riff* is a musical phrase that gets repeated throughout the 12-bar chorus, or whatever the song form. Thousands of songs in jazz have been derived from riffs, including "C-Jam Blues," "Bag's Groove," "Lester Leaps In, " and "Sonnymoon for Two," to name a few. Riffs also have their place in rock history.

Jack Bruce/Cream's "Sunshine of Your Love" and "Black Dog," by Led Zeppelin, are two classics that are based on riffs. Blues and R&B standards, such as "Night Train," and "Green Onions," are also built from riffs, as is T-Bone Walker's intro chorus's hook to his classic "T-Bone Shuffle." All three choruses of the melody/head to Albert Collins's "Don't Lose Your Cool" are riffs. (Check out his stellar performance of that, from his record *Truckin'*.)

Riffs can create a ton of momentum and energy, whether played as a melodic or chord-based background figure behind solos, so they're fun to play on the bandstand. Whenever I'm playing with horn, and/or keyboard players, I look forward to jumpin' in on whatever riffs they come up with on the spot.

To hear how much musical momentum that riffs can create, seek out Eddie "Cleanhead" Vinson's vintage recording of "Kidney Stew." The intro chorus hook and background parts behind Vinson's soulful vocals and alto solo were performed by Count Basie's horn section—and those guys knew how to play the blues.

Next listen to the rhythm part to "Like a Rocket" (figure 5.2), and notice how the rhythm and top (melody) note of the chords fit together, like simple lyrics through the 12-bar form. For example, in chorus 1, the rhythmic figure that's played as E9 chords in bars 1–3 is answered (as a rhythmic variation) over the A9 and E9 chords in bars 5–8, and then as another variation over the chords in bars 9–12, to wrap up the chorus. While I wasn't trying to recreate *exactly* the same rhythmic figure from line to line, the rhythms and top notes of the chords connect—like a riff, or simple lyric-through the song form.

Another term that applies to rhythm parts in this tempo and style is "comping," which means to accompany and complement the vocal part or solo. Comping is generally associated with jazz, but similar jazz-influenced rhythms and chord voicings sound right at home on this fast shuffle, as well. A comping pattern is often a 1- or 2-bar rhythmic figure that repeats. I played comping ("comp") patterns throughout all nine choruses, such as the rhythm in chorus 1, bars 1–2 over the E9 (I7). That rhythm was repeated in bars 5 and 6, over the A9 (IV7), etc.

Performance Tips

To demonstrate a wide range of sounds and textures behind the solo, I intentionally moved through various ranges, from chorus to chorus, as the track progressed. My roadmap for shaping this nine-chorus rhythm part—and the textures and momentum behind the solo—was to start in the higher register for the first two choruses, then go down low, and gradually work my way back up into the higher register as the track progressed. Chords within each chorus were generally played in a similar range, and often *voice-led*, which means to create a smooth transition from one chord to the next, with whole and half step motion and common tones, when possible.

Choruses 1 and 2

Choruses 1 and 2 revisit several chords from previous chapters, including the E9, Freddy King's "Hide Away" stop/break chord, that kicks off chorus 1, along with the sliding ninths in bar 4, and the A9 fingering in bar 5. The F♯–7, B7sus4, and E9 chords in bars 9–12 are voice led; from F♯–7 to B7sus4, only one note changes (C♯ to B). Likewise, only two notes change as B7sus4 resolves back to E9. Also note that in bars 21 and 22 the fingering for both the F♯–7 and Bsus4(9) chords is exactly the same. Keeping the C♯ note from F♯–7 creates Bsus4(9), and the root motion (F♯ to B) is provided by the other guitar and bass. Both B7sus4 and Bsus4(9) feature the tonic (E) on top and create a powerful V7sus4 sound, so they're perfect for riff-style comping. Other notes on top of the chord, such as the 3 (or ♭3), 5, 6, and 9, can also make for colorful and powerful rhythm chords. I used all of them in the choruses that followed.

Bars 4 and 16 introduce the first of many chromatic chords. Here, the C– triad is played as a chromatic passing chord on beat 2, between the C♯– and B– sliding ninths triads in beats 1 and 3. (Sliding ninths were discussed in detail in chapter 3.)

Also note that bars 17 and 18 introduce chromatic shifts in and out of the IV7 chord; the A9 shifts one-half step down and back up (twice) from A♭9.

Chorus 3

Chorus 3 begins down low on the neck with another comping figure, on (open-position) E, F♯–7, E chords, which is repeated for bars 27, 31, and 35. Particularly in the lower range, it's essential to play focused, clearly defined chords and rhythms to avoid muddying up the mix! Also, in bars 33 and 34, chromatic shifts come into play again, as the C9 chord approaches B9.

Chorus 4

Chorus 4 features more chromatic chords in bars 37 to 40, as the E♭7 approaches E7 from a half step below. Note that this top-three-strings fingering for E7 has the 5, ♭7, and the 3, which is the top note in the chord. Also, in bars 45 and 46, the C9 chord again approaches B9 chromatically, from a half step above.

Chorus 5

Chorus 5 begins with E9 chords (the James Brown fingering) on the offbeats, to create rhythmic kick and energy for the part. Note that the top note of the E9 chord, B, remains as the top note for most chords in this chorus. The B note on top creates an A9 sound for bars 53 and 54 and adds the colorful 11 over the F♯–11 in bar 57. It's also the root of the B13 chord. Sitting on the same top note, while the chords change throughout the 12-bar form, creates a strong thread that ties the rhythm part together, and that's one of the characteristics of riff-style playing. Chorus 5 also features several chromatic shifts/approaches into the E9 chord in bars 55, 56, 59, and 60, along with (another) chromatic shift between the sliding ninths in bar 52.

Chorus 6

Chorus 6 starts off with a jumpin' E6 voicing (on the top four strings) that was intended as a tip of the hat to Jimmy Rodgers' classic guitar part on the Little Walter instrumental, "Juke." Like chorus 5, much of this chorus features a repeated top note; this time, it's C♯ throughout the 12-bar form. The C♯ on top sounds bright and punchy as the 3 of the A7; it's also the 5 of the F♯–6(9) and the 9 of the B13, so it feels right at home throughout the progression.

Chorus 7

Chorus 7 features a simple but strong riff that repeats as a 2-bar pattern through most of the 12-bar form. It starts on beat 2 of bar 73, with E9—again, Freddy King's "Hide Away" fingering—with the 12th fret E as the top note. On beat 4, the top note moves down to C♯ (9th fret), forming a colorful E13 chord, and then the top moves back to the E9 on beat 1 of bar 74. This same riff melody string is played over the A7 in bars 77–78. The E and C♯ notes are the 5 and 3 of the chord, so they also sound great against the A7.

Chorus 8

Chorus 8 starts out with punchy, high register E13 chords on the top four strings. Also note the A passing chord on beat 2 of bar 86, which resolves back to E7 on beat 3. Bar 88 revisits the chromatic sliding ninths from chorus 1. The notes are exactly the same, only this time they're fingered differently, played higher up the neck on strings 4-3-2 instead of strings 3-2-1.

Chorus 9

Chorus 9 jumps out of the gate with high register E13 and A9 chords, most of which are played on the offbeats, to create as much forward momentum as possible. In bars 105–106, the C9 chord once again approaches B9 from a half step above. An open position descending E minor-pentatonic lick wraps up the track in bars 107–108, followed by a final E9 chord.

My approach to playing rhythm parts in this style has been strongly influenced by bands such as Count Basie and Duke Ellington, along with jazz-influenced R&B artists, such as T-Bone Walker, Bill Doggett, and Ray Charles. I encourage you to tap into their wealth of musical techniques. Emulate, adapt, and recreate the riffs, hooks, and background figures that the brass, woodwind, and keyboard players played on those classic recordings. Work their riffs out on the fretboard, to make them your own. They sound great on guitar!

Listen and practice along with the second part for "Like a Rocket." When you're ready, play along with the audio.

Like a Rocket
Rhythm Part

Mike Williams

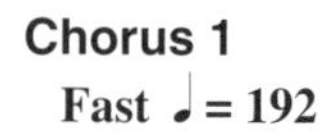

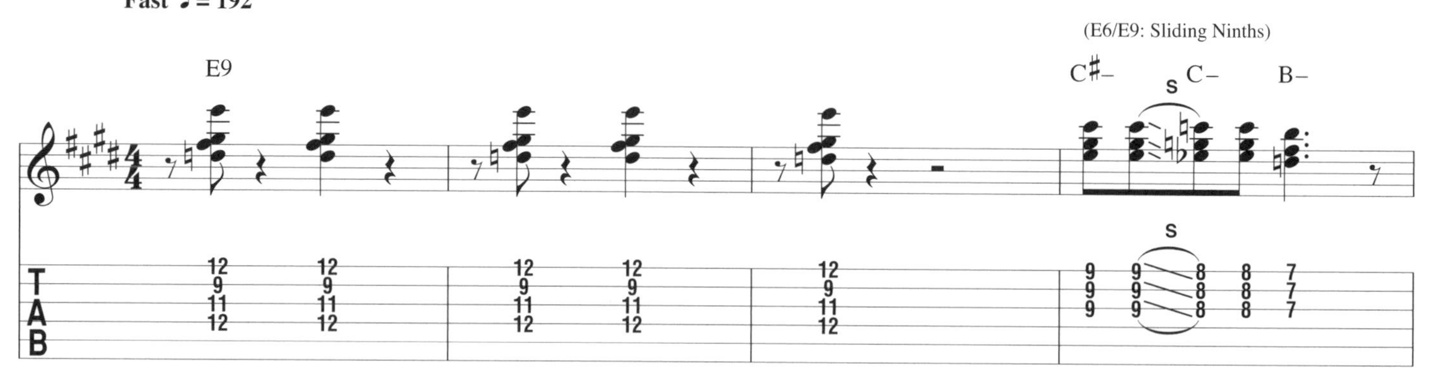

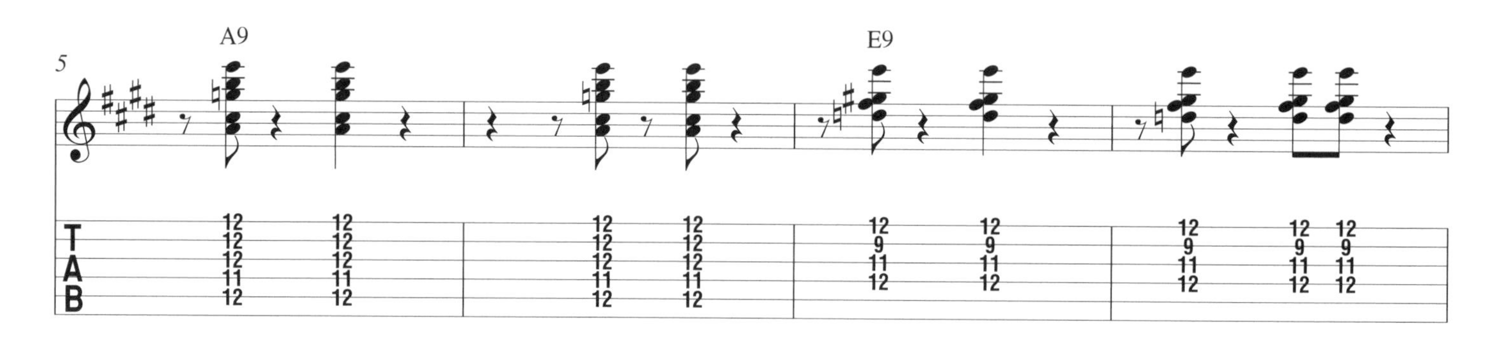

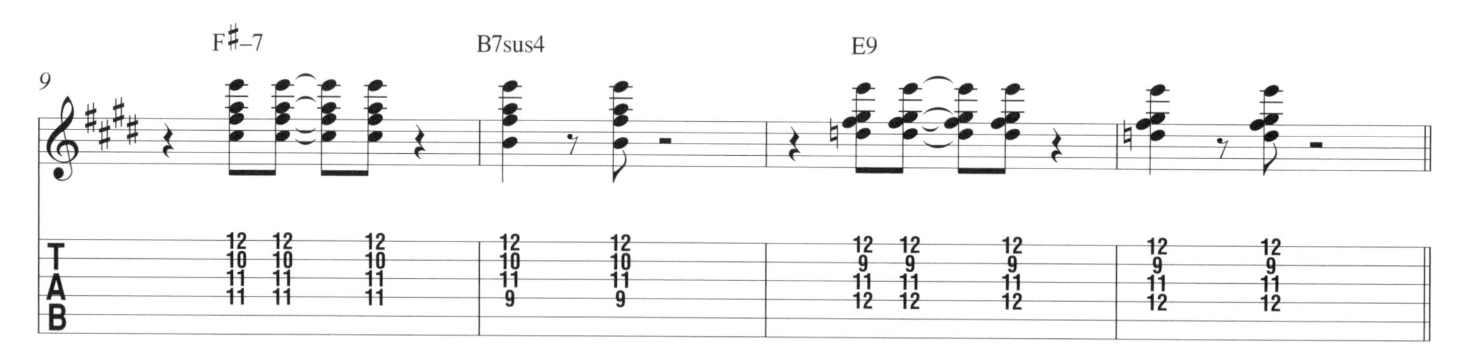

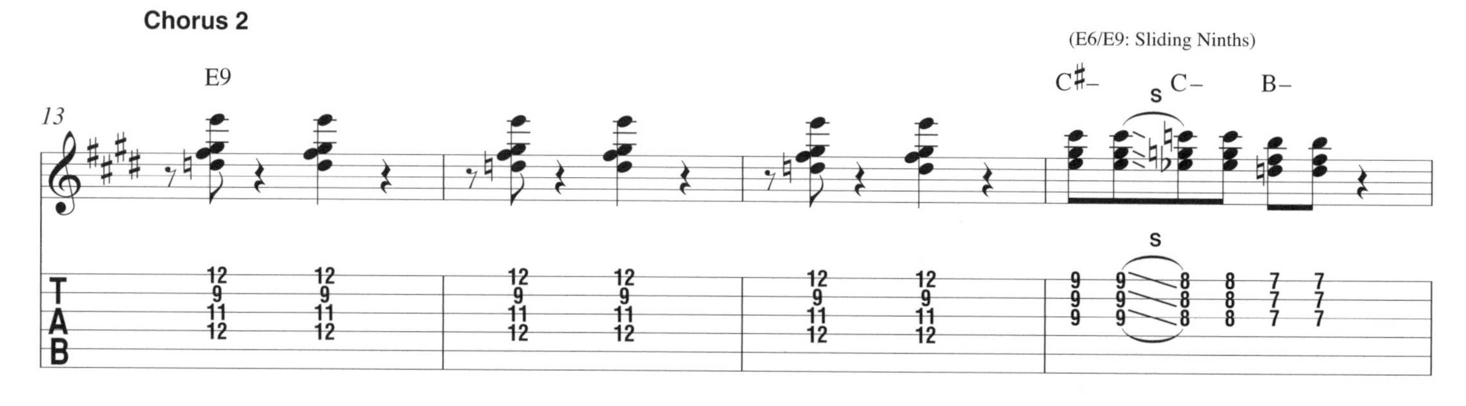

A9
A♭9
A9
A♭9
A9
E9
F♯–7
Bsus4(9)
E9
E
Chorus 3
F♯–7
E
F♯–7
E
A7
E
F♯–7
E
F♯–7
C9
B9
E
F♯–7
E
F♯–7
E

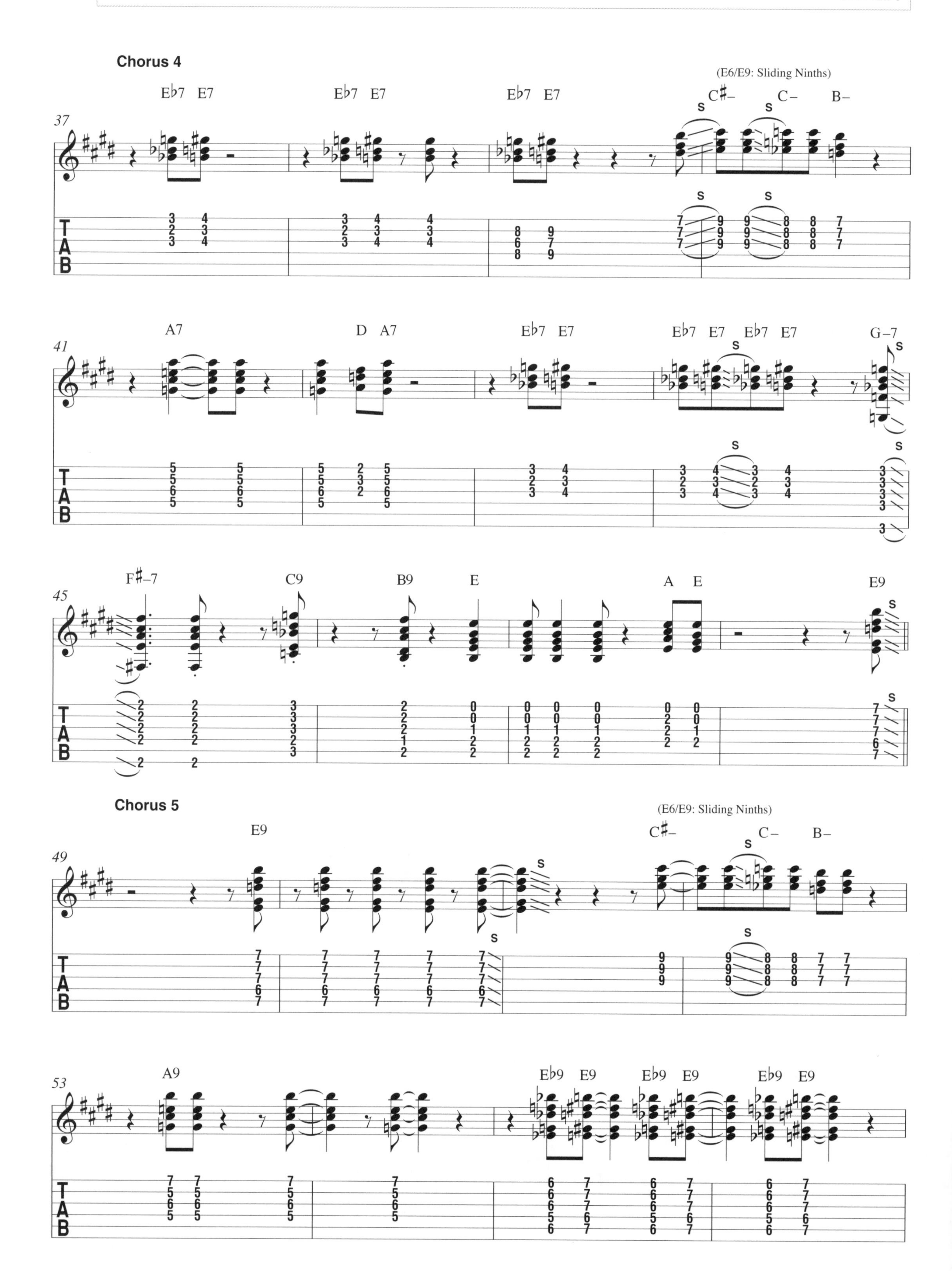
Chorus 4
(E6/E9: Sliding Ninths)
E♭7 E7
C♯– C– B–
A7
D A7
G–7
F♯–7
C9
B9
E
A E
E9
Chorus 5
(E6/E9: Sliding Ninths)
E9
C♯– C– B–
A9
E♭9 E9

57
F♯–9(11)
B13
E♭9 E9 E♭9 E9
E6
Chorus 6
61
E6
(E6/E9: Sliding Ninths)
C♯–
C–
B–
65
A7
E6
(E6/E9: Sliding Ninths)
C♯– C– B–
69
F♯–6(9)
B13
E♭6 E6
Chorus 7
73
E9
E13
E9
E13
E9

A9 A7 A9 E9 E13 E9
F♯–7 Bsus4 E9 E13 E9
Chorus 8
(E6/E9: Sliding Ninths)
E13 A E7 E13 C♯– C– B–
A9 A♭9 A9 A♭9 A9 E9
F♯–7 B9 E9

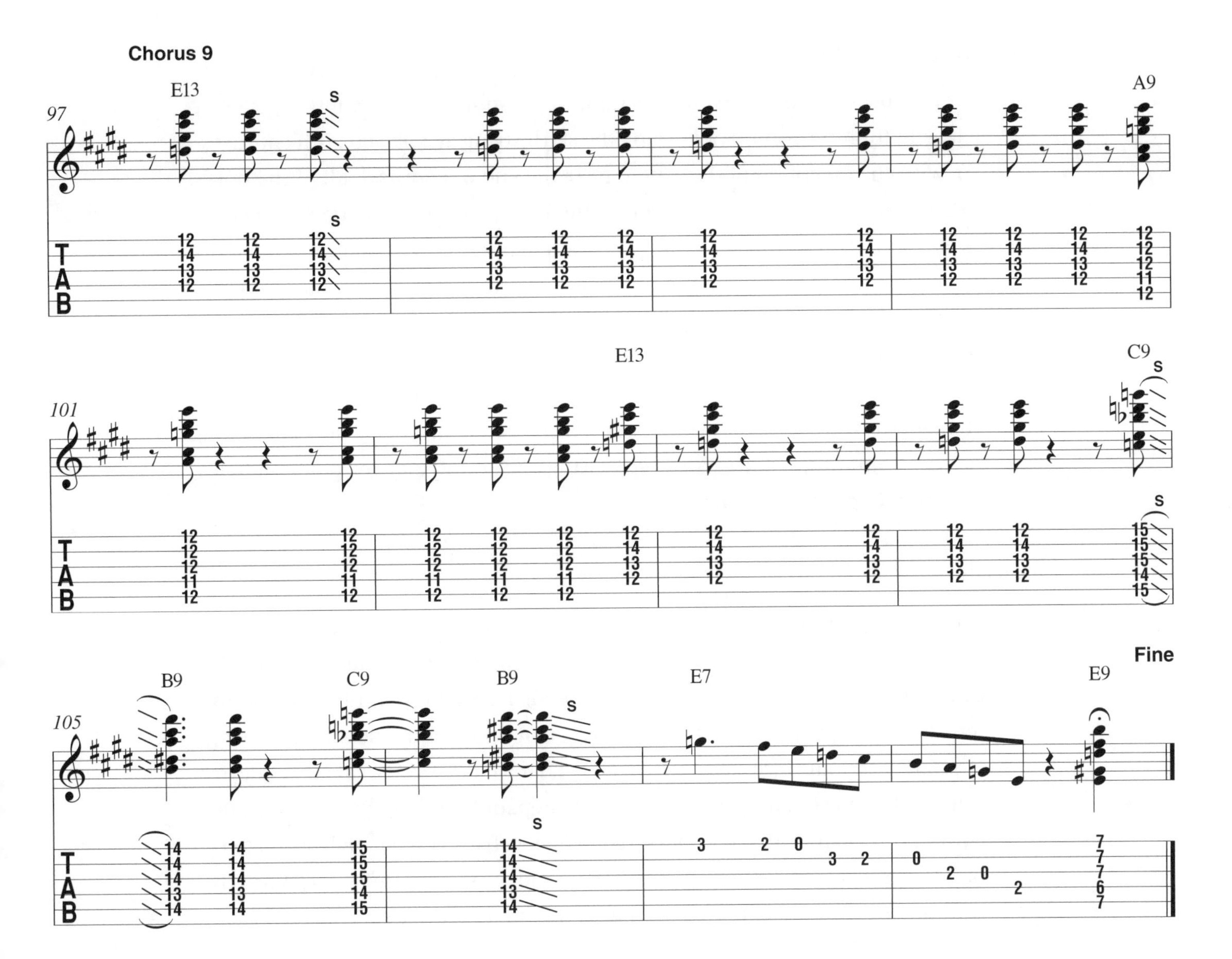

FIG. 5.2. "Like a Rocket" Rhythm Part 2: Chords

"LIKE A ROCKET" SOLO

A few objectives for this solo included playing with clarity and intensity, and varying the range (from low to high, etc.) as the solo progressed. Another goal on my "roadmap" for this track was to tap into vocal influences by leaving plenty of breaths between the phrases, and by playing with call and response through all nine choruses.

Performance Tips

About Choruses 1 and 2

This solo opens up with call and response over 4-bar phrases. The "call" slides up into chord tones B and D (the 5 and ♭7), which are sustained through bars 1 and 2. The same 2-note chord (dyad) answers the call, in the "response" in bar 5, and in bar 9 also, to cap off chorus 1. With the exception of two G♯ notes (the major third) on beat 3 of bars 7 and 11, choruses 1 and 2 are comprised entirely of notes from the E pentatonic or E blues scales.

Choruses 3 and 4

For choruses 3 and 4, the conversation moves down into the low register. It felt right to shift up and down along the sixth string as I played both choruses. So, with the exception of the A note near the end of chorus 4, all of the notes in choruses 3 and 4 were fingered on the low E string. Phrasing with clarity is particularly important in the lower range, in order to avoid muddying up the mix. With that in mind, the phrases in choruses 3 and 4 are fairly simple, yet the call and response helps them connect, to create a conversational feel through both choruses.

Working the bottom range of the instrument can provide a dramatic change in texture and sound during solos, and two of my big inspirations while "speaking in the low voice" are Freddy King and country singer/guitarist (with monster chops) Junior Brown.

Chorus 5

Chorus 5 taps into the open-position E blues scale with repeated string bends between A (4) and B♭ (♭5). Bars 54–57 shift up into the next higher position 2/3 fingering for E blues, with more string bends between A and B♭. To play the repeated string bends in bars 54 and 55, bend up from the note A (1st string, 5th fret) with your third finger. On beat 3 of bar 54, the A is "tweaked" a quarter step, and on beat 4, it's pre-bent one-half step, onto B♭ (♭5). Bar 55 continues with a pre-bent B♭ (♭5) that's released down to A (4) and then bent back up to B♭. Bar 57 introduces chromatic passing tones, and bars 58–59 finish the chorus by leaning into the E pentatonic sound with notes E F♯ E E G G♯ B C♯ B.

Chorus 6

Bars 61–66 are played in position 7. The half-step bend from C♯ into D that anticipates chorus 6 mixes in the color of the 6/13 from E pentatonic, with notes/phrases from E blues, which makes up most of bars 61–66. Bar 65 once again combines C♯ (6/13) and D (♭7) with bends and pre-bends before descending down (notes G E D B B♭ A E) from E blues, in bar 66. That phrase continues in bar 67 by shifting down to position 5 with notes G E A E (alternating between strings 4 and 5). Then, it wraps up with two slides up into the major 3 (with notes G G♯ G G♯) before ending on the root, E. Bars 69 and 70 are also played in position 5 with notes from the position 4/5 E minor pentatonic fingering, and then the G♯ (3) returns, right before the root on beat 1 of bar 71.

Chorus 7

Chorus 7 is fingered one octave (twelve frets) higher than the beginning of chorus 5, in the position 15/16 fingering for E blues. Bar 75 features a first-finger half-step bend from G (♭3) to G♯ (3), and bars 76 and 77 revisit the half-step bends between A and B♭. To play those notes, bend up from the A with the third finger. Beat 2 of bar 79 features another of B.B. King's classic slides down the B string, and it takes you down from position 15 to position 12 in a hurry. The last four bars of this chorus begin right before bar 81, with notes B C♯ E (5 6/13 root). To fret the A note on beat 1 of bar 81, slide up two frets (on the first string, 17th fret), then drop back down to the "home" E blues fingering in position 12, to finish the chorus.

Choruses 8 and 9

Chorus 8 kicks off with more repeated half-step string bends from A to B♭ in position 12. Bars 89–91 continue in position 12 with a big mix of E blues and E pentatonic. Also note a few jazzier connections throughout the rest of the chorus, such as the chromatic passage on beats 2 through 4 of bar 89 (notes G G♯ A A♯ B). The mix of E blues with the color of chromatic passing notes continues in bar 91 and throughout bars 93 and 94.

Chorus 9 closes out the solo with slides up into the high E (root), with lots o' tremolo picking, to kick up the intensity level a notch. Once again, call and response helps the phrases to connect, like a lyric through the song form. Jimmie Vaughan's influences are noticeable in this chorus, and throughout this solo, as are influences by longtime favorites B.B. King and Freddy King.

Also play chorus after chorus of your own solos over this track. Remember to breathe between your phrases, and focus on making your statements connect with call and response!

Listen and practice along with example 5.3, the solo to "Like a Rocket." When you're ready, play along with the audio.

26
Full Band

24
Rhythm Parts

Like a Rocket

Solo

Mike Williams

Chorus 1

Fast ♩ = 192

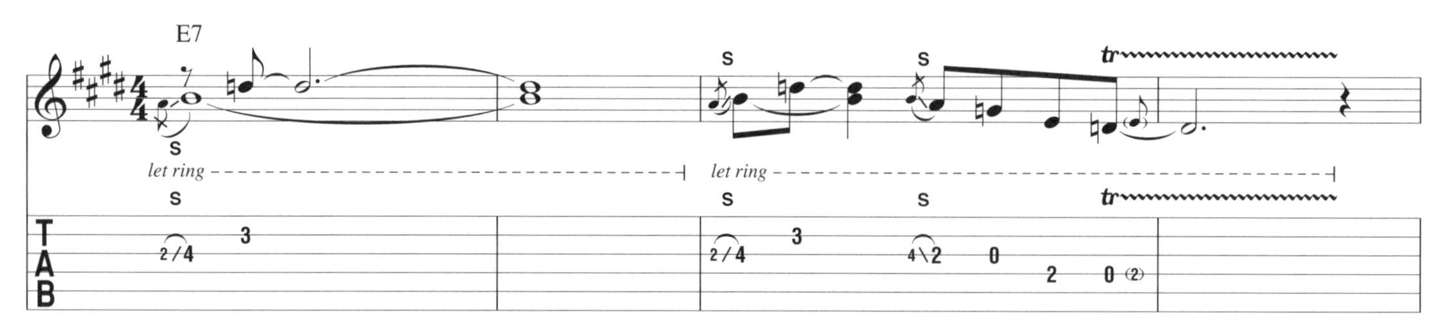

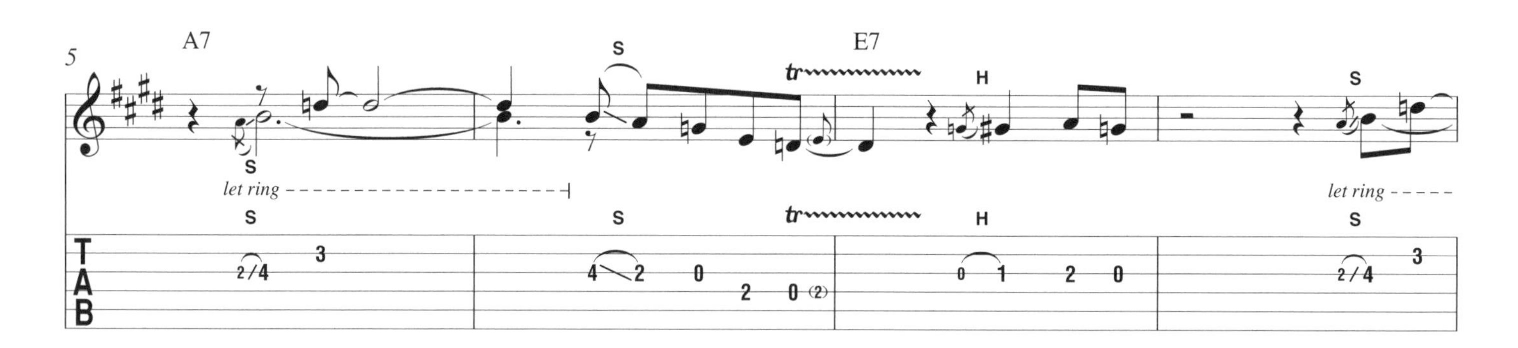

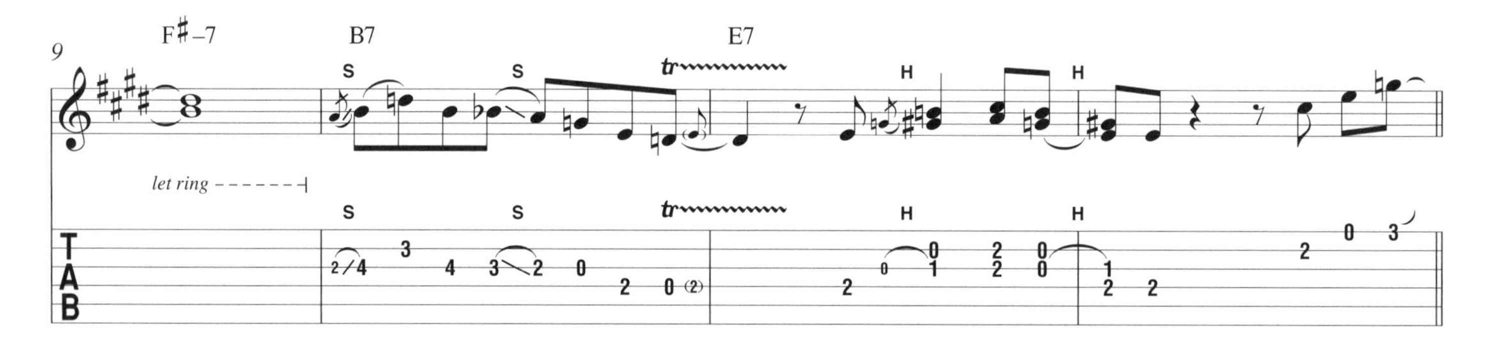

17
A7
E7
S
let ring
let ring

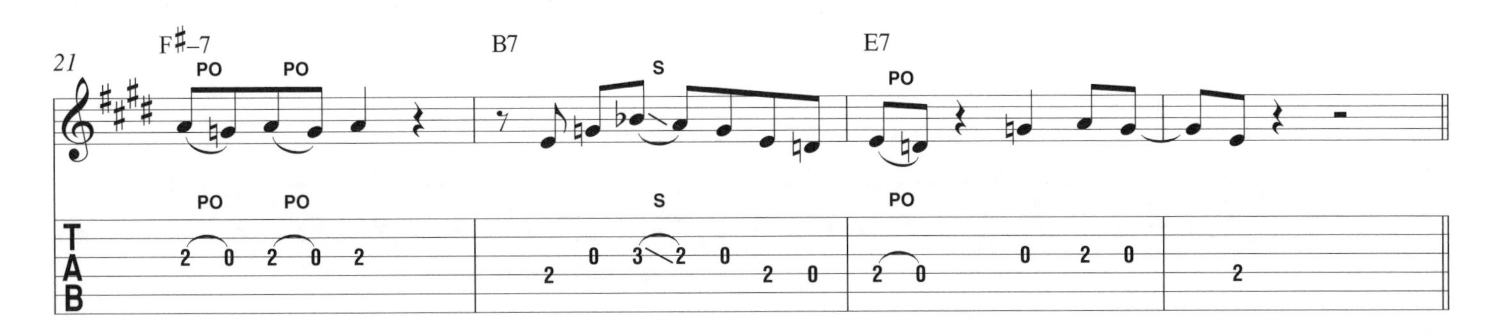
21
F♯–7
PO
B7
S
E7

Chorus 3

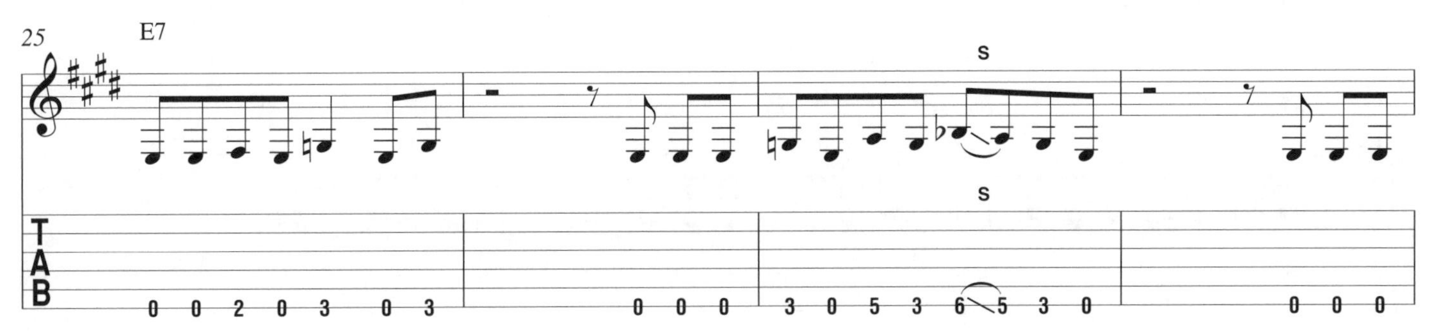
25
E7
S

29
A7
E7
S

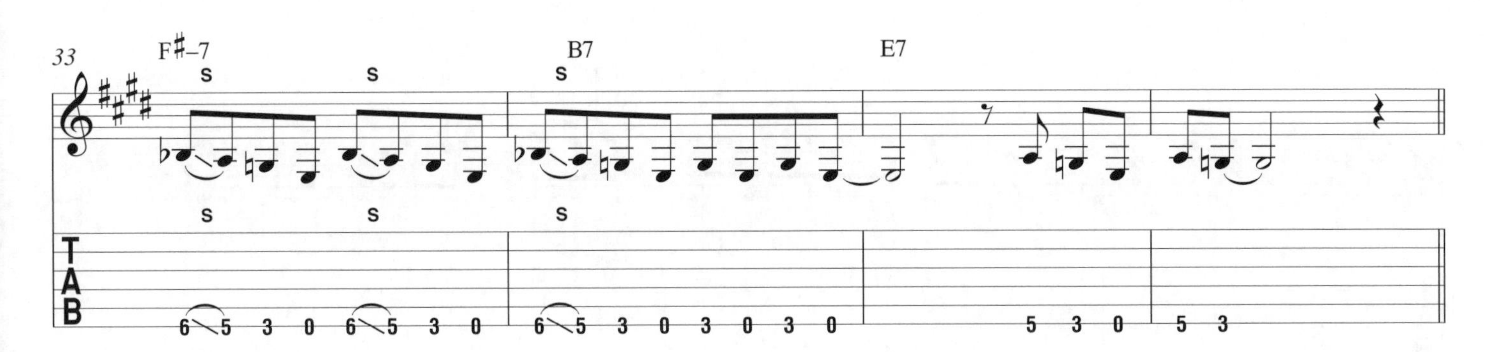
33
F♯–7
S
B7
E7

Chorus 4

Chorus 5

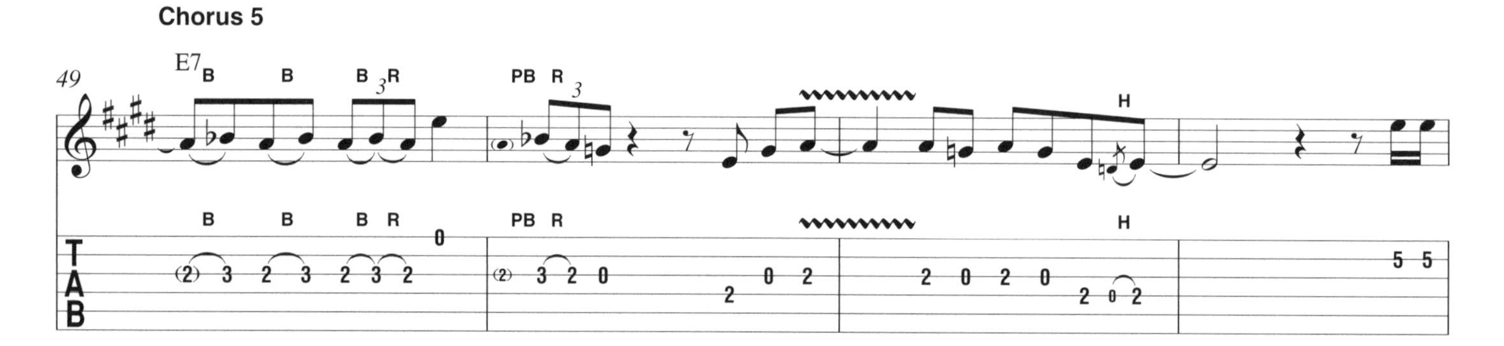

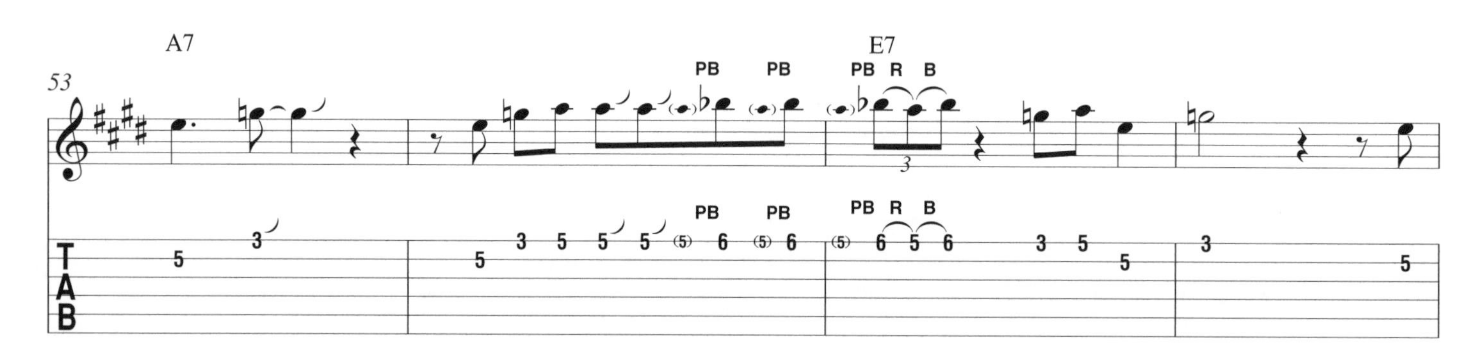

F#–7
B7
E7
S
B
Chorus 6
E7
B
A7
PB
E7
S
S
F#–7
H PO
B7
H PO
E7
S
Chorus 7
E7
B
B

Chorus 8

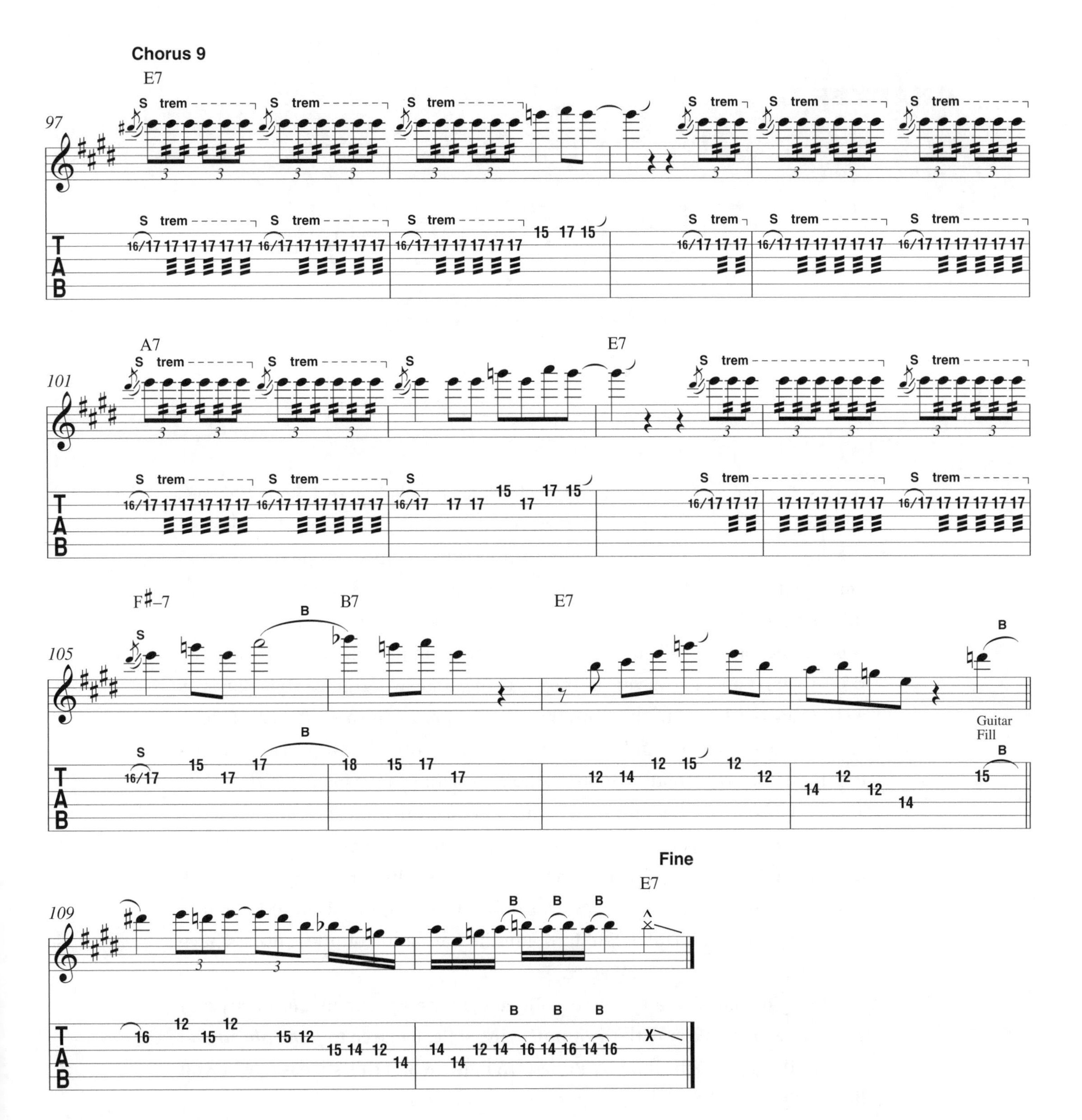

FIG. 5.3. "Like a Rocket" Solo

CHAPTER 6

T-Bone Swing Style: "Jumpin' Bones"

In this chapter, we'll work through techniques for playing in T-Bone Walker's classic jump style. T-Bone was born in Texas, and as a youngster, learned the language of Texas' brand of blues directly from one of its pioneers, Blind Lemon Jefferson. T-Bone was hugely influenced by jazz also, and that's evident in the legacy of recorded tracks that he's left us with. Records such as *T-Bone Blues* demonstrate Walker's mastery of singing and playing distinct and tasty rhythm parts and solos over shuffles, ballads, and swing/jump style blues, as well. Tracks such as "Strollin' with Bone," "Two Bones and a Pick," and "T-Bone Shuffle" have become standards for blues guitarists around the world. T-Bone's landmark "Stormy Monday" is one of the biggest hits in the history of the blues. T-Bone Walker's musical influences run deep throughout the world of blues guitar. Since the 1940s, T-Bone has left his mark on many of the greatest players in blues and rock. B.B. King, Clarence "Gatemouth" Brown, Buddy Guy, Chuck Berry, Wayne Bennett, Clarence Hollimon, Eric Clapton, Jimmy Vaughan, Stevie Ray Vaughan, Duke Robillard, Ronnie Earl, and countless others have "gone to school" on T-Bone Walker.

"Jumpin' Bones" is a tribute to T-Bone's jazzy and swinging jump style. If you're already familiar with the jump/swing style, feel free to *jump ahead* and start working through "Jumpin' Bones," in figure 6.3. If this style is new to you though, exercise 6.1 on the next page may be helpful.

FLAT-TIRE RHYTHM PARTS

One of the key components in vintage blues, R&B, and jump recordings by T-Bone Walker and others such as Louis Jordan and B.B. King, are the "jump chords" that sound nonstop on the upbeats. In tracks from the '40s, '50s, and '60s, the piano player often played the jump chords in the right hand, along with a boogie-woogie bass pattern in the left hand. On T-Bone Walker's classic "Strollin' with Bone," the piano's jump chords provide unrelenting forward momentum; they put the *jump* in the groove. On that track, the acoustic bass player doubles the piano's left-hand pattern, and that's typical for the vintage jump/swing style. To get the feel for the jump chords, I recommend T-Bone's tracks such as "Strollin' with Bone," "Papa Ain't Salty," "Two Bones and a Pick," and "T-Bone Shuffle." (The recording *T-Bone Blues* features some of Walker's best-recorded performances of blues in a variety of styles and tempos, so it's highly recommended.)

Jump chords sounding on the shuffle upbeats have been played for decades by guitarists, as well. These days, that rhythm style is commonly referred to as a "flat-tire" part, and it can be heard on tracks by Stevie Ray Vaughan, Robert Cray, and many other contemporary artists. In order for the flat-tire part to fire on all cylinders, the chords need to sound *unrelentingly* on the upbeats. If the triplet feel wanders (or gets even slightly out of sync), the groove will too, so rhythmic consistency is essential when playing the flat-tire part.

NOTE: The feel on the upbeats of this flat-tire part are similar to the marches in chapters 1 and 2. So, if you're having difficulty capturing this faster "dump-ty, dump" feel, refer back to those pages, if necessary.

Practice the flat-tire part over "Shuffle in B♭" in exercise 6.1. When you're ready, play along with the audio.

Shuffle in B♭
Flat-Tire Rhythm Part

Mike Williams

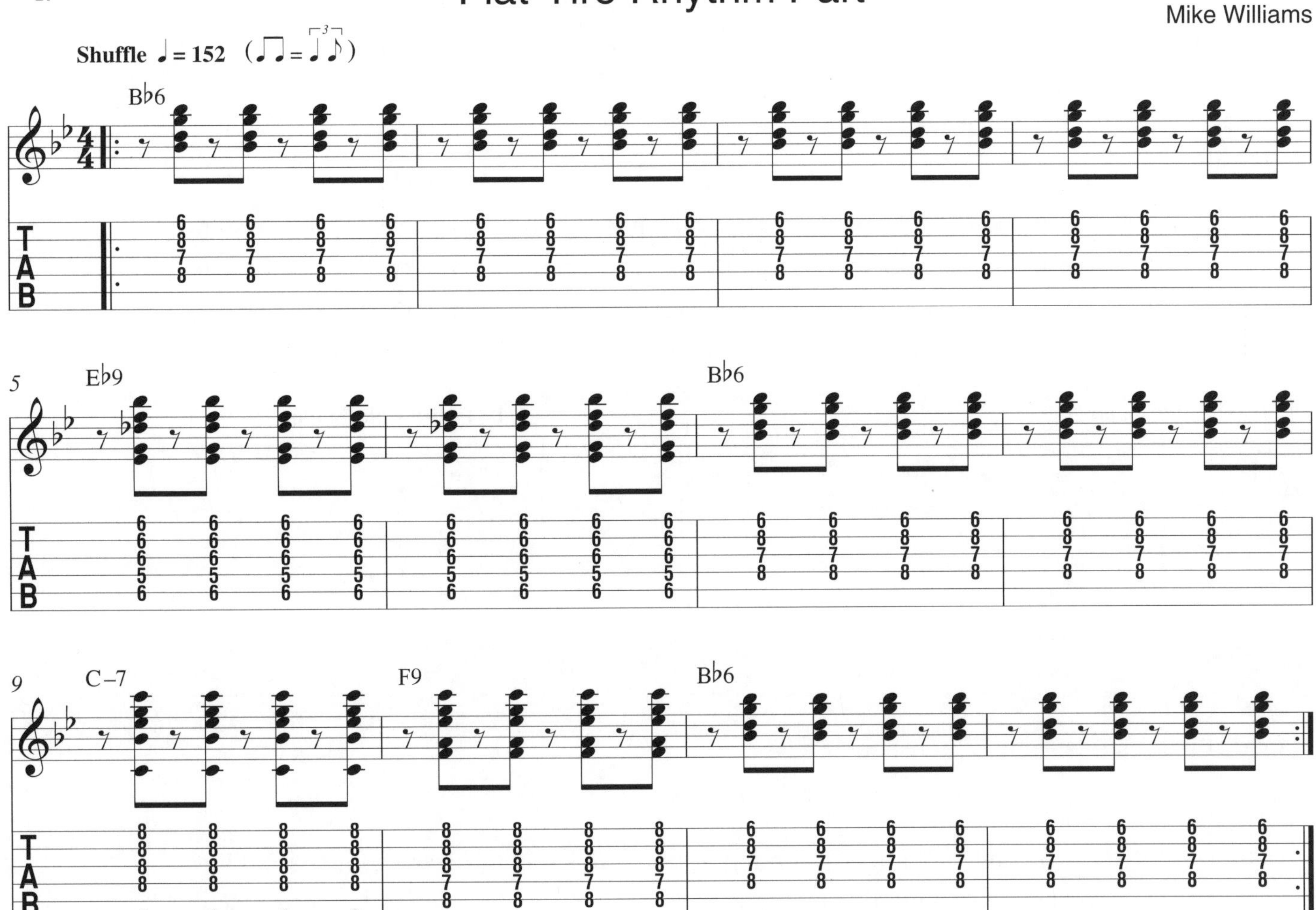

FIG. 6.1. "Shuffle in B♭" Flat-Tire Rhythm Part

"JUMPIN' BONES" SOLO

Performance Tips

The 2-bar guitar intro to "Jumpin' Bones" kicks off with a B♭9 (I7) chord, that's played in T-Bone's signature style. With the fifth in the bass, this voicing (with notes F, D, A♭, C, forming the 5, 3, ♭7, 9 of the chord) creates extra depth for the bottom end. T-Bone often played similar fingerings on slow blues tracks, such as "Blues for Marili," "Mean Old World," and "Stormy Monday" (see "Slow Bone," in chapter 7). As the opening B♭9/F descends chromatically down through A9/E, A♭9/E♭, G9/D, etc., it creates a ton of forward momentum into F9/C (V7) of bar 2, on the "and" of beat 2.

The chords in the intro can be picked/strummed a couple of different ways. Note that chords are strummed on the upbeats ("ands") throughout the bar, and each slides down (on the downbeat) to the next chord. Since the chords sound on the upbeats, it works well to pick/strum each as an upstroke. Or, as an alternative, you can strum each chord with a downstroke instead; that may make it a little easier to produce consistent sound and feel through the intro. Playing the descending chords as upstrokes tends to produce a slightly more high-end (treble) sound, and likewise, playing the chords as downstrokes emphasizes the lower, more midrange frequencies a bit. Try playing it both ways, and go with what works for you. Practice the intro at slower tempos at first, until you're able to play it with a relaxed and swinging feel.

Playing the Solo

To tap into T-Bone's vocabulary and influences on this track, I stayed as close to his "home base" on the fretboard as possible. So, with the exception of some of the chords, choruses 1 through 8 were played with notes of the B♭ blues scale (B♭ D♭ E♭ E F A♭) in position 6, combined with the major 3 (D), 2/9 (C), and 6/13 (G) from the adjoining B♭ pentatonic scale in position 5 (see figure 6.2).

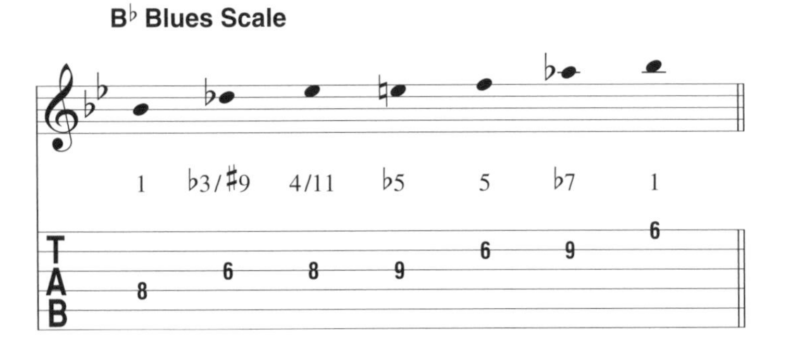

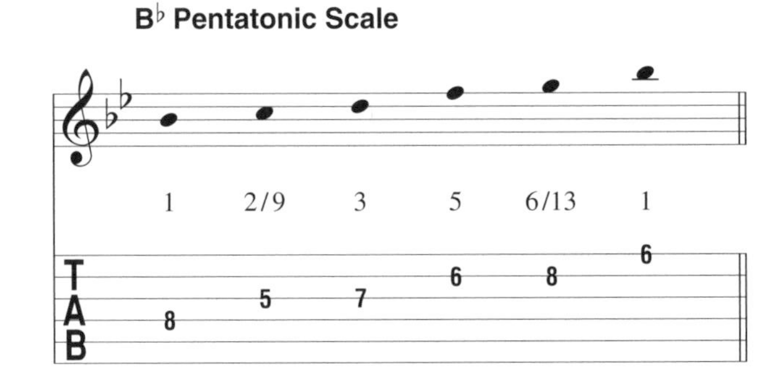

FIG. 6.2. B♭ Blues Scale and B♭ Pentatonic Scale

If you're not already familiar with the position 6 fingering for the B♭ blues scale and its adjoining major pentatonic fingering in position 5, I recommend working through chapter 12. Both fingerings are discussed and demonstrated there in detail, in positions 4 and 5, for the key of A. To play them in B♭, simply move them up one fret.

Chorus 1

The very first notes in this solo set the table for the choruses that follow, with a mix of B♭ pentatonic and blues that's served up "T-Bone Style." T-Bone had an impressive command of using call and response to link his phrases together, like a blues lyric through the chord changes. With that as a model, all solo choruses feature call and response. The brief 3-note opening call anticipates (plays across the barline) beat 1. That's answered with a longer reply that anticipates bar 4, with the C♯ (♯9), which bends up a half step into D (3), and then descends down the blues scale, with notes B♭ (root), F (5), E (♭5), E♭ (4), D♭ (♭3/♯9), B♭ (root). That phrase wraps up in bar 5 by leaning into the brighter sound of the major 3, with notes E♭ (4), B♭ (root), D (3), and B♭ (root).

Also, bar 13 (into bar 14) features a phrase that mixes mostly the major pentatonic sound, with D (major 3) and G (6), along with the note C♯ (♭3/♯9) from the B♭ blues scale.

One powerful technique in T-Bone's musical toolbox is his frequent use of repeated motifs to create forward push and momentum. Bars 10 and 11 feature a repeated 3-note phrase (♭5, 5, root) that's played as eighth notes. As you can see in the music, the phrase starts on "and" of beat 1. Then the next time it's repeated, it shifts to start on the downbeat, on beat 3. Since it's three notes in length, it sets up an interesting and challenging three-against-four feel. Repeated phrases like this can be difficult to count and feel, so don't be surprised if you get lost when you first practice it. Once you start repeating the lick, you may feel like you're stuck spinning on a musical merry-go-round, and after just a few beats, you're wondering how/when to jump off... (Give it a try, and you'll understand what I'm talking about!) I recommend counting through the phrase while listening to the track repeatedly. It may be helpful to count the five repeated high B♭ notes. Either way, this is one phrase that you'll probably need to practice repeatedly.

Choruses 2 and 3

Chorus 2 starts with another statement (call) in bar 15, that's again answered with a longer response in bars 17–19. Bars 20–26 cap off the chorus (paragraph) with a still longer follow-up/reply. T-Bone often started off with a short phrase (or phrases) that developed into longer responses as the chorus and solo progressed.

Chorus 3 picks up steam in bar 27 with three "blasts" of T-Bone's influential and often imitated "train whistle" chords. Whether played over the I7, IV7, or V7, this C♯ diminished triad on the top three strings packs a wallop for solos over blues in B♭. With notes E, G, and C♯, which are the 3, 5, and ♭7 of an A7 chord, this voicing can make the hair on the back of your neck stand up when played against a B♭7 chord. It works, though, and here's why: All three notes of the chord are bent, or "tweaked" up, almost (but not quite) a half step, so that it sounds somewhere between A7 and B♭7. So, when you play this bent C♯ diminished triad against the B♭7 chord, you're essentially playing an *out of tune* B♭7, with a bluesy top note that sounds somewhere between the ♭3 and 3. Try bending the chord gradually, then try bending it a little faster. Experiment with tweaking the chord with a slight quarter-step bend, and then also try bending it further up and down. Try rocking the strings back and forth, with some vibrato, as you sustain the bent chord.

To explore the range of "train whistle" sounds that this chord can produce, experiment with your volume knob on your guitar as you slowly bend the chord. Start with the volume off, and strike the chord, then gradually turn the volume up, as you bend the chord up, and then release the bend back down. Experiment with volume swells and decays as you slowly bend and release the bend. (I believe I hear the train right now—passing over the ridge, at a distance...)

This diminished chord may sound familiar. T-Bone played it on solo after solo with much success. Robert Johnson tapped into the chord's mojo back in the 1930s, even before it showed up on T-Bone's tracks. Jimi Hendrix's landmark intro on "Red House" starts off with it, and Stevie Ray Vaughan rocked it in many recordings, such as in his solo on "Love Struck."

As noted earlier, this voicing can sound great when played against the I7, IV7, or V7 chords, so try playing it in various places throughout the "Jumpin' Bones" progression. It can create a ton of raw energy and mojo for shuffles, jump tunes, slow blues, country blues, or rockin' blues, so have some fun with it!

Choruses 4 and 5

Choruses 4 and 5 are rhythm parts played behind the piano solo. For chorus 4, I jumped onto the comp figure that the keyboard player played for much of the recording, with rhythmic hits on beat 1 and on the "and" of 2. This is a great pattern to play over shuffles at various tempos, so move this to other keys and tempos!

Chorus 5 introduces another comp pattern, with a B♭7 (I7) that anticipates beat 1. That's followed by a passing E♭6 (IV) chord on beat 2, which returns back to B♭7 on beat 3. Note that the chord changes to E♭9 (IV7) for bars 55–56, but the comp patterns and rhythm remain the same. Bars 57 and 58 feature more colorful chord changes, played as half note rhythms, to complement the more rhythmically active piano solo. The harmony in bars 57–60 is a very popular reharmonization for blues, which can be heard on dozens of T-Bone's recordings, and on many of bebop great Charlie Parker's jazz/blues tracks, as well. You may also recognize them from the Allman Brothers Band's influential recording of "Stormy Monday," from *Live at the Fillmore East*. Bars 57–59 are analyzed as B♭7 (I7), C–7 (II–7), D–7 (III–7), D♭–7 (♭III–7), C–7 (II–7), etc.

Following that, the F9 (V7) in bar 60 is approached by G♭9 (a half step above), to create a little extra gravitational pull. In bar 61, the comp pattern from bar 51 returns, to wrap up the chorus.

Choruses 6 and 7

Another powerful technique in T-Bone's toolbox was his use of chords and fiery rhythms to create dramatic and explosive "shout choruses" on guitar. A shout chorus is another technique that's rooted in the jazz big-band style. Shout choruses are typically played at the climax of the arrangement, when all of the sections (woodwinds, brass, rhythm section, etc.) are playing figures together in unison and/or interacting with each other with strong call and response. Shout choruses can help to elevate a track's energy and intensity level right through the roof. T-Bone adapted momentum-building riffs—inspired or borrowed from the big band's horn section—to climax his tracks with powerful shout choruses.

Choruses 6 and 7 are played as shout choruses. Chorus 6 begins with a simple, yet effective 2-bar comp figure (or riff) that's played through the 12-bar form. Chorus 7 features another shout chorus that's based on a 2-bar riff. It kicks the intensity level up a few notches with rapid-fire triplets that are best played as alternating down/up strums. Powerful call and response between guitar riffs that alternate with drum fills throughout the chorus also raises the energy level, to help climax the track. Practice the triplet strumming patterns slower at first. Once you're comfortable playing them at a slower tempo, gradually work the shout chorus back up to full speed.

Chorus 8

Chorus 8 returns to single note phrases with a "call" in bars 87 and 88 that's "answered" with longer responses in bars 89–92 and bars 92–96. Finishing the chorus and the track are more of T-Bone's classic descending ninth chords in bars 97 and 98. Similar to the intro, the ending chords descend chromatically from B♭9/F (bar 97), down to F9/C on beat 1 of bar 98. On beat 2 of bar 98, B9 chromatically approaches B♭9, which is sustained for the rest of the bar. All of the descending chromatic chords are picked, so once again, try playing the chords on upbeats as up-strums, and chords on downbeats as down-strums. Also feel free to play all chords as downstrokes. Both methods can work, so use the technique that helps you produce the desired results.

The piece concludes with one of T-Bone's signature endings on the slow arpeggio/strum through the final B♭9 chord, which seemed like an appropriate way to conclude this tribute to his style and influences. I had a ball writing and recording this jump blues in the T-Bone style, and I hope you enjoy playing it!

Practice “Jumpin’ Bones” along with the music in figure 6.3 below. When you’re ready, play along with the audio.

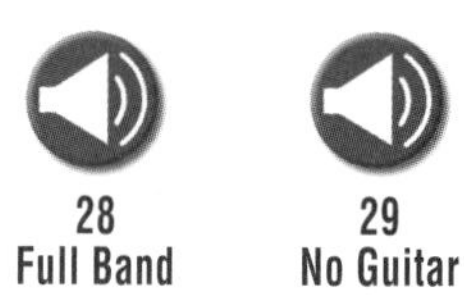

Jumpin’ Bones

Mike Williams

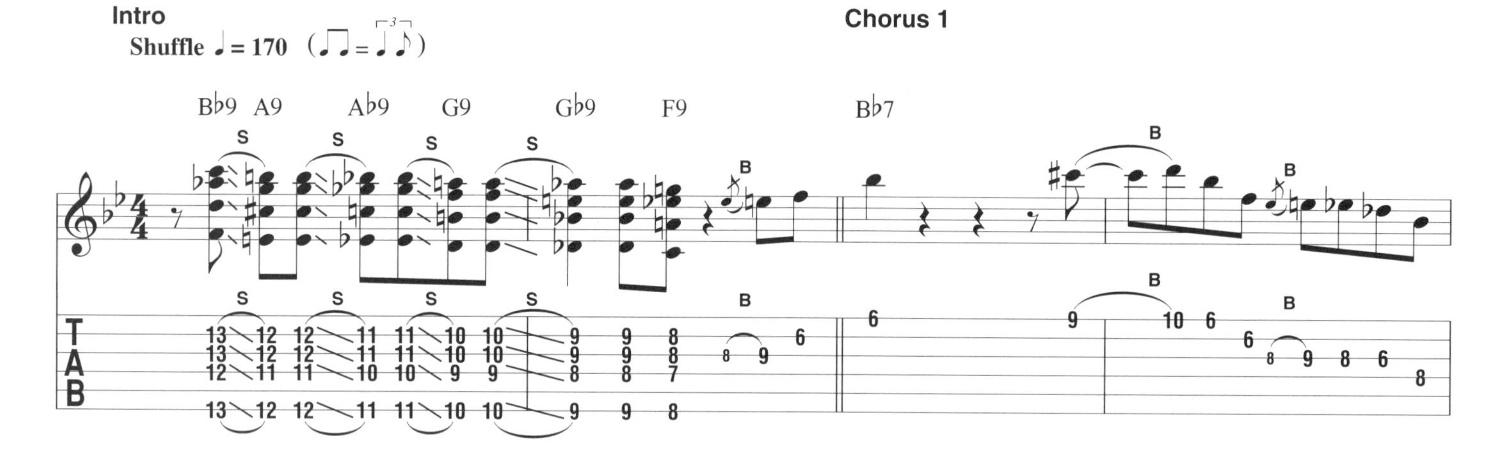

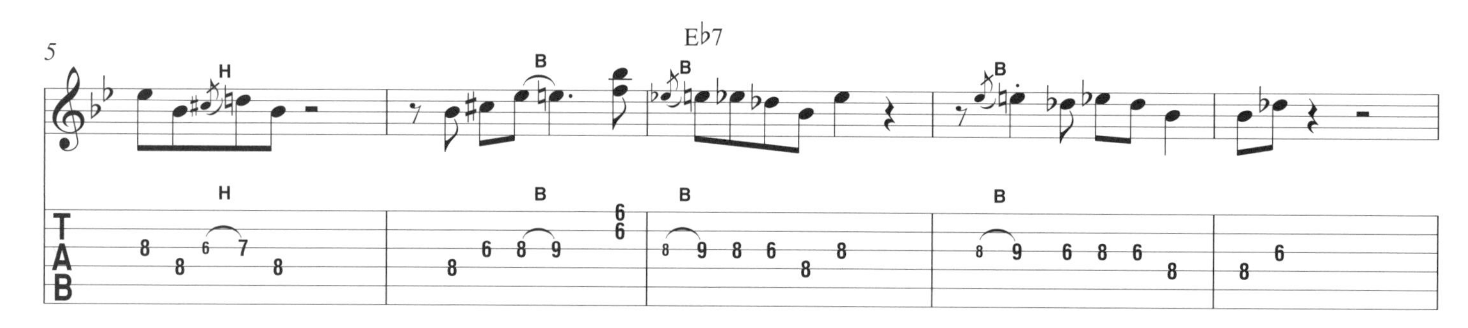

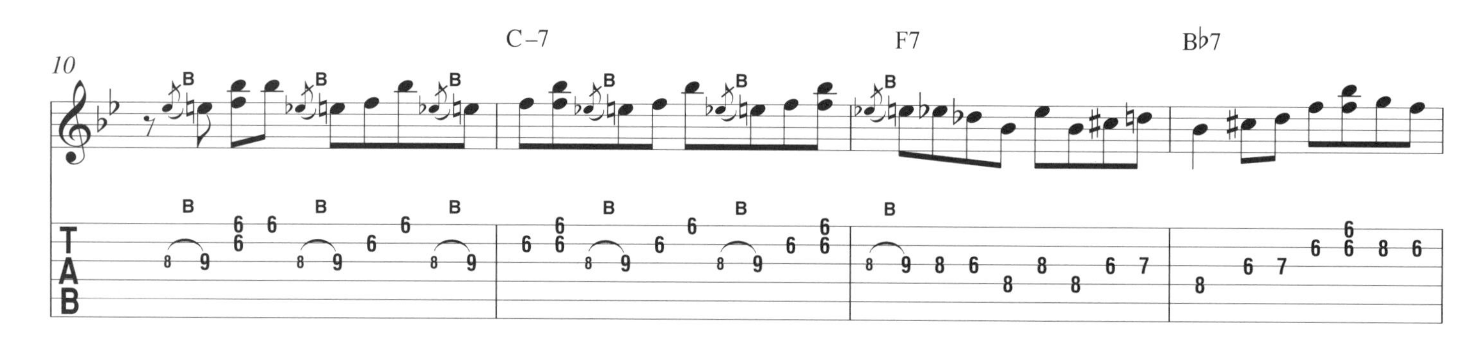

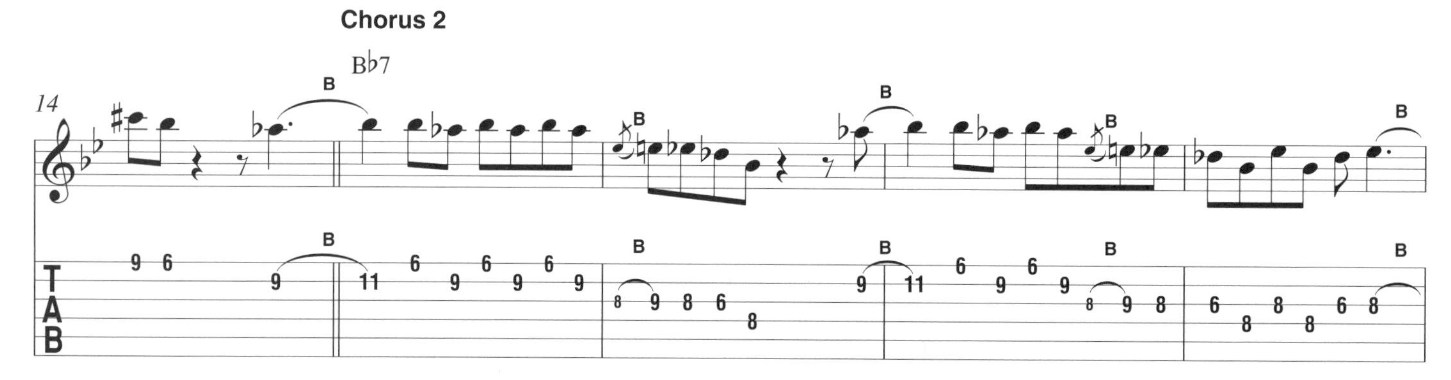

E♭7
B♭7
C–7
F7
B♭7
Chorus 3
B♭7
E♭7
B♭7
C–7
F7
B♭7

Chorus 4
Behind Piano Solo
B♭6
E♭9
B♭6
C–7
F9
B♭6
H
Chorus 5
Behind Piano Solo
B♭7
(E♭6)
B♭7
H
(E♭6)
B♭7
E♭9
H
B♭7
C–7
D–7
D♭–7
S
C–7
S
G♭9
F9
H
B♭7
(E♭6)
B♭7
B♭9

Chorus 6

(Shout Chorus 1)

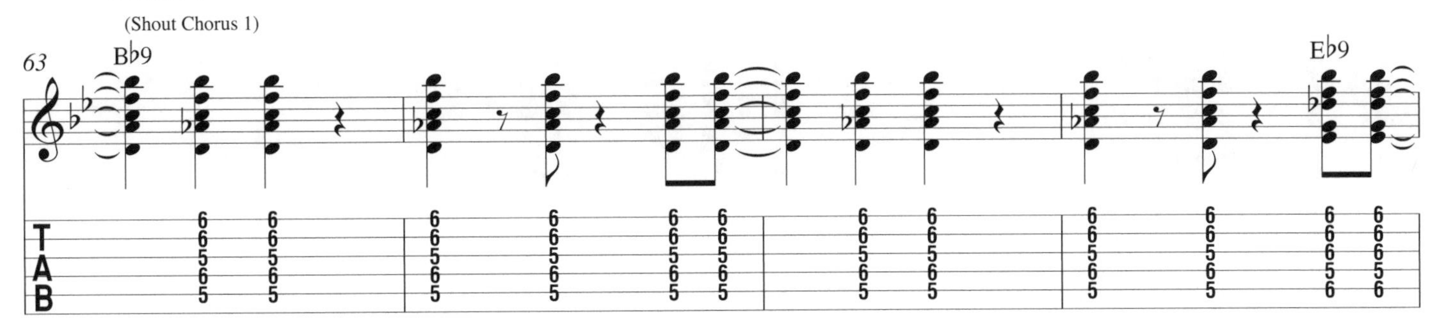

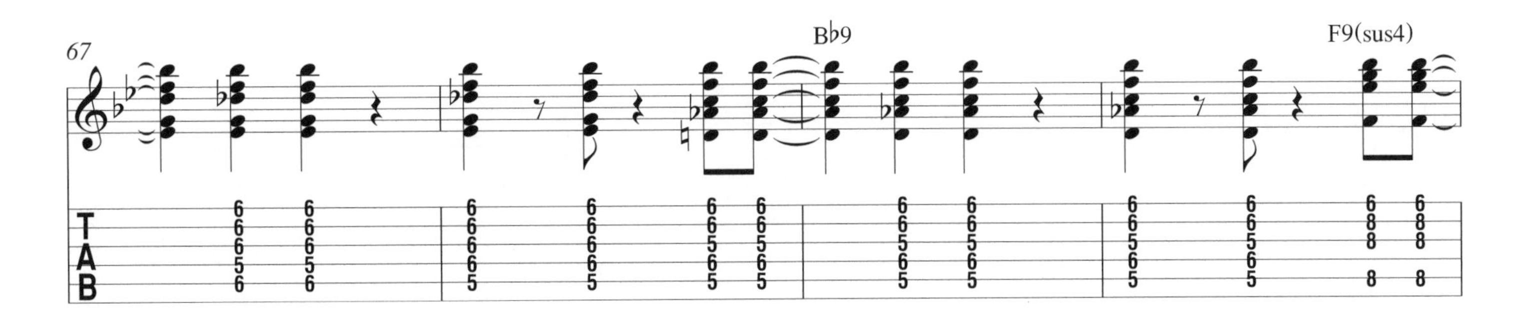

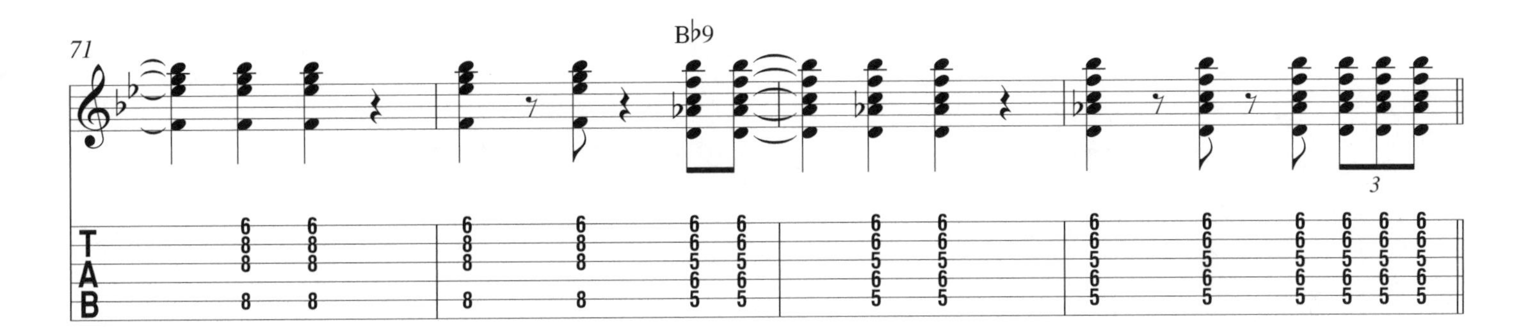

Chorus 7

(Shout Chorus 2, w/ drum fills…)

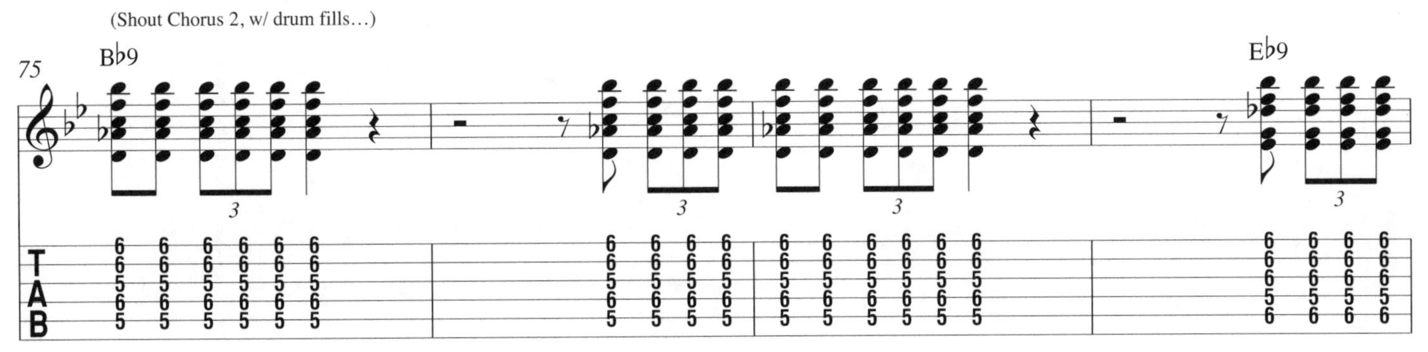

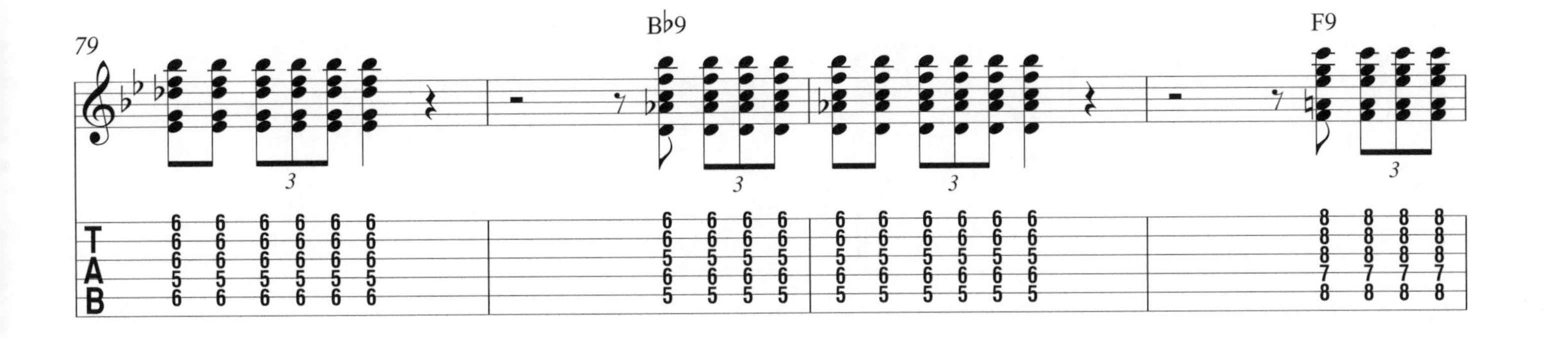

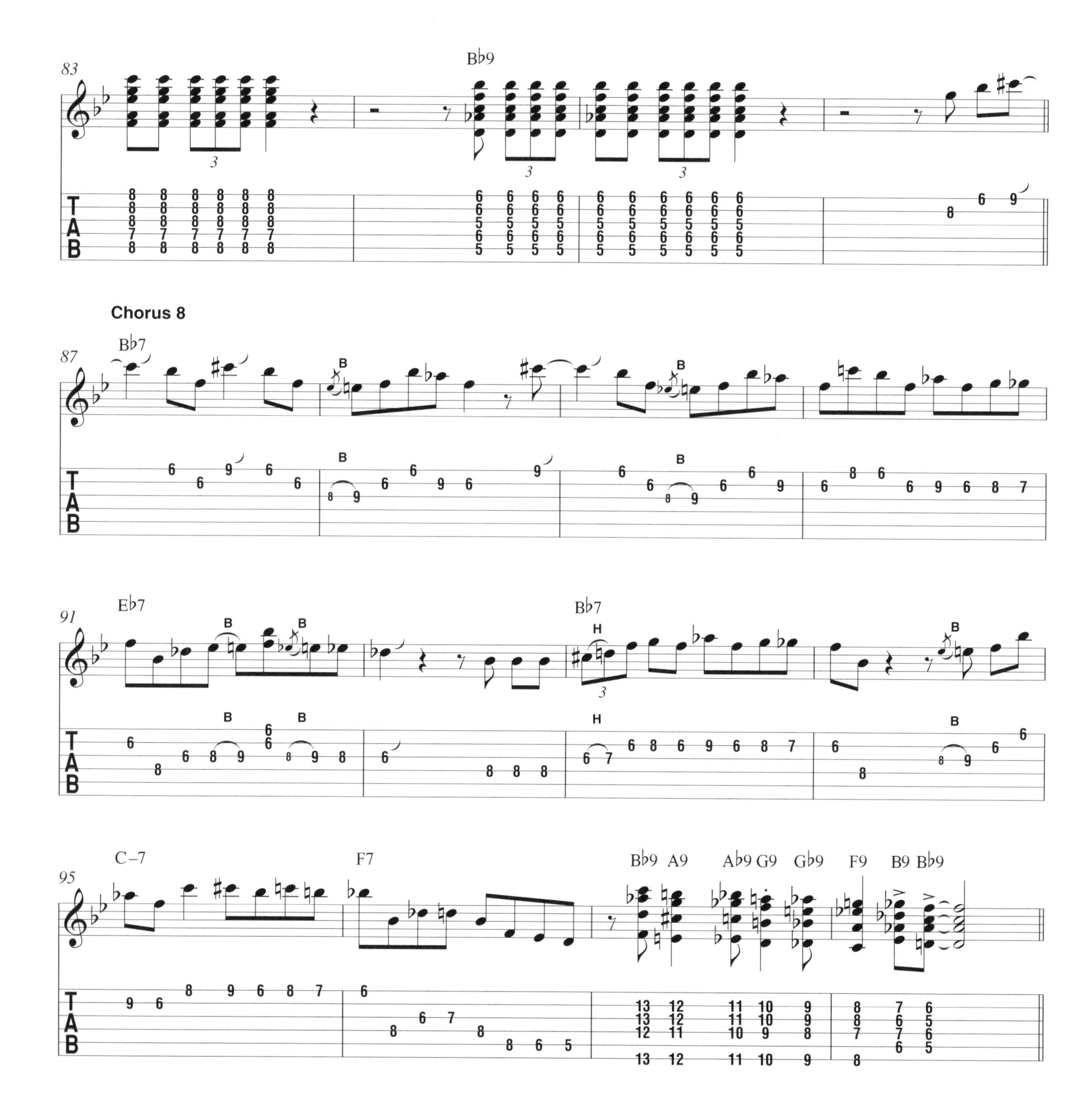

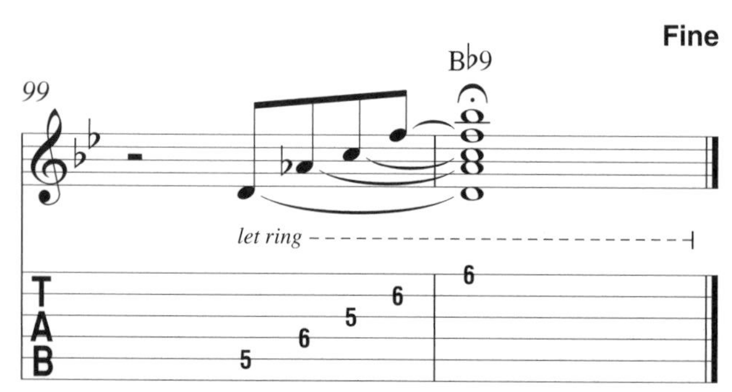

FIG. 6.3. "Jumpin' Bones"

CHAPTER 7

Slow Blues, T-Bone Style: "Slow Bone"

In this chapter, we'll work through few of T-Bone Walker's jazz-influenced rhythm techniques over "Slow Bone," a slow blues in G. Example 7.1 features a mix of T-Bone's signature ninth chords, chromatic shifts, and sliding-ninth fills, which can create colorful and jazz-influenced rhythm parts behind vocals and solos.

A few excellent examples of T-Bone's rhythm guitar style can be heard on his slow blues classics such as "Love Is Just a Gamble," from *The Complete Imperial Recordings 1950–1954*, along with "Blues for Marili" and "Stormy Monday," from *T-Bone Blues*. Both recordings are very highly recommended.

Listen to the "Slow Blues: T-Bone Style" rhythm part along with the music in example 7.1. Fingerings for the G9, C9, and D9 (I7, IV7, and V7) chords, along with the sliding-ninth chords on beats 3 and 4 of bar 5, were discussed and demonstrated in the sliding ninths section in chapter 3, so please refer back to that, if necessary.

Notice the chromatic half-step approaches from F♯9 and A♭9 into G9 in bars 3, 4, 7, 8, etc., along with the chromatic approaches from E♭9/B♭ and C♯9/G♯) into D9/A in bars 9, 10, and 12. If these chromatic shifts are new to you, they may require a little extra practice. So, count and play along with the audio (with guitar) repeatedly, if necessary, to get comfortable with the timing and feel through those sections.

Also notice that the 5 anchors the bottom of the D9/A (V7), E♭9/B♭, and C9/G chords in bars 8 through 12. T-Bone frequently included the 5 in the bottom in chords such as D9/A. They're referred to as *second inversion* chords, and they tend to create extra gravity and drama for the part, so they sound right at home over slow blues progressions such as this.

Practice the slow T-Bone style rhythm part along with figure 7.1. When you're ready, play along with the audio.

30

Slow Bone

T-Bone Style, Rhythm Part

Mike Williams

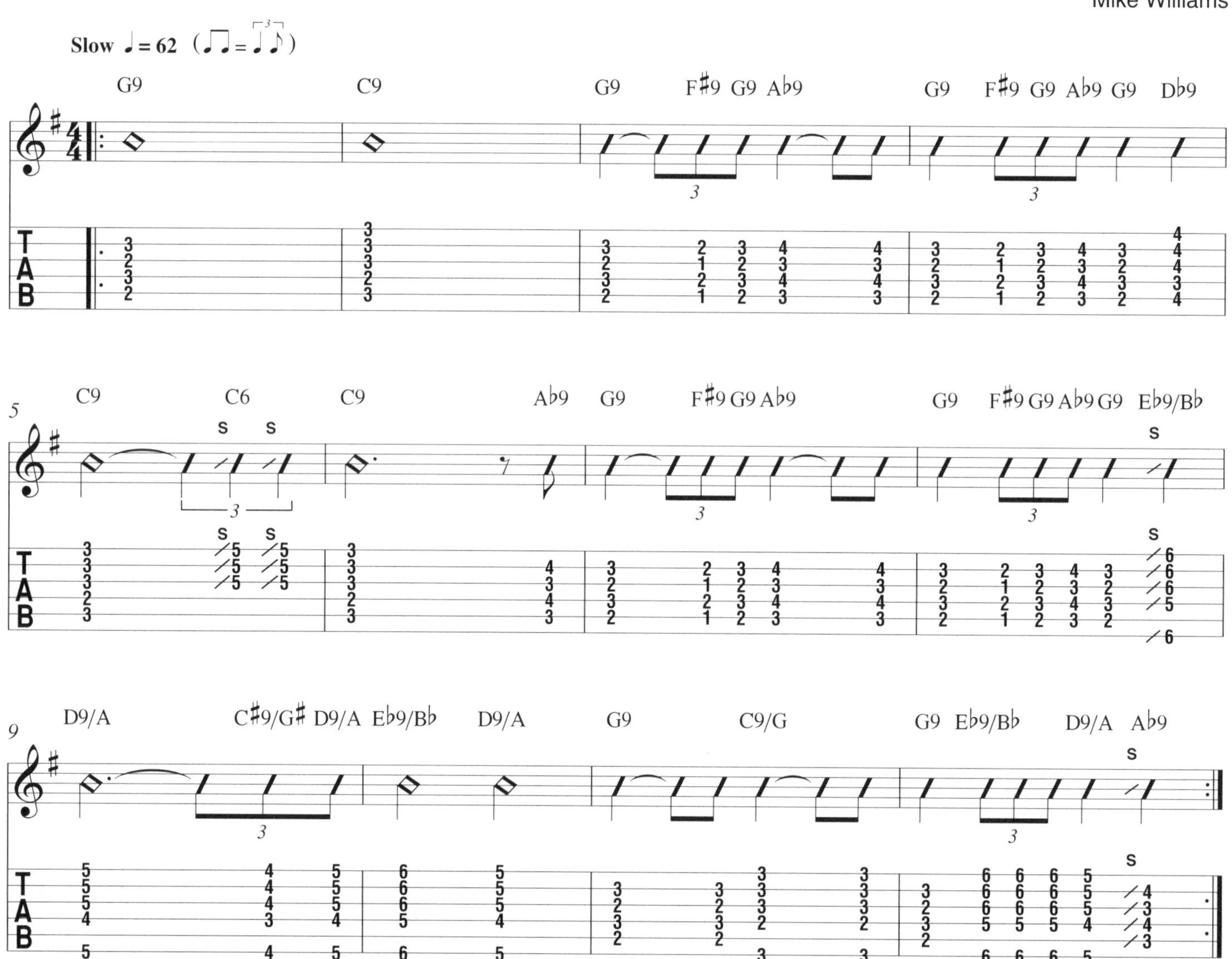

FIG. 7.1. Slow Bone: T-Bone Style Rhythm Part

"SLOW BONE"

Now, let's put the slow T-Bone style rhythm part to work in a performance setting. Listen to the track "Slow Bone," along with the music in example 7.2. The track is four choruses long. Choruses 1, 2, and 4 are guitar solos, and chorus 3 is a variation of the rhythm part in figure 7.1, played behind the piano solo. Guitar solos over chorus 1 and 4 (the last chorus), are included in the music notation and tab in figure 7.2, along with an intro and ending.

Performance Tips

The intro to "Slow Bone" was inspired by T-Bone's slow blues classics such as "Blues for Marili," "Love Is Just a Gamble," and "Stormy Monday." Beginning with guitar only, this intro reworks T-Bone's signature descending second-inversion ninth chords with the deep-sounding 5 in the bass. Bars 1 and 2 move down from G9/D, to F9/C, E♭9/B♭, and D9/A. The G9/D and other chords in the intro are embellished with a simple melody on the high E string. To play that, finger the G9/D chord with fingers 1–3, then add the E (6/13) at the 12th fret with your fourth (pinky) finger. Next, lift your pinky to play chord tones D and A (on strings 1 and 2). The F9/C, E♭9/B♭, and D9/A chords are fingered similarly, and then all four chords are repeated for bars 3 and 4.

One primary goal for this solo was to reflect/demonstrate T-Bone's rhythmic and melodic influences—to adapt and reuse some of his techniques and phrases and mix them with soloing vocabulary of my own. T-Bone's solos are typically anchored with notes of the blues scale (1 ♭3 4 ♭5 5 ♭7), mixed/colorized with the 2/9, 3, and 6/13 from the pentatonic scale. Most of his solos were based in the world's favorite (or "home base") blues fingering, so that's how I approached soloing over "Slow Bone."

Chorus 1

Most of the phrases in both choruses are played on top of the ("home base") G blues scale in the third position. At times, T-Bone's phrases were sparse and relaxed, with lots of room to breathe between statements. Then, as the track progressed, his solo phrases often became more densely packed, with double-time lines, and with groups of triplets, sixteenth notes, or quintuplets crowded into each beat.

T-Bone's phrases over slow blues were often very similar to the lines that he played at medium and faster tempos. For solos over slow blues, T-Bone frequently reworked/adapted his classic eighth-note and triplet-based phrases from faster tempos into more crowded sixteenth-note based lines, which he played more or less at double-time tempos.

My solo on "Slow Bone" mixes slower phrases in places with faster, more crowded rhythmic groupings of quintuplets and sixteenth-note triplets in other places. As is typical for solos over slow tempos such as this, several of the phrases fall rhythmically between the cracks, so they were difficult to transcribe.

T-Bone often added color and texture to his single-note lines by mixing them with 2- and 3-note fills. Bars 9 and 10 create C13 chord sound (with a little added spice) from the sliding ninth fills played in the T-Bone tradition. (Again, if necessary, refer back to chapter 3, where sliding ninth chords are discussed in detail.)

The phrase on beats 1–3 of bar 13 is a quote from some T-Bone solo. (As of this writing, I can't remember the track, but I know it's out there somewhere...) Bar 14 features several funky quick/repeated slides up the D string. That lick was influenced (or instigated) by solos from great sax players, such as King Curtis, Clifford Scott, and Stanley Turrentine.

The solo phrases in bars 15 and 16 are intentionally slower and more relaxed. After playing several faster, more crowded phrases, it felt like it was time to slow it down—to close out the first chorus.

Last Chorus

The last chorus kicks off with a 4-bar phrase ("call") from T-Bone's vast playbook. To finger it, slide up into the B♭, and fret the repeated D and B♭ notes on the top (E and B) strings with fingers 1 and 2. Slightly tweak the B♭ notes, with quarter-step bends, and pick the D and B♭ notes as alternating eighth-note triplets. Keep 'em comin' throughout most of bars 17–19. Then, on the last triplet of beat 4, slide up into the big/fat G9/D chord. Really accent the triplets on beats 1 and 2, to notch up the intensity level a bit. Finally, slide down off of another big/dramatic G9/D chord hit on beat 3, to set up the "response" in bars 21–24.

T-Bone had a natural flair for creating drama and intensity in a solo, and an opening call-and-response phrase such as this can leave the listener wondering, "What's coming next?"

To answer that question (or call), another quote from one of T-Bone's solos surfaced in bars 21 and 22. (Again, I don't remember where it came from, but I'm sure that I heard him play it more than once, and I learned it long ago by listening and singing along with his solos.)

Bar 23 starts with a 3-note motif (D F G) that's repeated a few times. As it develops, it leads into longer, more complex phrases in bars 24 and 25. T-Bone frequently employed that technique in his solos. He would start with a simple, short phrase, which would develop into longer, more complex phrases as the solo unfolded. An example of that can be heard in his solos on "Papa Ain't Salty," from his record *T-Bone Blues*, which is analyzed and discussed in detail in the *Berklee Blues Guitar Songbook* (Berklee Press, 2010).

Bars 23–26 continue with more phrases based on G blues, combined with added A (9) and E (13) notes from G pentatonic. Notice the call and response from one bar to the next, and also note that each statement starts before and plays across the barline. Again, that helps the phrases to have more of a conversational and less compartmentalized (or rhythmically boxed-in) feel, overall. Listen for that quality in solos by T-Bone Walker, B.B. King, and others.

The track concludes in bars 27 and 28 with one of T-Bone's influential and often imitated endings. Start on beat 1 by picking the root (G) on the 4th string (third finger), followed by three big eighth-note hits on a B♭ diminished triad (D♭ E B♭) on strings 3-2-1. This type of diminished triad (the "train-whistle" chord) was discussed in detail in chapter 6, "Jumpin' Bones," so refer back to that, if necessary. On beat 3, hit the C9 (IV7) chord, followed by three more hits on the B♭ diminished triad. On beat 1 of bar 28, play G9, followed by A♭9, and finally back "home" to G9 on beat 3. A final arpeggio through the G9 chord wraps up the track "T-Bone style" with notes B F A D, and with a G (root) added as the top note. To play that, lay your pinky across the top string (3rd fret) and pick the final G note, as the chord continues to ring.

Good luck with this rhythm part and solo. If you've enjoyed this style of slow blues, keep listening and tapping into the wealth of ideas, techniques, and inspiration from T-Bone's recordings. Play chorus after chorus of your own solos over this progression. Adapt T-Bone's rhythm parts and phrases; rework/ change them around to make them your own.

Practice "Slow Bone" along with the music in figure 7.2. When you're ready, play along with the audio. Refer to figure 7.1 for the exact rhythm guitar part in bars 7–8, 11–12, 43–44, and 47–48.

FIG. 7.2. "Slow Bone" Solo

CHAPTER 8

Two Rhythm Parts in the Style of Robert Lockwood Jr.: "Shuffle in A"

FILLS AND TURNAROUNDS IN "SHUFFLE IN A"

With a style that encompasses a vast range of influences—from Robert Johnson and the Mississippi Delta, to jazz—Robert Lockwood Jr. is recognized as one of the greatest blues guitarists of all time. "Shuffle in A" is a tribute to his unique and powerful performances on recordings as a leader, as well as with artists such as Sonny Boy Williamson, Little Walter, Otis Spann, and many others.

This "Shuffle in A" was influenced/inspired in a big way by Lockwood's classic rhythm parts on tracks with Sonny Boy Williamson, such as "Keep It to Yourself."

Performance Tips

Choruses 1 and 2

Choruses 1 and 2 begin with the guitar holding down a tight low-end bass pattern on top of an A7 barre chord in position 5, for the first three measures of each chorus. The repeated triplets in the fourth measure (beats 1–3 of choruses 1 to 3) create a powerful A7 chord sound, along with plenty of gravitational pull toward the IV7 (D7) chord. To finger this 3-note A7 chord, slide up with triplets into chord tones E G C♯ on the top three strings, on frets 9-8-9. (**NOTE:** this chord also forms a C♯ diminished triad, and similar voicings are discussed in more detail in chapters 6, 7, and 9, so refer to those pages if necessary.)

The fifth and sixth measures of all four choruses feature variations of Robert Lockwood's classic fills over the D7 (IV7) chord. Lockwood probably adapted/created these riffs from parts that he learned first-hand from Robert Johnson, who's been referred to over the decades as Lockwood's stepfather. It's a shame that Lockwood never took patents out on these fills, because they've been adapted and rerecorded countless times by others, since he first invented them.

There are a number of options for fingering these fills. They can be played as 3-note fills on three strings, or as 2-note two-string fills. As notated in figure 8.1, they can be fingered on the top (E and B) strings, or on the G and B strings. I used both fingerings on the audio. In choruses 1, 3, and 4, the fills were fingered higher up the fretboard, on strings G and B; in chorus 2, they were fingered lower, on strings B and E. In every chorus, the fill creates a little extra forward momentum by starting *before* beat 1 of bar 5 with a slide up into F♯ (the 3 of D7). With steady triplets throughout the bar, beat 1 outlines D7 with chord tones F♯ and C (3 and ♭7). Beat 2 is played as a "passing" G7, with chord tones F and B (also the 3 and ♭7). Beats 3 and 4 return to the D7 sound with chords tones F♯ and A (3 and 5).

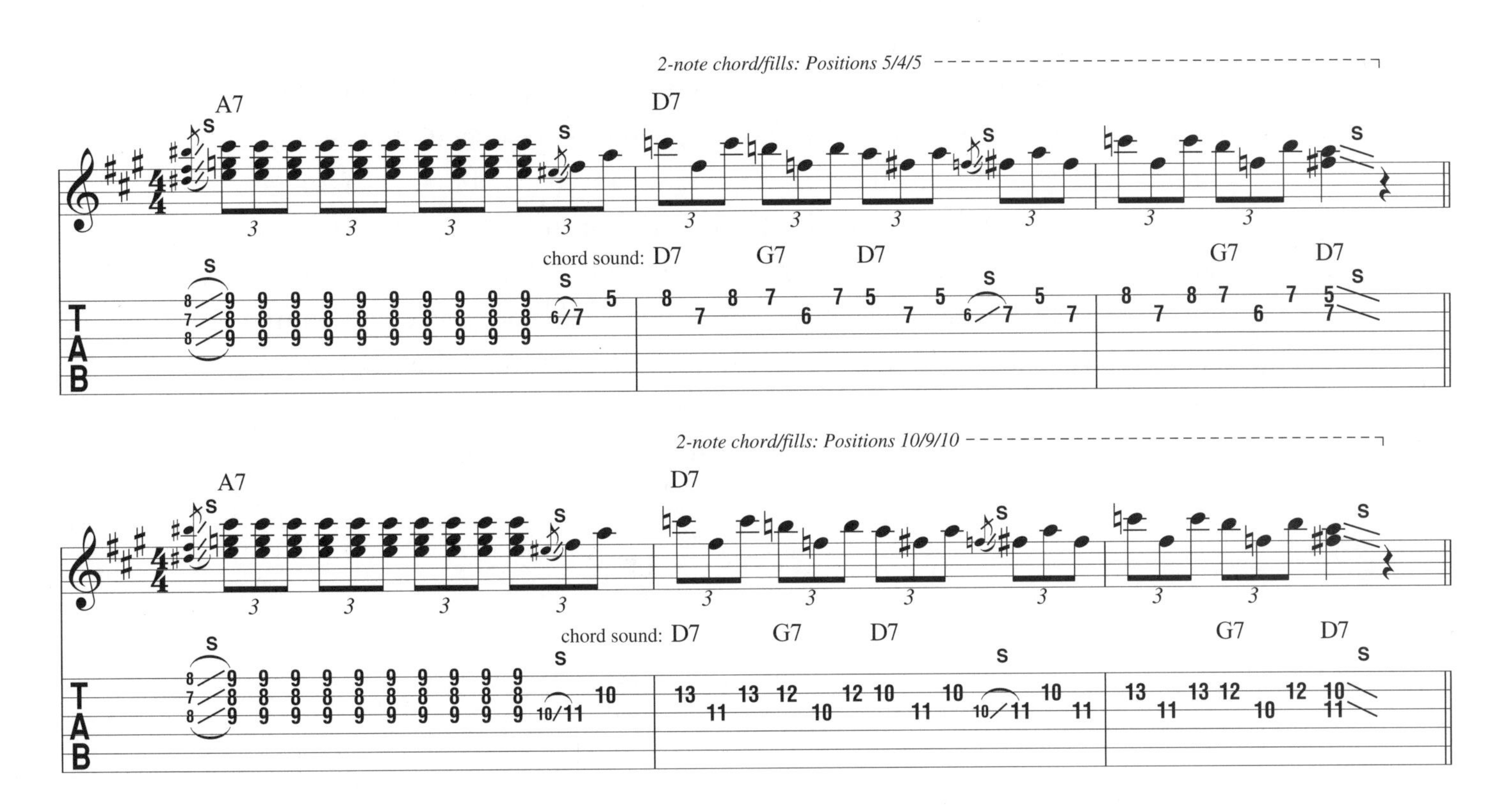

FIG. 8.1. Chord tones (3 and ♭7) Outline Alternating D7 G7 Sound through Bars 5 and 6

The seventh and eighth measures of choruses 1–3 return to mostly continuous triplets and more forward momentum from the chord tones of A7 (E G C♯), similar to bar 4. Bars 9 and 10 are once again played as triplets on chord tones 3 and ♭7, to outline alternating E7 and A7 chords in bar 9, and D7 and G7 chords through beat 3 of bar 10.

The fills in bars 9 and 10 are fingered just like the fills over D7 in bars 5 and 6. Both sit right on top of D7 and E7 chords. I played them on the top two strings in choruses 2 and 4, and higher up the fretboard, on strings G and B, in choruses 1 and 3.

Choruses 3 and 4

Choruses 3 and 4 begin by varying from the (low-end) bass pattern over A7 from choruses 1 and 2. Bars 1 and 2 instead feature A7 D A7 chords on beats 1–3. This 3-note A7 is fingered in position 5, and it's simply a smaller version of a standard/full A7 barre chord. The D "passing" (IV) chord on beat 2 is played with a third-finger barre in the 7th fret across strings 4-3-2.

Bar 27 features another classic fill from Lockwood's vast "library" of rhythm techniques. To play it, fret the E and C♯ notes on the G and E strings with fingers 2 and 3. (Note that the E and C♯ notes form a major sixth interval.) Next, move that fingering/shape (major sixth) down two frets to play notes D and B. Then, to finish the fill, "tweak" (bend) the note C, so that it sounds somewhere between C (♭3/♯9) and C♯ (the major 3).

Robert Lockwood's rhythmic and melodic influences come through "loud and clear" in the turnarounds on choruses 3 and 4. Lockwood's turnarounds are often based on a sophisticated (and jazz influenced) combination of triplets, sixteenth notes, and sixteenth-note triplets. They also tend to include colorful and melodic 9s and 13s, mixed with notes from the blues scale. Lockwood's mix of 9s and 13s, combined with jazzier rhythms, provide extra color, texture, and pizzazz for his rhythm parts and solos. Both are essential components of his unique and personal sound. Lockwood's fills and turnarounds can be challenging to get under the fingers, but they're well worth the extra practice.

Listen to example 8.2, and practice the part. When you're ready, play along with the audio.

A7
D7
E7
Rake
Chorus 3
(D)

FIG. 8.2. "Shuffle in A" with Lockwood-Style Fills

WALKING TENTHS ON "TAKIN' A STROLL"

"Takin' a Stroll" (figure 8.5) showcases another side of Robert Lockwood Jr.'s rhythm guitar style, with three choruses of his innovative "walking tenths" over a shuffle in E.

Robert Lockwood's "walking tenths" provide extra harmonic motion, and a welcome variation in texture and sound, behind vocal parts and solos on many recordings, such as "Take a Little Walk with Me," "C. C. Rider," "Lonely Man," and "Worst Old Feeling." Lockwood's parts such as this were influenced or derived from the left-hand (bass) patterns of stride and/or boogie-woogie pianists, and that's a reflection of the vast range of styles and instruments that influenced his musical development over the decades.

Performance Tips

Listen to "Takin' a Stroll" while following along with the notation. Notice that with the exception of the (larger) E7 chords on beat 1 of bars 1–4, etc., much of the track is played as 2-note chords that are constructed on the interval of a tenth (hence, the name "walking tenths"). **NOTE:** A tenth is an octave plus a third. (If these terms are new to you, I recommend learning about intervals, as part of an in-depth study of ear training and theory.)

Chorus 1

Bars 1–4 of "Takin' a Stroll" consist of a very similar pattern of walking tenths over the E7 (I7) chord. Bars 1–8 of all three choruses are anchored by a bass pattern of steady eighth notes along the low E string. The bass pattern in bar 1 begins with notes E E, F♯ F♯, G♯ G♯, F♯ F♯ 1 1, 2 2, 3 3, 2 2). A second note, fretted on the G string, sounds a tenth above each bass note, to form the walking tenths in bars 1–8. Lockwood often played parts such as this finger-style, but the walking tenths can be played with a pick, or with pick and fingers also. I played choruses 1–3 finger-style, mostly because the turnarounds in choruses 1 and 2 seem to work better that way.

Example 8.3 is a brief excerpt from chorus 1. It illustrates the bass pattern described above, along with the harmony that the walking tenths create over the E7 (I7) and A7 (IV7) chords in bars 3 though 5.

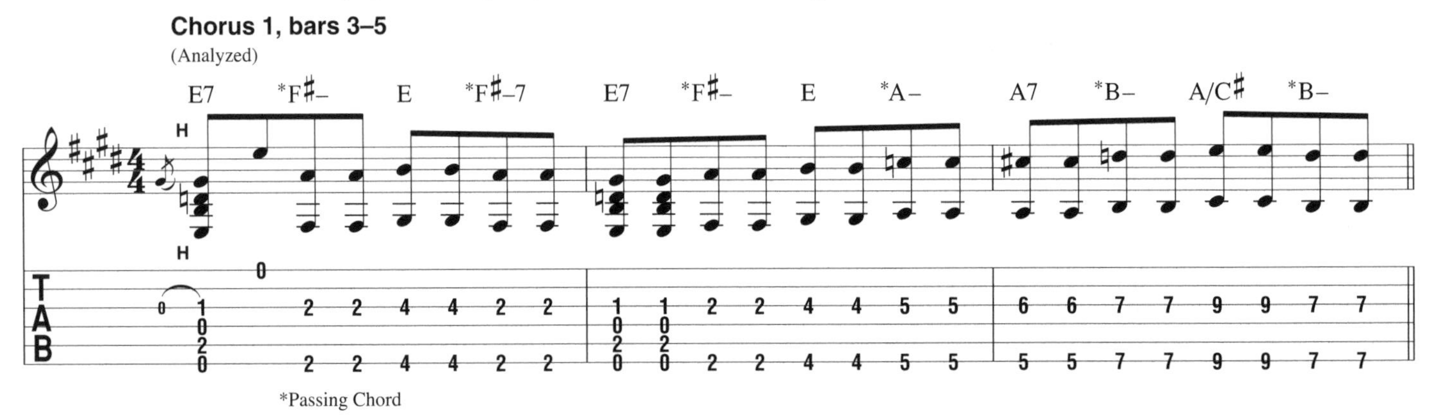

FIG. 8.3. Chorus 1, Bars 3–5

Note the asterisks (*) in figure 8.3. On beat 2 of bar 3, the notes F♯ and A create either an F♯ minor or B7 passing chord sound. F♯ and A can be analyzed as the root and ♭3 of F♯ minor, and they're also the 5 and ♭7 of B7. Either way you hear it, it works as a passing chord. And the same applies to the B– chord on beats 2 and 4 of bar 5, which can be analyzed as either B– or E7/B. On beat 3 of bar 3, notes G♯ and B are chord tones 3 and 5 of E7. Beat 4 returns to notes F♯ and A, analyzed the same as beat 2. On beat 4 of bar 4, the upper note C approaches C♯ (the 3rd of A7) on beat 1 of bar 5. Beat 4 of bar 4 is analyzed as an A– passing chord. And while it sounds a bit odd (to my ear) in this context, it works, because it connects chord tones G♯ and B of E7 on beat 3, with half step motion, to notes A and C♯ of A7 in bar 5.

Bar 5 outlines harmony that's similar to bars 1–4, but transposed to the IV7 (A7) chord. Beats 1–4 are analyzed as: A7, B– (or E7/B), A/C♯, B– (or E7/B). Bar 6 is fingered similarly to bar 5, and bar 7 returns to E7, with chords that are similar to bar 1.

Example 8.4 illustrates the harmony in bars 8 and 9. Note that beats 1 and 2 of bar 8 are similar to beats 1 and 2 of bar 3. On beat 3 of bar 8, note the E triad that's followed by C7/G on beat 4, which is a chromatic approach into the B7/F♯ in bar 9.

FIG. 8.4. Chorus 1, Bars 8–9

Bar 10 of "Takin' a Stroll" sets the turnaround up with a classic Lockwood/Chicago style ascending line of eighth notes (A A, C C♯, D D, E♭ E). Lockwood's influences are all over the turnaround phrase in bars 11–12 also. It starts with two eighth notes on the low open E (on beat 1 and "and" of 1). On beat 2, finger a standard open-position E7 chord with fingers 2 and 1 on notes B and G♯ (A string, 2nd fret, and G string, 1st fret). Pick chord tones B, G♯, and open E as triplets, as notated in the music and tab. For beats 3 and 4, the 2-note E7 fingering/shape moves up chromatically by half steps through beat 1 of bar 12, where it resolves on chord tones D B and E (♭7 5 and root) of E7. Next, on beat 2 of bar 12, is an ascending triplet (notes A A♯ B), which is a double chromatic approach into the B7/F♯ (V7), to wrap up chorus 1.

As discussed earlier, I've found that it's easier to play this turnaround finger-style, in order to skip strings while picking the ascending triplets on strings 5,

3, and 1 (open E) in bars 11 and 12. Pick and fingers (or pick-style) can work for that also, so use whatever picking method works for you!

Choruses 2 and 3

Bars 13–20 of chorus 2 are similar to bars 1–8 in chorus 1. Notice the E and A notes filling in the triads on beat 3 of bars 16 and 17, which create a subtle change—a little extra depth to the chorus. Also note the Lockwood-style fill over A7 in bar 22 that sets up the turnaround in bars 23 and 24.

Chorus 3 presents another variation for bars 25–28. On beat 3 of bars 25–27, notes G and B♭ (A♯) function as chord tones of E diminished, which "passes" chromatically to the E triad on beat 4. Bar 28 features one of Lockwood's vintage E7(♯9) chord fills on the top 3 strings. To nail it with as much of his "deep-blues" feel as possible, tweak/bend the G note (B string, 8th fret), so that it sounds somewhere between G natural and G♯. Really lean into those triplet-based strums. Play them with as much conviction and intensity as you can tap into.

Bars 29 and 30 are similar to bars 25–26. Here, they're transposed to play over the A7 (IV7) chord; beat 3 functions as a passing A diminished chord, which leads to an A triad on beat 4. Bar 31 is similar to bars 25–28, etc., and the C7/G in bar 32 approaches the B7/F♯ (V7) in bar 33, just like it did from bar 20–21 in chorus 2. Bar 34 features another triplet based phrase—on loan from Robert Lockwood's "school of the arts." This one's a jazzy sounding mix of notes from the open E minor pentatonic (E G A B D) that's been colorized with notes F♯, G♯, and C♯ (2/9, 3, and 6/13) from E pentatonic. Like choruses 1 and 2, chorus 3 wraps up in bar 36 with a return to the (V7) B7/F♯ chord. Lockwood must have preferred the deeper sounding 5 in the bass for his turnarounds (i.e., the F♯ that anchors the B7 chord), because he recorded them on track after track.

During his lifetime of ninety-one years, Robert Lockwood Jr. left his unique and indelible signature on the blues. He helped invent the language as it's played today. So seek out and learn from his recordings. Take apart his fills and turnarounds. Adapt and reuse his phrases in your own way!

Listen to example 8.5, "Takin' a Stroll," and practice the part. When you're ready, play along with the audio.

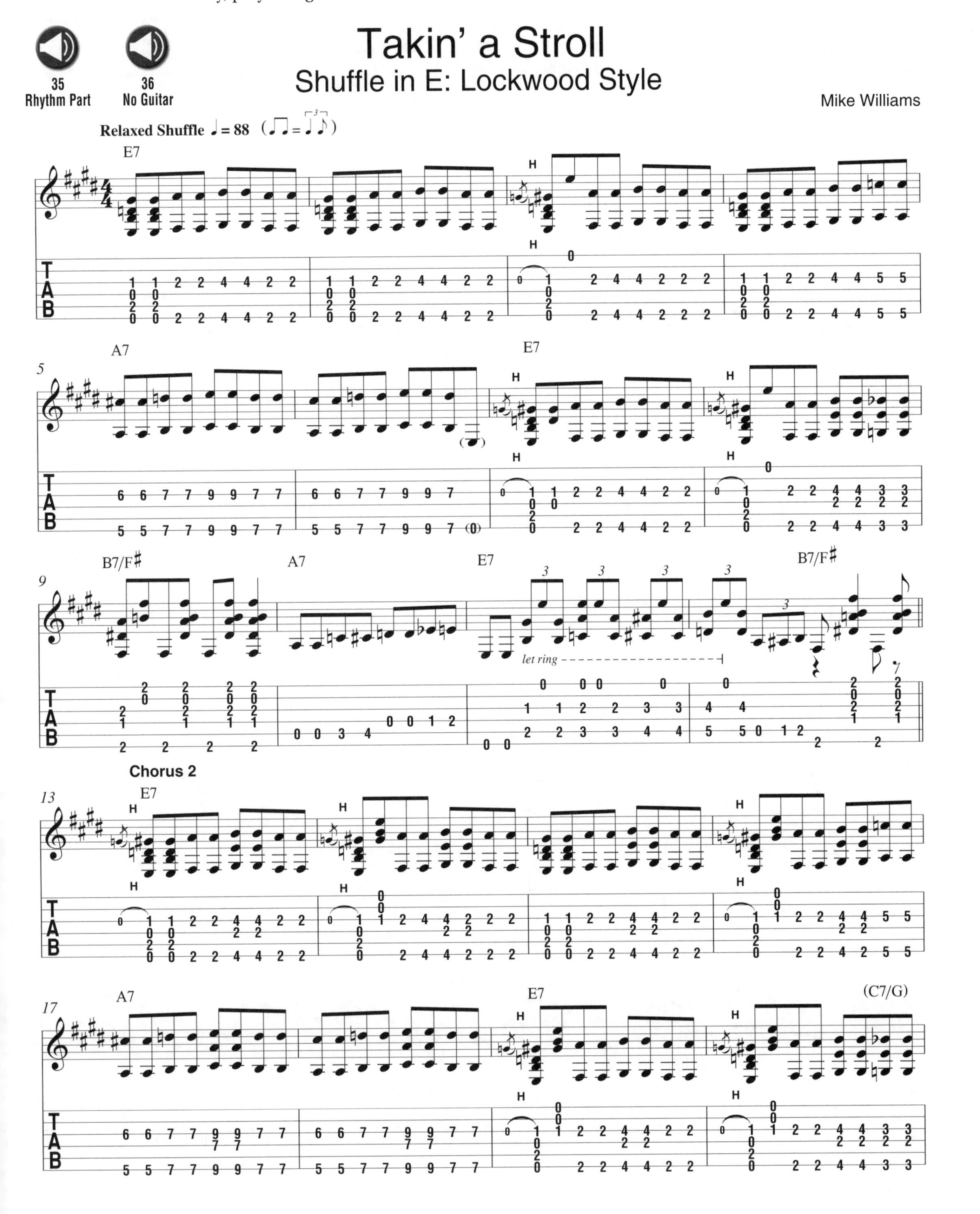

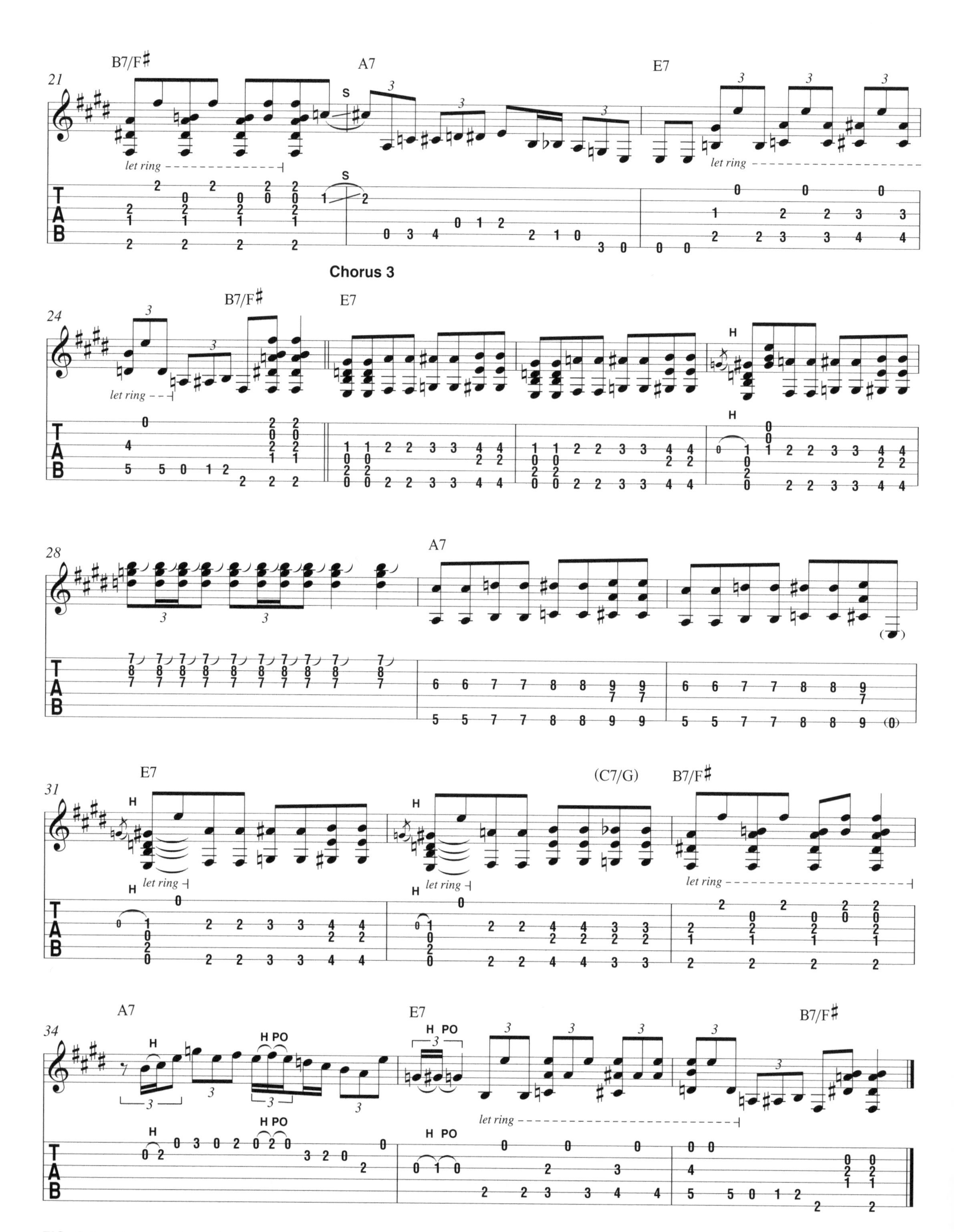

FIG. 8.5. "Takin' a Stroll"

CHAPTER 9

Quick Takes on Two Rhythm Parts: "Slow Blues in E"

"SLOW BLUES IN E"

In part 1 of this chapter, you'll work through a rhythm part for "Slow Blues in E." The solo, tempo, and overall feel was inspired by B.B. King's stellar live performances on tracks such as "Sweet Little Angel" and "Worry, Worry," from *Live at the Regal,* along with "Night Life" and other tracks from *Blues Is King.* I recorded the solo first, then overdubbed the rhythm guitar part after that. The goal while recording this rhythm part was to provide momentum, interaction, and support for the solo, and to leave plenty of room (i.e., to stay out of the way), at the same time. That may sound easy, but it's an ongoing challenge for most of us.

"Slow Blues in E" is four choruses of a standard 12-bar blues in E, with a quick IV, so bar 2 is played as A7. The basic form is as follows:

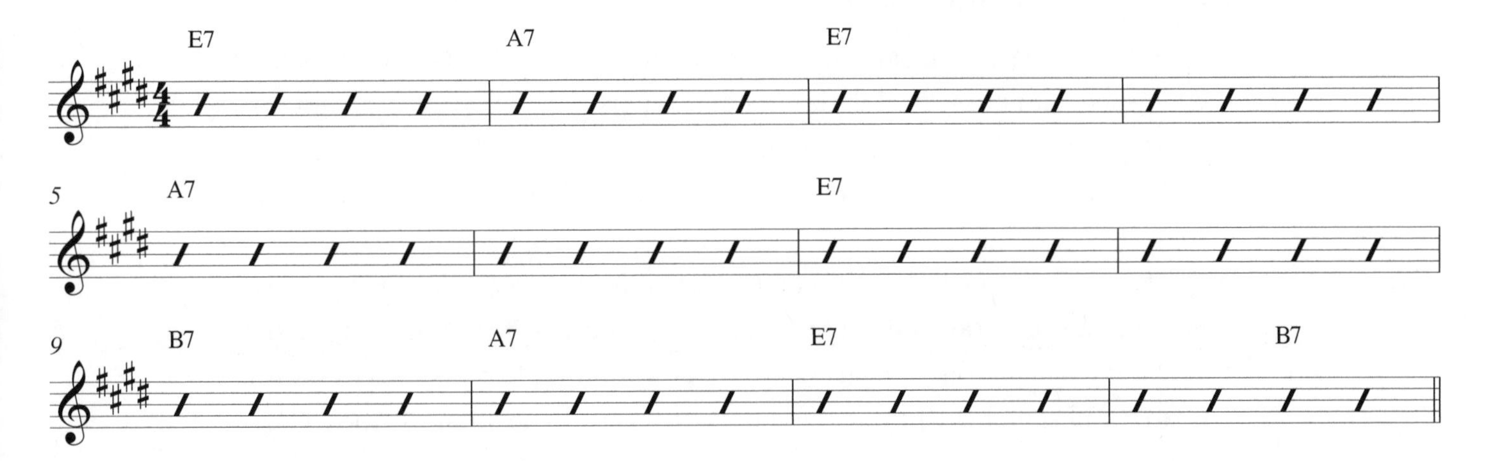

FIG. 9.1. "Slow Blues in E" Basic Form

Performance Tips

Take a look and listen to the variations for the chords in choruses 1–4 of example 9.2. Right from the opening E9 chord in bar 1, tensions such as 9s and 13s provide added color and depth for the I7, IV7, and V7 chords throughout the track. Other voicings, such as E13sus4 in bar 1 and E13 in bar 4, also provide texture and depth. Sliding ninth chords (such as the A6/A9 in bars 5–6, and E6/E9 in bar 8) are played frequently throughout all four choruses, and they also provide 9 and 13 color and harmonic momentum behind the solo. **NOTE:** Most of the chords on this track—including the sliding ninths—were played (and analyzed/discussed in the same key) in "Like a Rocket," from chapter 5. They were also explained in detail in chapter 3, so refer to those pages if necessary.

Chromatic passing chords provide a jazzier texture and smooth, half-step voice leading between chords in several places throughout the track. B♭9 approaches A9 (IV7) in bars 5, 29, and 41. Also note the C9 that approaches B9 (V7) in bars 9, 21, 33, and 45.

Bars 25–27 feature classic Chicago-style chords that were inspired/influenced by Muddy Waters and Jimmy Rodgers. Bar 25 begins with a 3-note voicing of E7, with chord tones B D and G♯ (5, ♭7, 3) on the top three strings. (Those notes also form a G♯ diminished triad.) In bar 26, that same fingering shifts down one fret, to tap into some serious Windy City "mojo" over the A7 chord. This is the diminished "train whistle" chord, discussed in the T-Bone style "Jumpin' Bones," from chapter 6. Next, in bar 27, the G diminished fingering shifts back up to E7 (G♯ diminished), and that's followed by more sliding ninths in bar 28, which leads to the IV7 (A9) chord in bar 29.

The same 3-note chords are played in the turnarounds for choruses 1, 2, and 4. Beat 2 of each of those turnarounds begins with E7 sound (G♯ diminished). Then, the chord shifts down chromatically on beats 3 and 4, and resolves on an open position E7 chord on beat 1 of bar 12.

Brief Notes about the Solo

Slow blues progressions are the perfect vehicle to take the listener through a wide spectrum of musical dynamics and intensity. So, they're fun, and very challenging to play over, at the same time. My solo over the slow blues is not written out, but as noted earlier, that track was inspired by some of my favorite solos by B.B. King.

If you want to play along by ear, here's a brief outline of where the solo was played: Chorus 1 starts up in the "home base" fingering for E blues, in position 12. Bars 1–5 of chorus 2 are also played in position 12. Bar 6 of chorus 2 shifts up to the next higher E minor pentatonic fingering, in position 15. And then, in bar 8, it shifts back to position 12. The turnaround before chorus 3 drops down into the open position, and bars 1–7 (of chorus 3) are also played down there. Around bar 8, the solo works its way back up into the higher regions. The first half of chorus 4 begins way up in position 15, and then the solo wraps up back at "home," in position 12.

While I wasn't intentionally copying B.B.'s phrases note-for-note, my hope was to tap into at least a small portion of his feel and intensity. And while on the subject of conveying intensity and feel, B.B. King's recordings *Blues Is King* and *Live at the Regal* are essential listening for anyone that's into electric blues. B.B.'s intensity level on the track "Night Life" (from *Blues Is King*) sails right though the roof; his performance on that track (and record) has been a huge inspiration over the years. In the words of Chicago bluesman Jimmy Rodgers, "If you ain't got it, go out and get it."

First listen to the solo and rhythm part in example 9.2. Then practice the rhythm part along with the audio. (Also play your own rhythm parts and solos along with this track!)

Chorus 2
E7
A9
E7
E6
E9
A9
A6
A9
trem
E7
E6
E9
C9
B9
B♭9
trem
A9
E7 (G♯°)
(G°)
(F♯°)
E7
B7/F♯
tr
Chorus 3
E7 (G♯°)
A7 (G°)
E7 (G♯°)
trem
T
A
B

E6
E9
B♭9
A9
A6
A9
E7
E6
E9
C9
B9
trem
A9
E7
B7/F♯
Chorus 4
E7
A7
E7
B♭9
A9
A6
A9
TAB

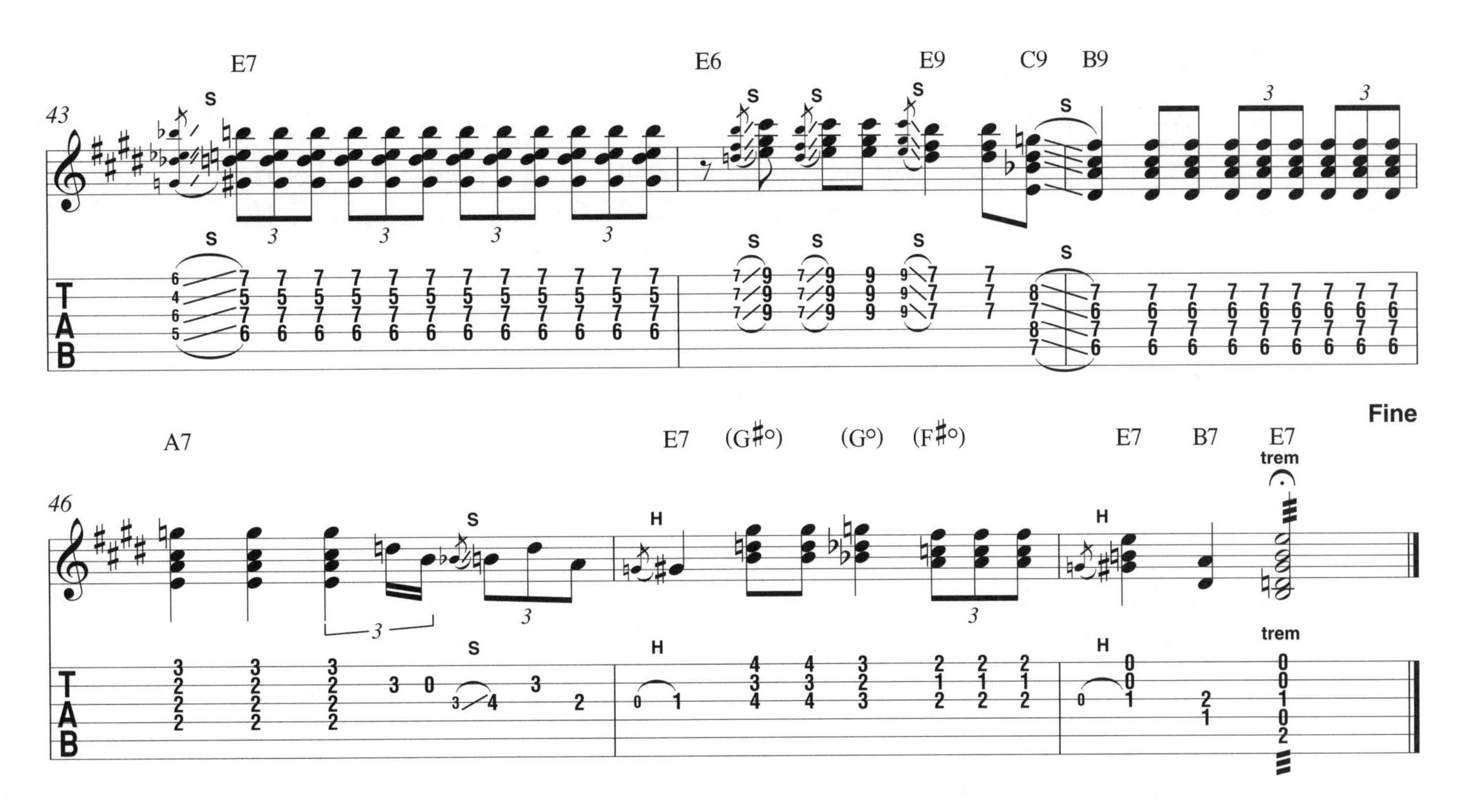

FIG. 9.2. "Slow Blues in E" Rhythm Part

RHYTHMIC HITS OVER A "SHUFFLE IN F"

Next, we'll change up the tempo and groove, and introduce few a other variations for a "Shuffle in F" that are well worth having under the fingers. Choruses 1 and 2 of example 9.3 feature vintage rhythmic hits that have been played on hundreds of recordings by the likes of B.B. King, Eric Clapton, Jimmy Vaughan, Robert Cray, and many others. The rhythmic hits in choruses 3 and 4 lean more toward the Albert Collins sound and feel–so they would sound right at home on instrumentals such as "Don't Lose Your Cool," "Backstroke," "Frosty," or most shuffles at this tempo.

Performance Tips

Choruses 1 and 2

Choruses 1 and 2 feature punchy rhythmic hits on beats 1 and the "and" of beat 2 that provide tons of forward momentum and drive for the rhythm section. To nail the feel for this part, smack all of the chord hits with a punchy, staccato, and aggressive picking attack, as demonstrated in the audio.

Choruses 1 and 2 sound pretty similar, since the rhythmic hits are the same for both. Chorus 1 is anchored by the F6 fingering in position 1, while chorus 2 features a higher F9 up in position 7. The B♭9 (IV7) and C9 (V7) chords also shift up the neck for chorus 2. In the first chorus, the B♭9 is played in position 1 with notes (from bottom to top) B♭ D A♭ C F (root, 3, ♭7, 9, 5). The B♭9 in chorus 2 is played on the inside strings in position 5 instead, with notes D A♭ C F. (Notice that these are the same notes as the previous B♭9 fingering, minus the low B♭/root.)

Chorus 3

Chorus 3 also packs lots of drive and attitude, and these chord hits are also played with punchy/staccato picking attack. Here, the hits sound on beats 2 and on the "and" of beat 2. Notice that bars 25–28 feature a passing B♭ triad (IV), which resolves to F7 (I7). Bars 29, 30, and 34 feature a B♭ passing triad that moves to A♭, which sounds great over the B♭7 (IV7) chord. Bar 33 similarly features passing C to B♭ triads over the V7 chord.

Chorus 4

Chorus 4 is very similar to chorus 3, with the subtle addition of the F (root) on beat "and" of 1, which somehow creates even more momentum and attitude for the part. As you'll notice in the notation for chorus 4, I played the note F every other bar (G in bar 9), but feel free to vary and experiment with the placement of subtle additions such as this. At the same time, keep in mind that for rhythm parts like this that are sittin' in the pocket, less is more!

Listen to example 9.3, and practice the rhythm parts in choruses 1–4. When you're ready, play along with the audio.

17
B♭9
F9
21
C9
B♭9
F9
Chorus 3
25
(F7) B♭ F7
B♭ F7
B♭ F7
B♭ F7
29
(B♭7) B♭ A♭
B♭ A♭
(F7) B♭ F7
B♭ F7
33
(C7) C B♭
(B♭7) B♭ A♭
(F7) B♭ F7
B♭ F7

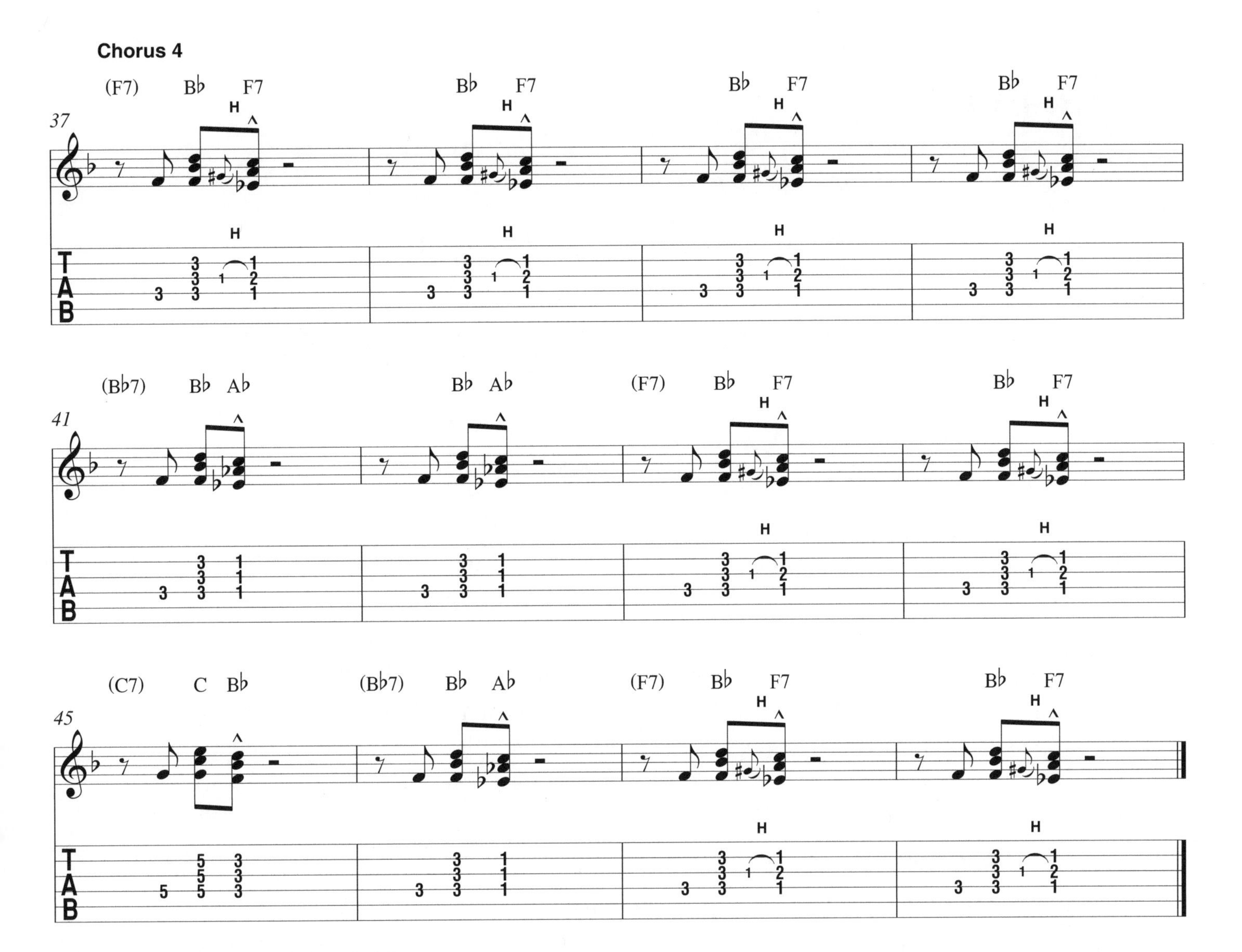

FIG. 9.3. "Shuffle in F" Rhythmic Hits

CHAPTER 10

Rhythm and Solo Workout over a Shuffle in G: "Doggin' It"

In this chapter, you'll learn a lead-sheet style arrangement to "Doggin' It," a shuffle in G, along with two choruses of the guitar solo and two choruses of rhythm guitar.

Example 10.1 is a lead sheet for the head (melody) to "Doggin' It." That's followed by two choruses of the guitar solo in example 10.2 and two choruses of rhythm guitar in example 10.3. Listen to "Doggin' It" on the audio, and follow along with the notation. The track is ten choruses long, and the arrangement is as follows:

Choruses 1, 2: In Head (see example 10.1)

Choruses 3, 4, 5: Guitar Solo (see example 10.2)

Choruses 6, 7: Piano Solo (two choruses of rhythm guitar are written in example 10.3)

Choruses 8, 9: Bass and Drums Solo Together: Trading 4s

Chorus 10: Out Head, to Coda; the song ends with an improvised guitar fill, followed by three final chromatic chords, F9, F♯9, G9 (see example 10.1)

Performance Tips

About the Lead Sheet Arrangement

Many of the rhythm section players that I perform with can sight-read lead sheets, so my original reason for writing this shuffle was to come up with another tune that I could call during unrehearsed live performances. "Doggin' It" was written in the key of G, since that's one of my favorite keys for rhythm parts and solos over blues, and it works well for keyboard players also. Another intention while writing this head was to include rhythmic hits and stops (such as in bars 8, 9, and 12), to lend a few jazzier influences, while keeping it simple (and greasy) at the same time. When playing in a trio setting, the hits and stops can be played by bass and drums. The keyboard part adds quite a bit of color and support to the track, though, so I'm happy to play tunes such as this with piano or organ whenever possible.

I originally had a cleaner/jazzier vintage Blue Note tone and concept in mind for guitar, when I set out to write this. However, somehow, I ended up with the ol' white Strat in my hands, along with a dirtier Fender tweed amp tone, as I hit the "Record" button. This solo popped out in the first take, so my concept of the tune—less clean, more dirt—changed right then and there.

As notated in example 10.1, the head to "Doggin' It" lays in position 3, on top of the "home-base" G blues fingering (G B♭ C D♭ D F). B and E notes from the 2nd position G pentatonic scale add "major" sound/color (the 3 and 6/13) to the mix.

FIG. 10.1. "Doggin' It" Lead Sheet

About the Solo

The first chorus of the guitar solo (chorus 3 of the track) is also played in position 3, and it's mostly rooted in the G blues tonality. Bars 6, 7, 8, and 12 tap into G pentatonic sound with the addition of the note E (the 6/13), and bars 3, 7, 10, and 11 feature the B (major 3), also from G pentatonic.

Most of the second chorus of the guitar solo is played in position 3 also, with the exception of bars 14, 15, and beat 1 of bar 16. Those phrases lay in the next higher position 5/6 G minor pentatonic fingering. Note the B.B. King–inspired quick pull-off/slide combination on beat 1 of bar 16, which shifts from the higher 5/6 position, back to the "home-base" fingering in position 3. (If you've worked through other solos in the book, this should already sound familiar.) Start by fretting the B♭ note with your first finger on the top string (6th fret). Next, strike the G note with your third finger (B string, 8th fret), then immediately pull off to F (first finger, 6th fret), then slide down from F, to D (3rd fret) to finish the phrase. (Thanks again for this one, B.B.!)

Also worth noting are the repeated string bends that are played as eighth notes through beats 2, 3, and 4 of bar 14. (This is essentially one long string bend, that's notated as pre-bends through beats 2–4.) Once again, this phrase lays in the position 5/6 G minor pentatonic fingering. Play up the notes G, B♭, and C, then *slowly* bend/tweak the C (third finger, 8th fret) on beat 2, up a half step, to C♯ (and beyond) for beats 3 and 4. The bend(s) finally resolve up into the note D, written as a whole step pre-bend from C to D, on beat 1 of bar 15.

Take a look at the phrase that begins on beat 3 of bar 16. It begins with notes E, G, E in position 3, in the "home-base" G blues fingering. Also, note the high D on beat 1 of bar 17. To catch that high D, quickly slide your pinky or third finger up to the 10th fret; then slide immediately back down to the "home" box in position 3, to finish the phrase and the rest of the chorus. Clarence "Gatemouth" Brown is the inspiration for lots o' funky sounding slides like that. If you're not familiar with his playing, check out his recordings, such as *San Antonio Ballbuster*, or his *Original Peacock Recordings*.

Chorus 3 and 4 of my solo are not written out, but feel free to play along with them by ear. (If you've played through the other solos in the book, you've already learned all of the licks anyway!)

FIG.10.2. "Doggin' It" Choruses 1–2 of Guitar Solo

Choruses 6 and 7 Rhythm Guitar

The punchy rhythmic hits (on beat 1 and the "and" of 2) in chorus 6 create a supportive pocket behind the piano solo. That's the same rhythmic figure that was played in choruses 1–2 of example 9.3 (in the key of F), and it's also the same rhythmic figure that the pianist played for much of the head and other parts of "Doggin' It."

Note the A– passing chords on beat 2 of bars 13, 15, 19, and 23. The A– triad sounds very similar to a C passing (IV) chord, since the notes (A C E) are also chord tones (1 3 6) of C6. Also note that the same A– triad creates a sliding-ninth C6/13 sound over the IV7 chord in bar 17. This more active rhythm part sets up a welcome variation in sound and texture as the piano solo develops.

Doggin' It

Rhythm Guitar (Behind Piano Solo)

Mike Williams

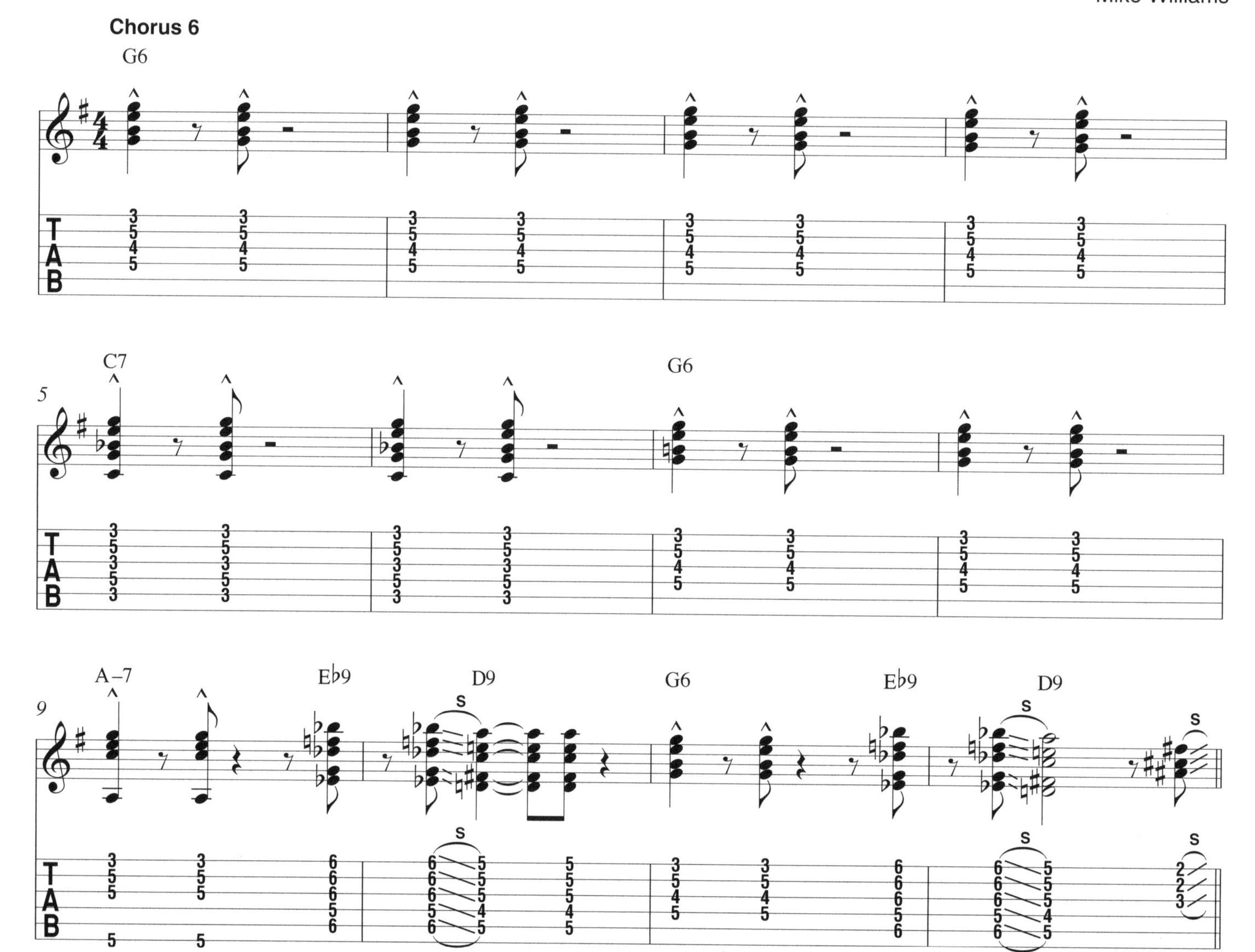

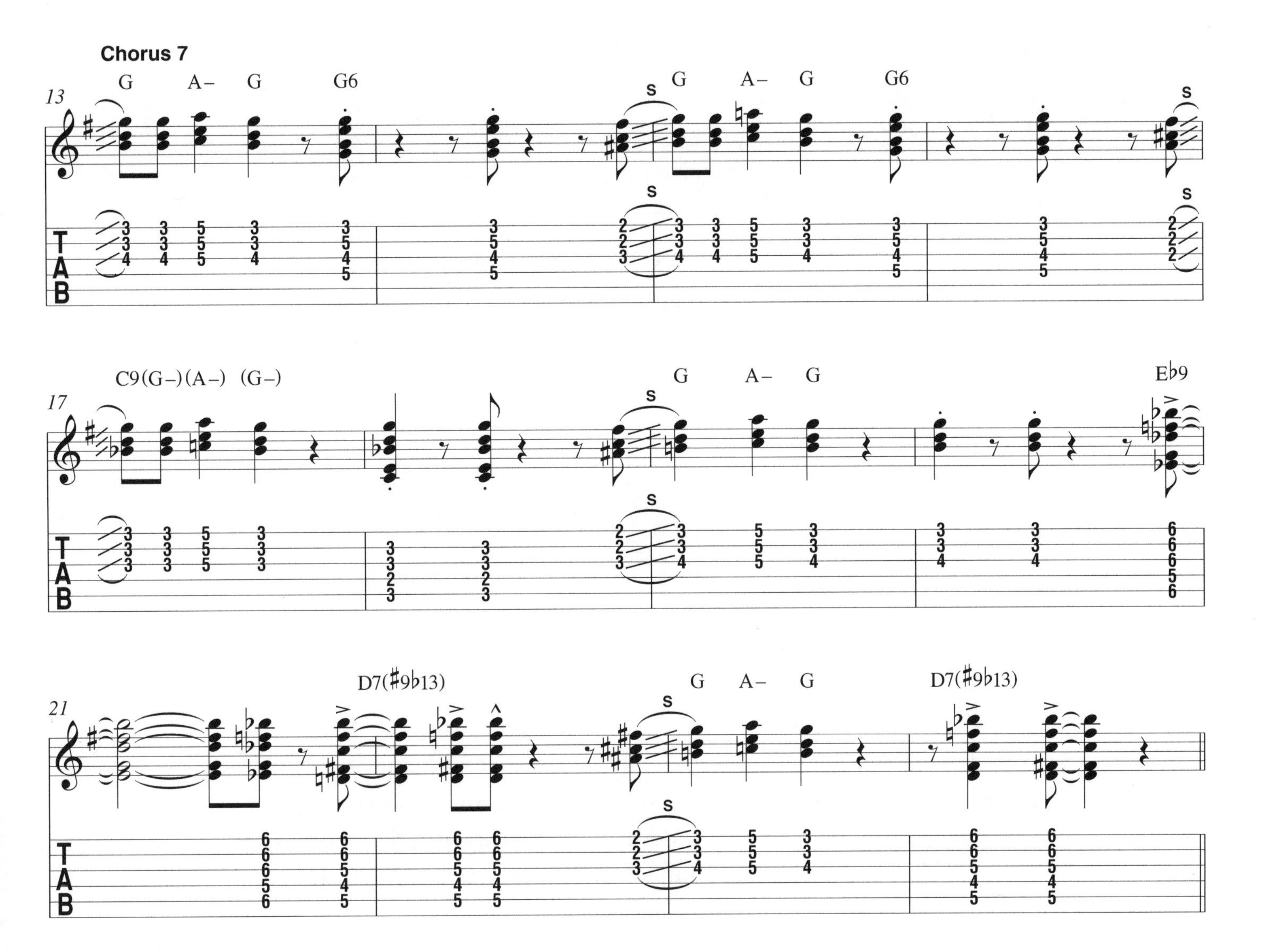

FIG.10.3. "Doggin' It" Two Choruses of Rhythm Guitar

Choruses 8 and 9 Bass/Drums Solo

The bass and drums *trade 4s* through choruses 8 and 9, taking turns soloing for four bars apiece through the 12-bar song form. In the first chorus, the bass takes the first four, drums takes the next four, and then bass the last four, to complete chorus 8. Drums solos over the first four bars of chorus 9, bass takes the next four, and then drums completes the last four bars. **NOTE:** the drums "sets up" the out head with a big, essential hit and stops on beat 1 of chorus 10.

Practice following the bass and drums solos through choruses 8 and 9. Count along with the solos, if necessary. These guys are great players, so you should be able to follow the form. Also practice coming back in on the out head right after the drums hits on beat 1. After you've practiced all parts (the head, rhythm, and solo, etc.) individually, play along with the audio.

And one final reminder: Keep the talking to a minimum during the bass solos!

CHAPTER 11

Locking In with the Backbeat

The term *backbeat* refers to beats 2 and 4, which are accented to provide essential rhythmic drive and momentum in blues, jazz, funk, and other styles. In swing and jazz, drummers accent the backbeat by closing the hi-hat on beats 2 and 4. In blues, R&B, and funk, drummers smack the snare drum with explosive hits to mark the backbeat.

If you're unclear about the role of the backbeat in the musical styles that you're playing, listen and count along with any of the play-along tracks from this book. Notice that drummer Mark Teixeira slams the backbeat on all tracks, including "March in E," "Like a Rocket," "Downtown in F," "Funky Albert," as well as on the "Slow Blues in E," and "Jumpin' Bones."

Practicing along with a metronome (or click) on 2 and 4 works great for learning styles of music that have a prominent backbeat, such as jazz, blues, or funk. If you've never played with the metronome on 2 and 4, it may be very challenging, at first. You may find yourself turning the beat around, so that the click sounds on 1 and 3, instead. This exercise should help you to get on the right track.

FEELING THE BACKBEAT

To get the feel for locking in with the backbeat, first practice playing steady quarter notes on the high open E (1st) string along with the metronome on 2 and 4. Track 43 demonstrates example 11.1 at three different tempos: 50, 75, and 100 bpm. Since the click sounds on 2 and 4 (every other beat), the tempo for quarter notes in 4/4 time is 100, 150, and 200 bpm.

Counting your way in with a click on beats 2 and 4 can be tricky, until you get used to it. To start the count off, *count between the clicks*, as demonstrated in the audio. A typical 2-bar count off sounds like this: "1, click, 2, click, 1, 2, 3, 4," and then, you're in!

Once you count yourself in, play steady quarter notes on the open E (or 1st) string. Listen carefully, and count 1, 2, 3, 4, as you play it, to make sure that your tempo stays in sync with the click that's sounding on beats 2 and 4. If you feel yourself getting in front of the beat ("rushing"), slow down, and let the metronome catch up. Likewise, if you're a little behind the metronome ("dragging"), speed up just a bit until you're back in sync with it. You'll need to adjust your time (speed up or slow down) as necessary to stay in sync with the metronome, because it's not going to adjust to play your tempo!

While working through the exercises that follow, you may find that you've gotten out of sync with 2 and 4, and turned the beat around. When that happens, simply count yourself back in, and start the exercise again. Slow the tempo down if necessary. Once you're able to "lock in" with the backbeat at a slow tempo, you'll find that it's easy to gradually increase the tempo, over the days ahead. Play quarter notes on the open E string along with the metronome on beats 2 and 4.

43

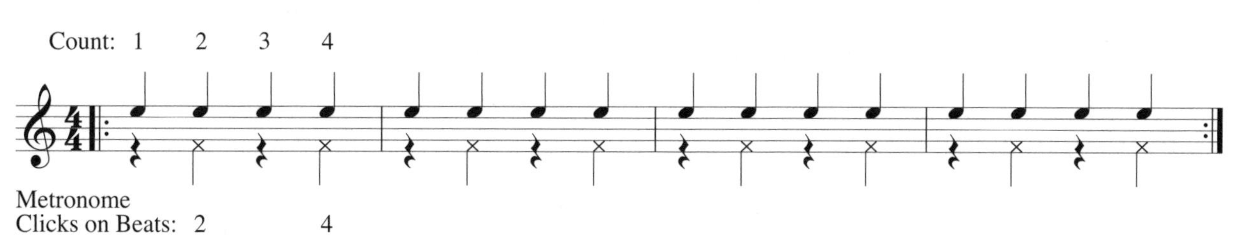

FIG. 11.1. Exercise: Feel the Backbeat

The metronome has perfect time, and yet it conveys no soul whatsoever; that's our department, as musicians. That said, practicing along with the backbeat on the metronome is a great way to strengthen your chops and time. It allows you to gradually increase your tempo as you're working up more challenging phrases, parts, and techniques. Practicing along with the backbeat will also heighten your awareness of the backbeat and the groove, so it can greatly improve your ability to hear and "lock in" rhythmically with the drums and other instruments during live performances.

PRACTICING WITH THE BACKBEAT

44

45

46

To take playing with the backbeat to the next level, let's work through a few of the rhythm parts from the book along with (just) the backbeat on 2 and 4.

First, listen to the audio, which are rhythm parts "March in E," "Like a Rocket," and "Funky Albert" (from earlier in the book), along with just a metronome click on 2 and 4. Then, practice each part along with the demo example.

Note that the Funky Eighth- and Sixteenth-Note Feel Exercises (figures 4.2 and 4.3) were recorded along with only a backbeat click, on beats 2 and 4. So, they're also studies in playing with the backbeat.

WALKING BASS/COMP PART: JAZZ/BLUES IN B♭ WITH BACKBEAT

Here's another rhythm part that sounds great at various tempos along with just the backbeat.

During lessons and labs around Berklee, and also in live performances, I frequently play in duos with another guitarist, or with a saxophone, or other instrument. Having the ability to comp changes and play walking-bass lines over varied chord progressions (at the same time) is very useful for accompanying other instruments. It's also a great vehicle for strengthening your soloing chops, since once you've recorded a bass/comp part over a set of chord changes, you can practice soloing over it for chorus after chorus. (Having at least a fundamental knowledge of how bass lines work is valuable for guitarists, also!)

The walking bass line and comping part in example 11.2 on page 122 was written over a typical jazz/blues progression in the key of B♭.

Performance Tips

Listen to the "B♭ Blues" Walking Bass/Comp part on track 47. Practice it slowly, at first. Once you've got it under your fingers in a steady tempo, practice it along with the metronome on 2 and 4, as demonstrated. (This may take a while to get under your fingers, so be patient and keep working at it.)

Left-hand fingering suggestions are included in example 11.2. For a bass/comp part such as this, it works well to have the second finger covering ("skating along") most the bass notes, since that leaves the first, third, and fourth fingers free to continue the bass line, and to outline the harmony with guide tones (3 and 7 of the chords) on adjacent/nearby frets. The opening B♭7 chord in bar 1 is an example of that. Fingering the B♭ (root), A♭ (♭7), and D (3) on strings 6-4-3 (with fingers 2-3-4) frees up the first finger, so that it can easily walk up to the note C on beat 2. Using all four left-hand fingers for the walking bass and chords makes faster tempos, such as the version in track 48, *much* more playable.

On bass/comp parts such as this, there's typically more than one option for fingering the chords, so a few alternative fingerings are noted and included at the bottom of the chart.

Two versions/tracks of the walking bass part are included on the audio. One is slow, with the backbeat at 50 bpm. The other is much faster, with the backbeat at 100 bpm; to demonstrate the rhythm part in context, it also features an overdubbed solo.

Brief Suggestions for Solos

Walking bass/comping examples such as these work well over a wide range of tempos. They're fun to play over, since they offer the soloist several options and levels for improvising, from basic, to advanced. It's a blues progression, so you can solo over it by using notes/phrases from the B♭ blues scale, and/or with a mix of B♭ pentatonic and B♭ blues. However, since the progression features chord changes with more harmonic complexity, it works great to approach it more from the jazz perspective, also. The soloist might choose to play more into the chord changes using chord scales, arpeggios, approach notes, substitutions, and other techniques associated with jazz improvisation. For a deeper understanding of soloing in the jazz/blues style, I recommend extensive listening and garnering ideas, influences, and soloing vocabulary from the greats such as Grant Green, Kenny Burrell, Wes Montgomery, George Benson, Pat Martino, Joe Pass, and John Scofield, along with horn players, such as Cannonball Adderley, Charlie Parker, Stanley Turrentine, Sonny Rollins, Sonny Stitt, John Coltrane, and others.

For a follow-up to these exercises, listen closely to drum parts in funk, jazz/swing, and in shuffles at varying tempos and grooves. Notice that the drummer clearly accents beats 2 and 4. Practice rhythm parts and solos with just the backbeat. And when you're on the bandstand, lock in "like a junkyard dog" with that backbeat!

FIG. 11.2. "B♭ Blues" Walking Bass/Comp

CHAPTER 12

Pentatonic and Blues Scale Fingerings

The greatest blues guitarists from current and past generations (T-Bone Walker, B.B. King, Freddy King, Albert King, Albert Collins, Magic Sam, Jimmy Vaughan, Stevie Ray Vaughan, and Robert Cray, to name just a few) have each found their own unique/distinct sense of phrasing—their own "voice" for solos over the blues. After hearing just a few notes, it's easy to differentiate one soloist above from the others, since each of them have developed their own unique "signature" phrases, vocabulary, and feel. Yet, all of the artists above share common vocabulary that's been passed along from one generation to the next. All draw upon a similar harmonic/melodic source as the foundation for their solos. Their phrases often are comprised exclusively of notes from the blues scale (1 ♭3 4 ♭5 5 ♭7), combined with notes from the major pentatonic scale (1 2 3 5 6).

The phrase in figure 12.1 illustrates just how typical it is to mix notes from the A blues scale (A C D E♭ E G) with the 3 (C♯), the jazzy/colorful 6 (F♯), and the 2/9 (B) from the A pentatonic scale. This lick should sound at least somewhat familiar, because T-Bone Walker and so many of the greats that followed have soloed with a similar combination of notes from both scales, for decades.

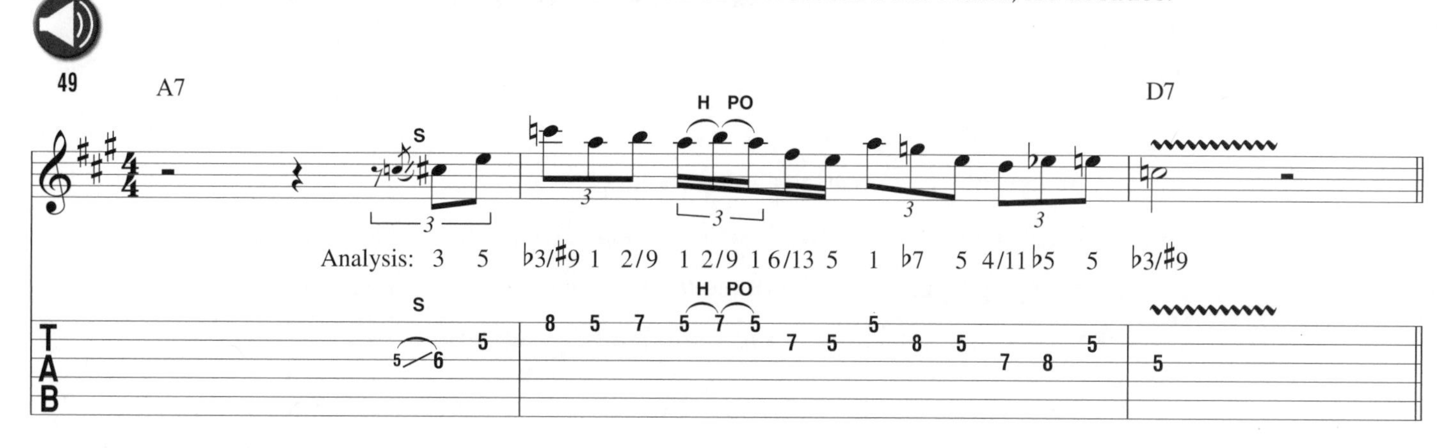

FIG. 12.1. Pentatonic/Blues Phrase

The analysis (1 3 5 ♭7...) in figures 12.1 and 12.2 illustrates the relationship to both scales.

FIG. 12.2. A Blues and A Pentatonic Scales

Learn Classic Blues Guitar Solos

Ten classic electric blues solos, by many of the artists above, are analyzed and demonstrated in detail in my other book, the *Berklee Blues Guitar Songbook* (Berklee Press, 2010). For a note-for-note study of their phrasing, and methods for mixing notes from the major pentatonic and blues scales, please refer to that publication.

The examples that follow are a series of scale fingerings and exercises to help you hear, visualize, and understand how the major and minor pentatonic and the blues scales share common tones and intersect/connect with each other up and down the length of the fingerboard.

The examples in this chapter are in the key of A, since that's a very popular key for blues. They're organized in seven sections:

1. A minor pentatonic fingerings, five positions along the neck
2. Understanding the major/relative minor relationship between the C major and A minor scales
3. Five positions along the neck for A minor and C pentatonic, along with A minor and C major scales
4. A blues scale, five positions along the neck
5. A blues scale, connecting/shifting through five positions along the neck
6. Mixing A pentatonic and A blues scales, five positions along the neck
7. Phrases that mix A pentatonic and A blues, five positions along the neck

If you're already familiar with the scale fingerings presented in sections 1 to 5, feel free to jump ahead to exercise 7. That's where we'll combine notes and phrases from the scales, to create phrases that sound more like real music. Keep in mind that learning the scale fingerings below is just a first step; *it's a means, not an end.* Once you've learned the fingerings (the mechanics), the real work begins! For solos over the blues, the goal is to create a conversation that makes musical sense, by mixing the notes/phrases from the scales together in your own way, to create your own blues "lyric" over the song form.

SUGGESTIONS ABOUT TONE AND SOUND

We've got electronic tuners to get us in tune, and frets that define pitch, so most of the work of tone production is already taken care of... Agreed? *Not true!* The bottom line is that we guitarists need to work diligently on producing great tone and sound, just like those who play trumpet, sax, violin, and so many other instruments do.

To reap the maximum benefits from these exercises, practice all fingerings at a steady tempo, along with a metronome, as demonstrated. Whether your tempo is slow, medium, or fast, strive to produce the very best tone and sound on every note you play. The quality of your tone, sound, and feel should take priority over the tempo at which you practice the scales and exercises on the following pages, or whatever you're playing.

While practicing technique exercises, it's most beneficial to feature the tone and sound that comes from your hands on your instrument, instead of your effects rack, so I recommend playing with a clean tone, with minimal or no distortion or effects, such as reverb, on your guitar. The goal is to hear how precisely your hands are working together, so a clean, "transparent" tone will help to expose the quality of sound that's projecting directly from your hands. Excess reverb, delay, or other effects tends to mask and/or overshadow the tone/sound that's coming from your technique. I love reverb and varying degrees of natural tube/amp overdrive for rhythm parts and solos over the blues, but for technique exercises, it's best to keep the reverb, delay, and crunch, etc. down.

STOP THOSE OPEN/RINGING STRING NOISES!

Listen *carefully* for any unintended open string noises, as you play up and down the scale fingerings that follow. Dampen any/all noises immediately by touching the ringing string for just an instant, with either your picking-hand palm and/or fingers, and with your fretting-hand fingers, when necessary. You'll need to adjust your hand position and posture a bit, so it may take weeks or even months to get the hang of damping the noises. Keep experimenting and working to develop a damping technique that works for your hand position, posture, guitar (size), and playing style.

To *really* hear how your technique sounds, record yourself playing each exercise, and then carefully listen back to your track. Note what's working for you, as well as the areas that need improvement. Adjust your technique/hand position slightly, then record the exercise again and again, until you get it right. Stopping those unintended open ringing strings is essential, so it's worth the extra efforts.

EXERCISE 1. A MINOR PENTATONIC IN FIVE POSITIONS

Getting command of the pentatonic scale fingerings is a great place to begin for soloing over the blues, so we'll start with the minor pentatonic scales in figure 12.3 below. Practice each scale fingering "full-range," as written and demonstrated below. Start each scale on the lowest root in that position. Play up to the highest note (in position), and then work your way back down, to the lowest note in position. Finish by playing back up to the root. Each exercise is played twice (repeated). When you're ready, play along with the audio, which demonstrates the A minor pentatonic scale in positions 2 and 5, at a medium tempo (quarter note = 100 bpm).

FIG. 12.3. A Minor Pentatonic in Five Positions

Understanding Relative Major and Relative Minor Scales

The C major and A minor scales share the same key signature, which has no sharps or flats. Because of that, the keys of C major and A minor share a special musical association, referred to as the *relative major/relative minor* relationship. To describe relative major and relative minor in its simplest terms, we need to get into a bit of music theory. Let's use a diagram of a piano keyboard to help visualize and understand the theory.

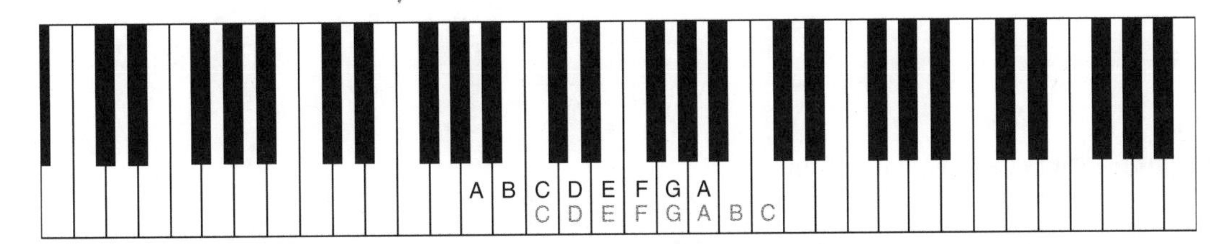

Fig. 12.4. C Major/A Minor Scales on a Keyboard

The C major scale is played by striking seven consecutive white notes (in any octave), starting from the note C and moving up: CDEFGABC. The key of A natural minor consists of the same seven notes as the key of C. To play a one-octave A minor scale, play up the keys from the note A: ABCDEFGA.

Since C major and A minor share the same key signature and consist of the same seven notes:

- The C major pentatonic (a.k.a. C pentatonic) scale has the same five notes as the A minor pentatonic scale: CDEGA (C pentatonic) and ACDEG (A minor pentatonic).
- The C major pentatonic scale uses five of the seven notes in the C major scale: scale degrees 1, 2, 3, 5, and 6 (CDEGA). You might recognize the sound of the notes in the major pentatonic scale as the hook to the Motown hit "My Girl," by the Temptations.
- The minor pentatonic scale has scale degrees 1, ♭3, 4, 5, and ♭7 (CE♭FGB♭). The minor pentatonic scale creates "darker," bluesy (minor) sound, as opposed to the (major) pentatonic scale, which creates a "brighter" country (major) sound.

EXERCISE 2. C MAJOR AND PENTATONIC WITH A NATURAL MINOR AND A MINOR PENTATONIC FINGERINGS

Next, practice the fingerings on the next page for "C Pentatonic and A Minor Pentatonic with C Major and A Natural Minor Scales in Five Positions." I strongly recommend eventually memorizing all fingerings, so repeat these scales as many times as necessary. Practice all scales "full-range" in each position, as in the notation. Start on the low root, then play up to the high note, then down to the lowest note, then return to the root. When you're ready, play along with the audio, which demonstrates the scales in the 2nd and 5th positions.

51

2nd Position: A Minor Pentatonic Scale

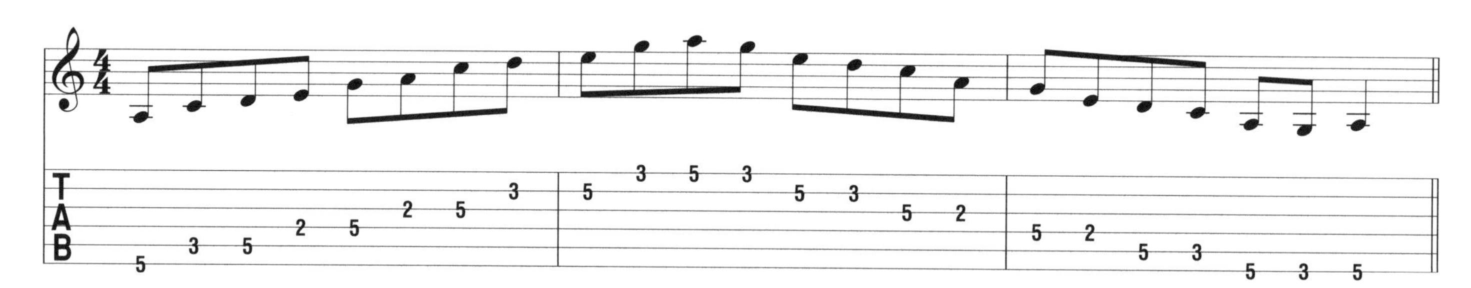

2nd Position: C Major Pentatonic Scale

5th Position: A Minor Pentatonic Scale

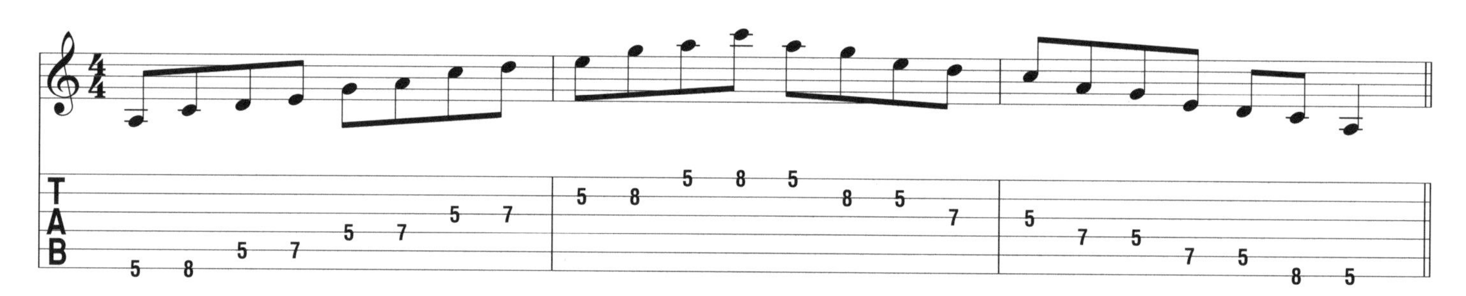

5th Position: C Major Pentatonic Scale

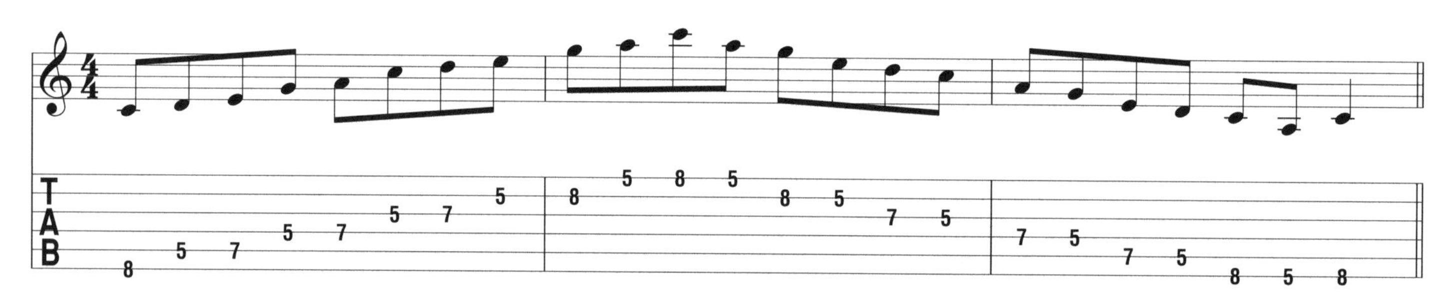

7th Position: A Minor Pentatonic Scale

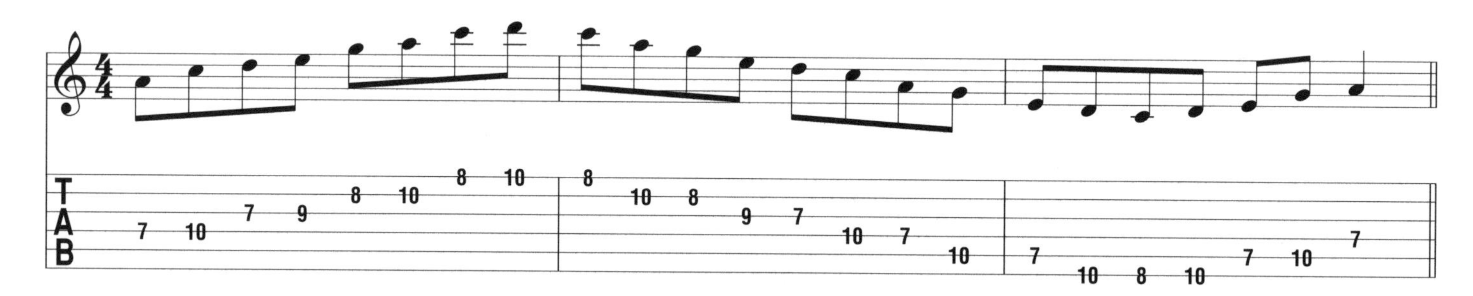

FIG. 12.5. A Minor and C Major Pentatonic in Five Positions

EXERCISE 3. FINGERING POSITION DIAGRAMS

This next diagram (figure 12.6) illustrates five positions along the neck for C major and A natural minor, along with five positions for the corresponding C pentatonic and A minor pentatonic scales. All low C (roots) are diagramed as solid black circles, and all low A (roots) are diagramed as solid black squares. Also note the alternate fingerings that are included in parenthesis—(1), (3), etc.—on some strings for the 2nd, 7th, and 9th position pentatonic scales. While the standard fingerings illustrate the notes that are common to the major and pentatonic scales, blues players often prefer to solo using the alternate fingerings (played with fingers 1 and 3, instead of 2 and 4).

52

The audio demonstrates C major and C pentatonic scales in the 2nd and 5th positions. Listen, practice, and when you're ready, play along with this track.

2nd Position: C Major/A Natural Minor Scale

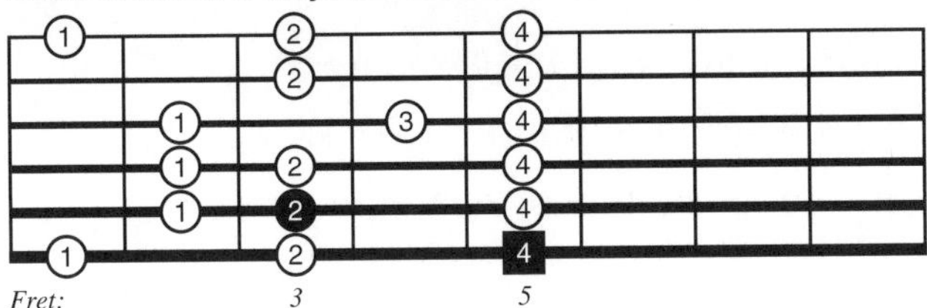

2nd Position: C Pentatonic/A Minor Pentatonic Scale

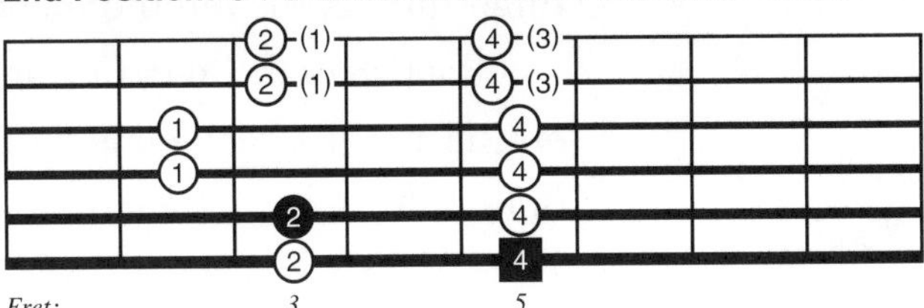

5th Position: C Major/A Natural Minor Scale

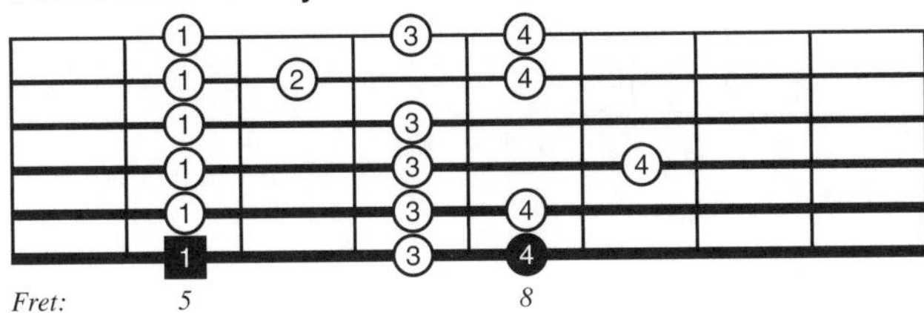

5th Position: C Pentatonic/A Minor Pentatonic Scale

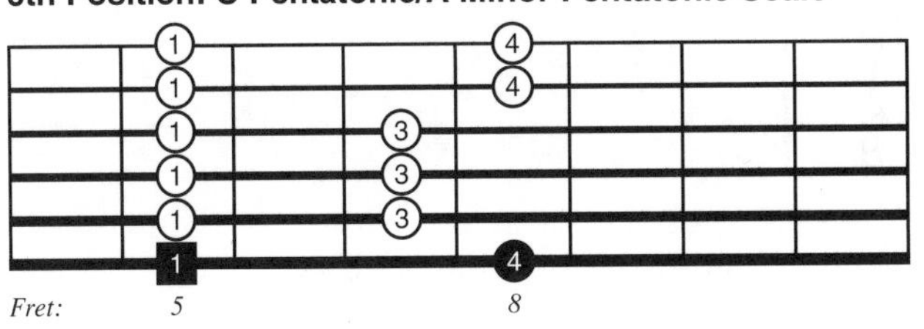

7th Position: C Major/A Natural Minor Scale

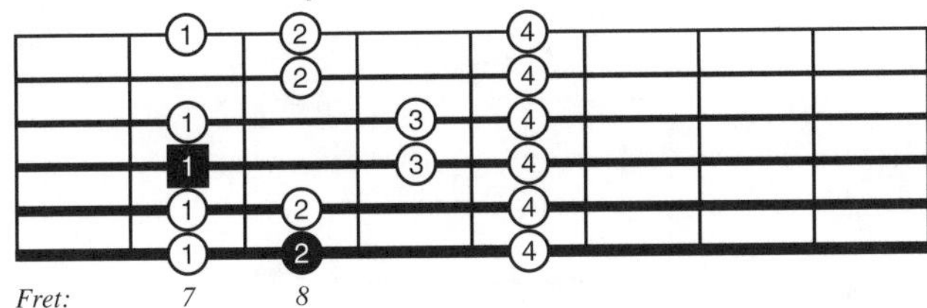

7th Position: C Pentatonic/A Minor Pentatonic Scale

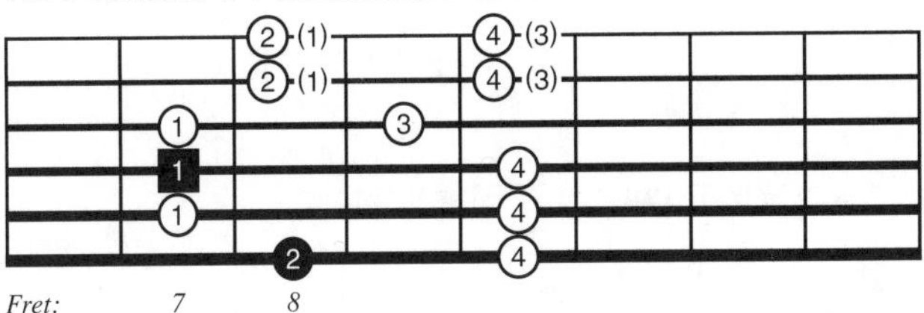

9th Position: C Major/A Natural Minor Scale

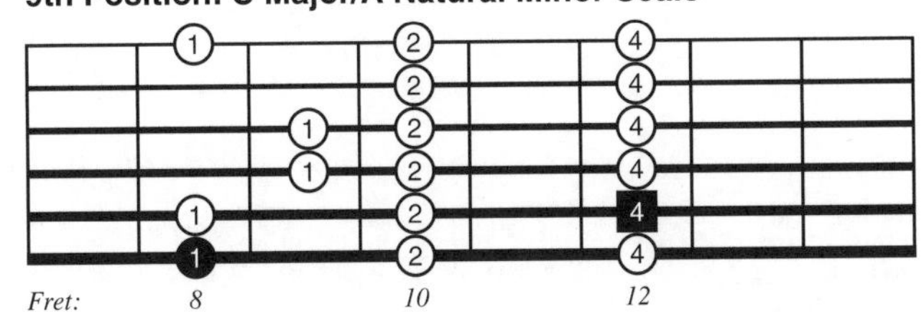

9th Position: C Pentatonic/A Minor Pentatonic Scale

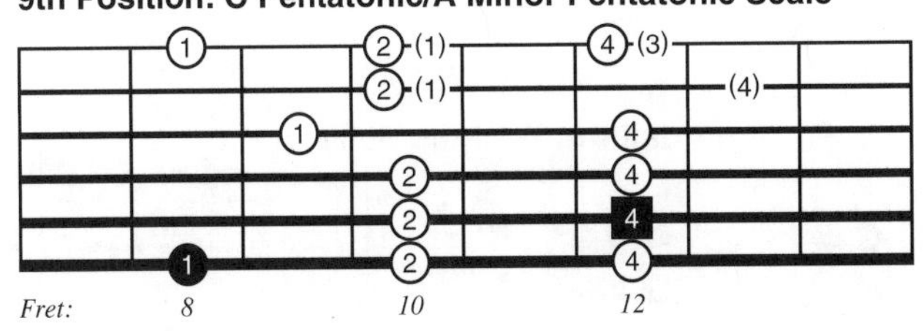

12th Position: C Major/A Natural Minor Scale

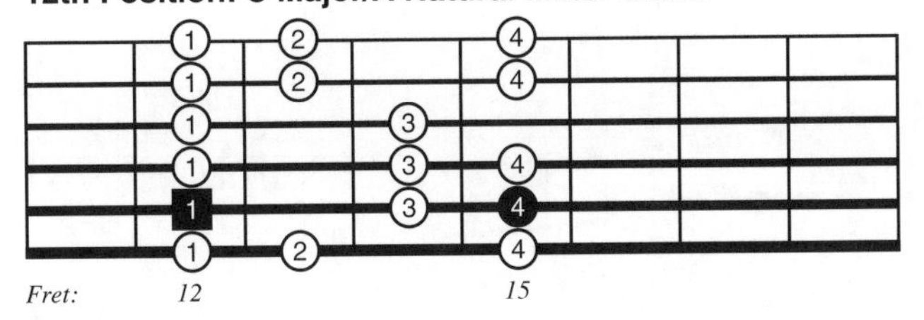

12th Position: C Pentatonic/A Minor Pentatonic Scale

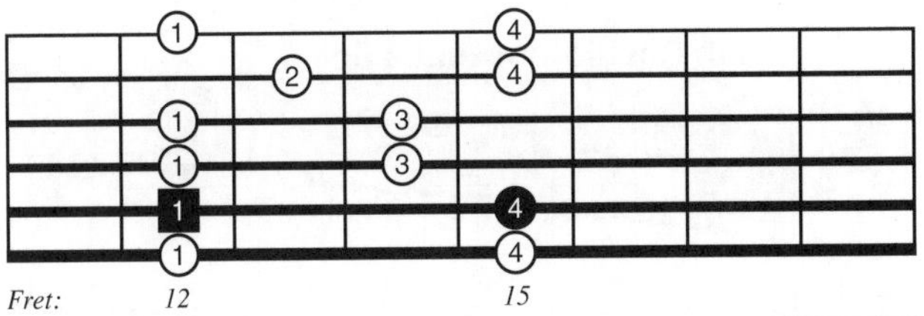

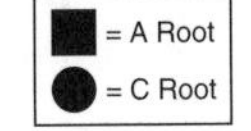

FIG. 12.6. Five Positions of C Major, A Natural Minor, C Pentatonic, and A Minor Pentatonic Scales

EXERCISE 4. A BLUES SCALE IN FIVE POSITIONS

The blues scale adds one note (the ♭5) to the minor pentatonic scale to form a 6–note scale. Note in figure 12.7 how similar these fingerings are to the five fingerings for the A minor pentatonic scale.

Practice each fingering, and when you're ready, play along with exercise 4 on the audio, which demonstrates the A blues scale in the 5th and 12th positions. (**NOTE:** Both fingerings sit right on top of A minor chords, as diagramed/explained later in this chapter, in figure 12.13.)

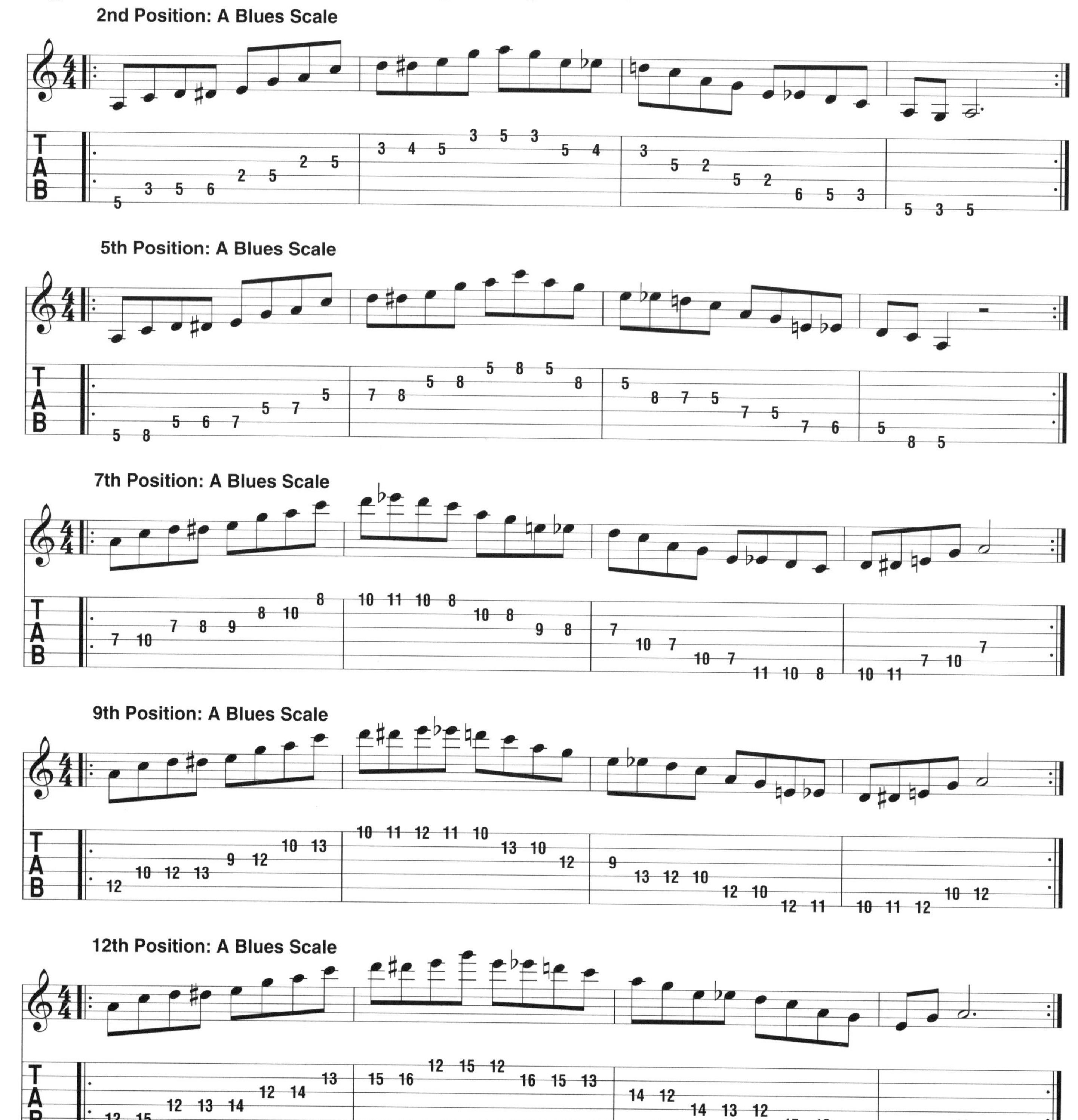

FIG. 12.7. A Blues Scale in Five Positions

EXERCISE 5. A BLUES SCALES: SHIFTING THROUGH FIVE POSITIONS

Notice how the A blues fingerings connect with each other from one position to the other along the neck. Listen to and practice each phrase below. When you're ready, play along with the audio. And for a long-term follow-up to this exercise, study solos by the blues greats, and notice how they shift from one fingering to the next. Experiment with creating your own phrases that similarly shift between positions up and down along the neck!

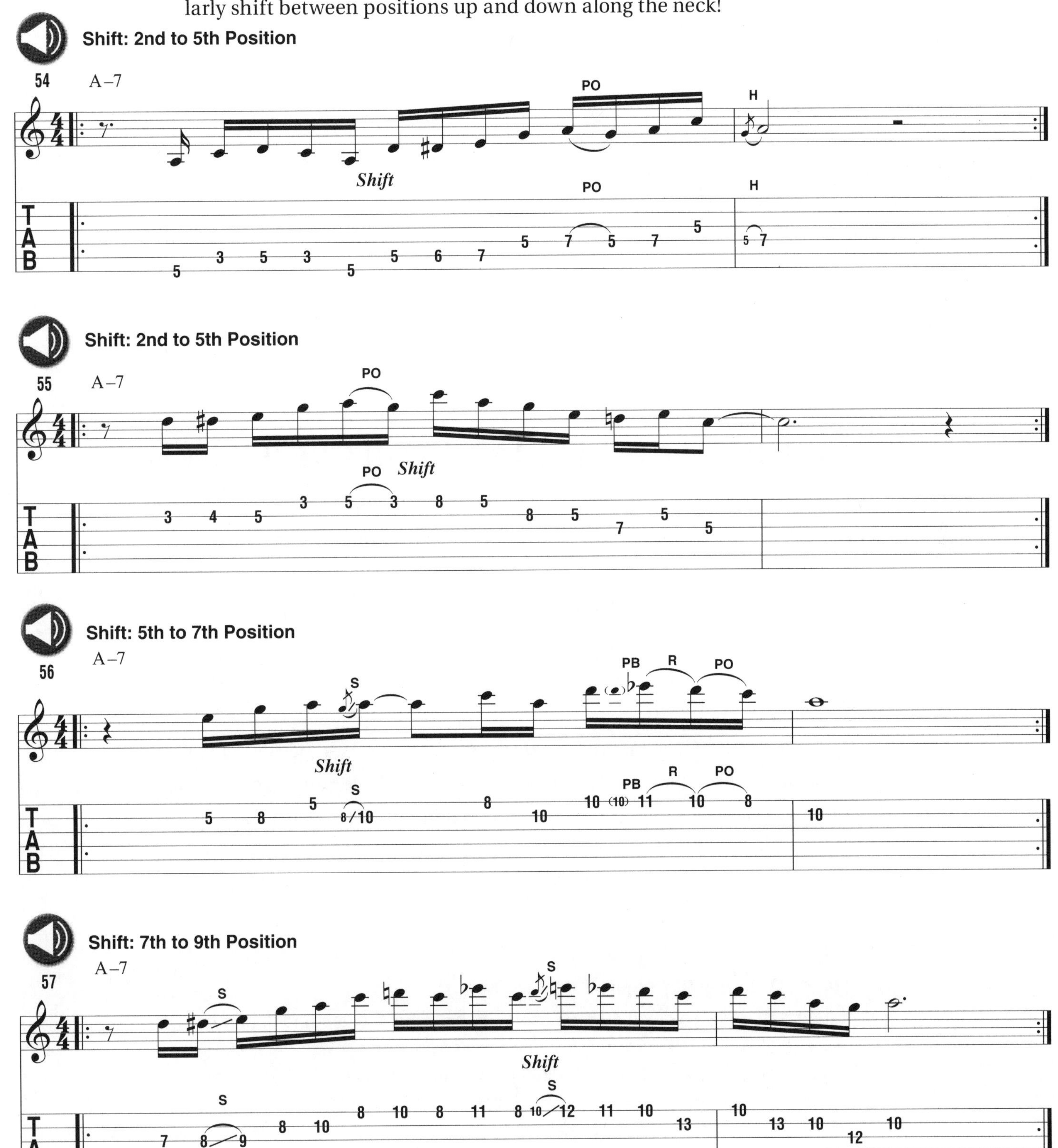

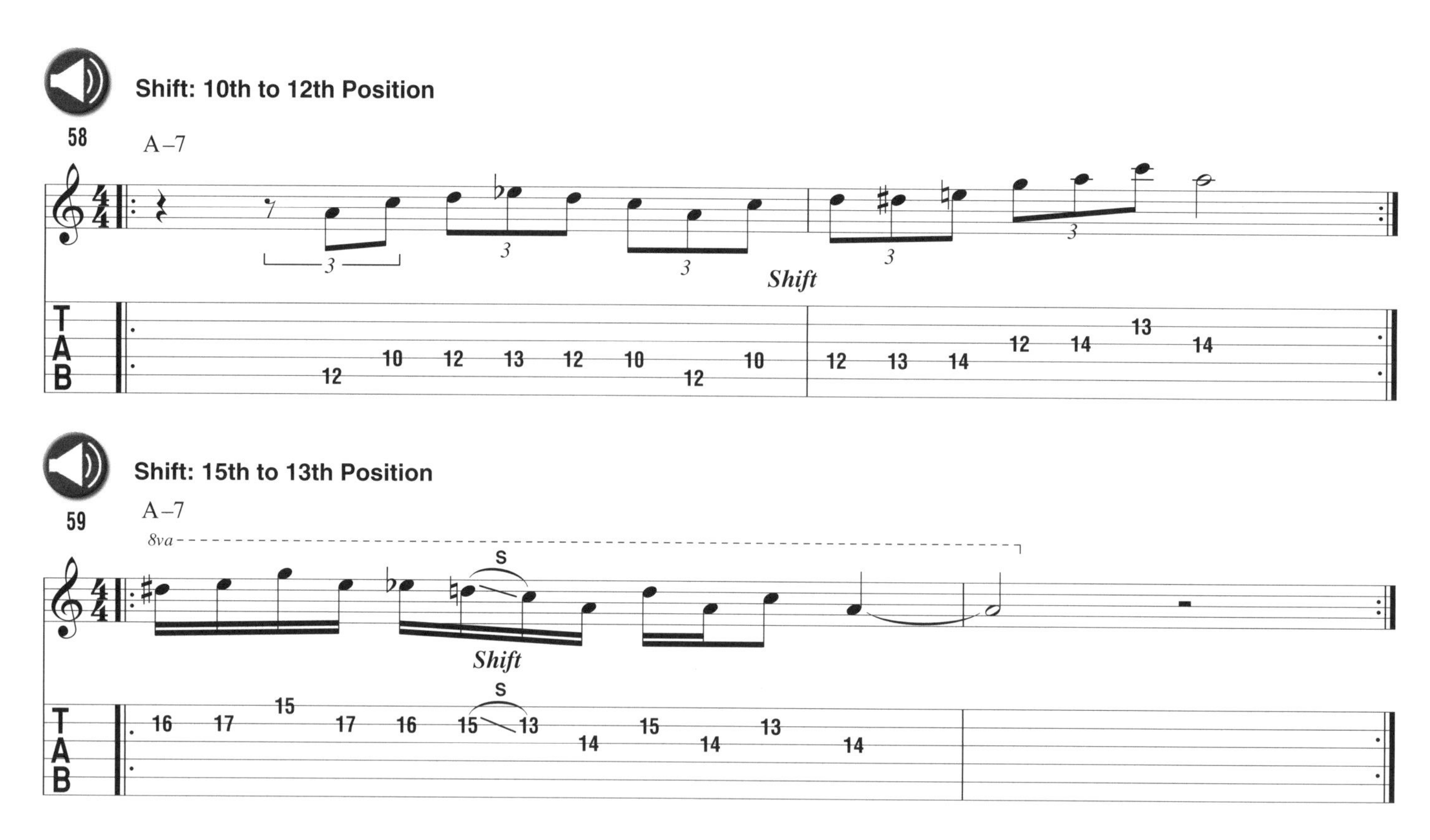

Fig. 12.8. A Pentatonic and Blues: Shifting Positions

EXERCISE 6. MIXING A BLUES WITH A PENTATONIC IN FIVE POSITIONS

Now that you've practiced shifting between positions of the A blues scale, let's look at how it combines with the A pentatonic scale along the neck.

a. A Pentatonic and A Blues: Positions 4 and 5

Since it's *so* user-friendly, the position 5 fingering on the next page is the most common/popular fingering for the (5-note) minor pentatonic and (6-note) blues scales, so we'll start there. This fingering for the blues scale is considered to be "home base" for most blues soloists, and so it tends to be the scale that new blues and rock players learn first. Thousands of blues and rock players combine notes from the major pentatonic and blues scales (a.k.a. "boxes") in positions 4 and 5. Practice (and eventually memorize) the A pentatonic and blues scales in positions 4/5, and when you're ready, play along with the audio.

About the Fingering Diagrams

The root and 5 are common (shared) notes in both the A blues and A pentatonic scales. To illustrate how the two scales overlap/intersect with each other along the neck, the root is a solid square and 5 is an open circle. The rest of the notes in the A pentatonic scale are solid circles, and the rest of the notes in the A minor pentatonic and A blues scale are gray.

4th Position: A Major Pentatonic Scale

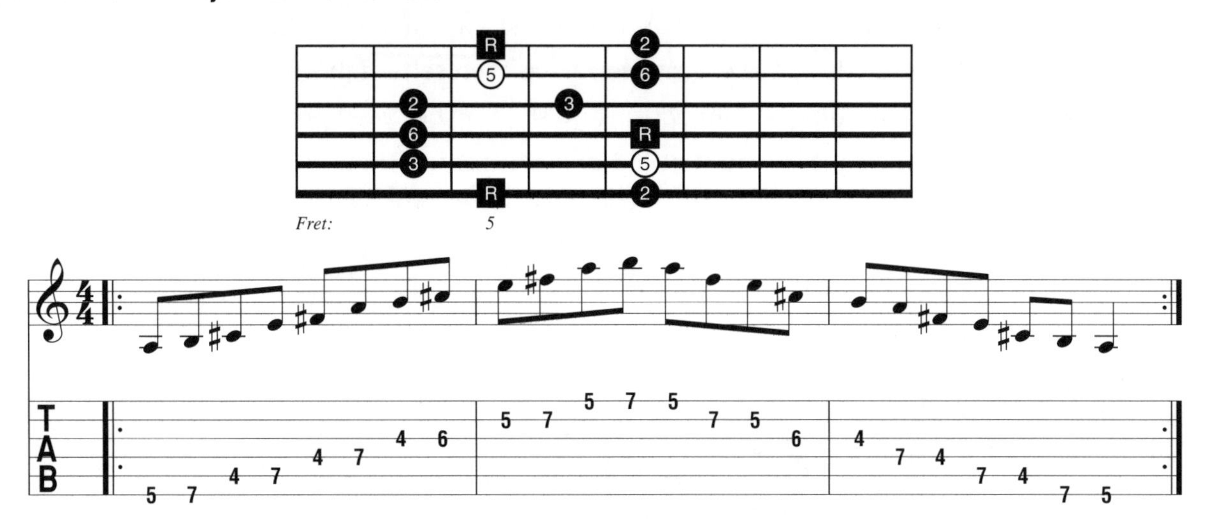

5th Position: A Blues Scale

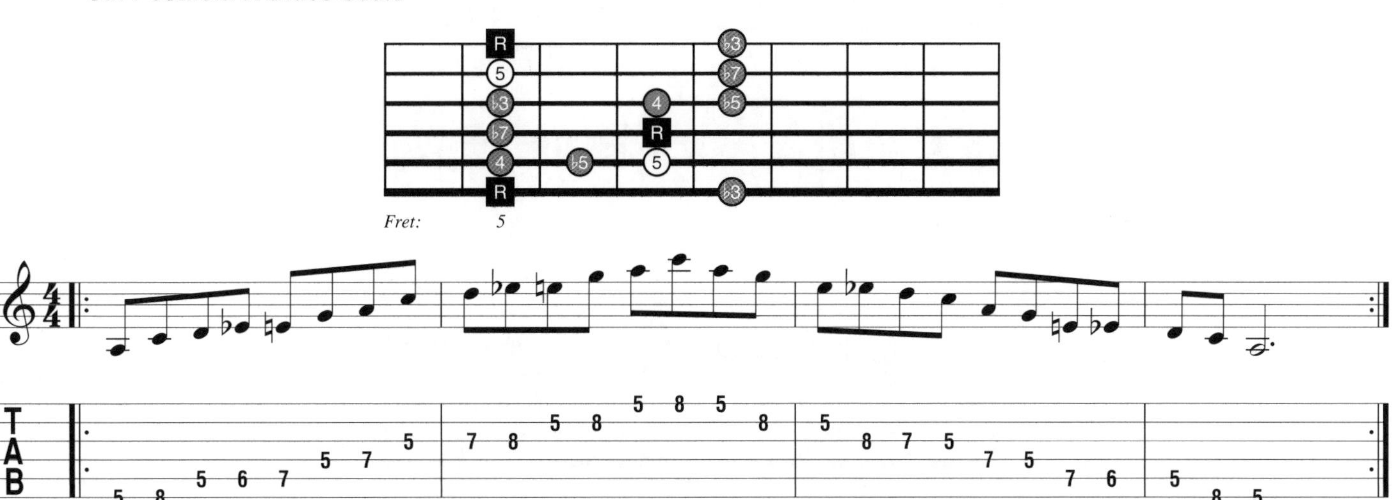

4th and 5th Positions:
A Major Pentatonic and A Blues Scales Combined

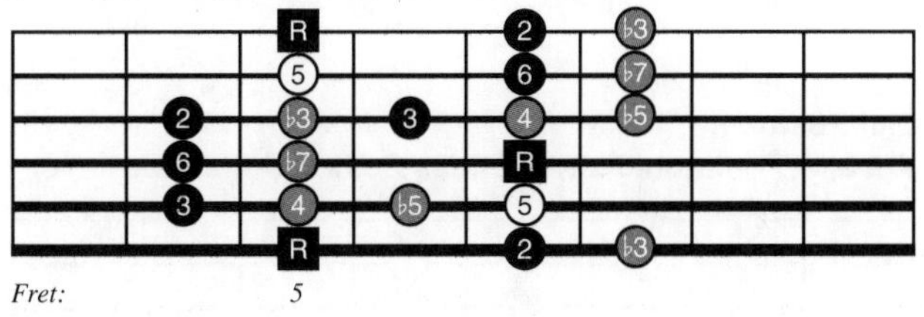

FIG. 12.9. A Major Pentatonic and A Blues Scales: Positions 4 and 5

b. Mixing A Pentatonic and A Blues: Position 2

Now move down three frets, to play the A major and A blues scales in position 2. It's very common to shift between the 4th and 5th position boxes that you just played, to (and from) the 2nd position boxes shown in figure 12.10. Many of the greatest blues, rock, and jazz guitarists have been self-taught. They discovered phrases and methods for connecting and shifting between positions by experimentation and by ear, and that led to each finding their own voices on the instrument. So, keep experimenting and working to discover your own ways of connecting the pentatonic and blues boxes up and down the neck!

Practice and eventually memorize the A pentatonic and blues scales in position 2. When you're ready, practice them along with the audio.

61

2nd Position: A Major Pentatonic Scale

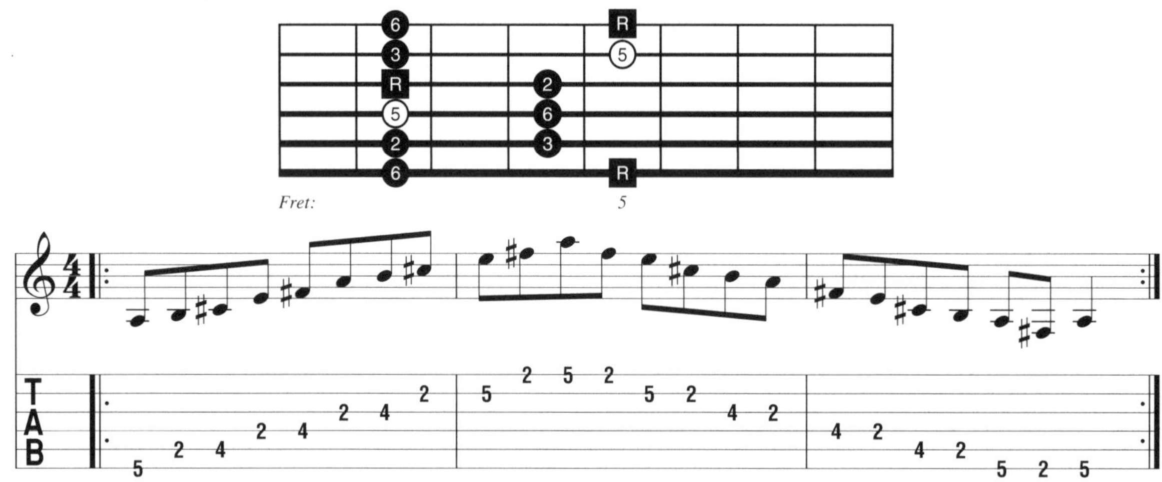

2nd Position: A Blues Scale

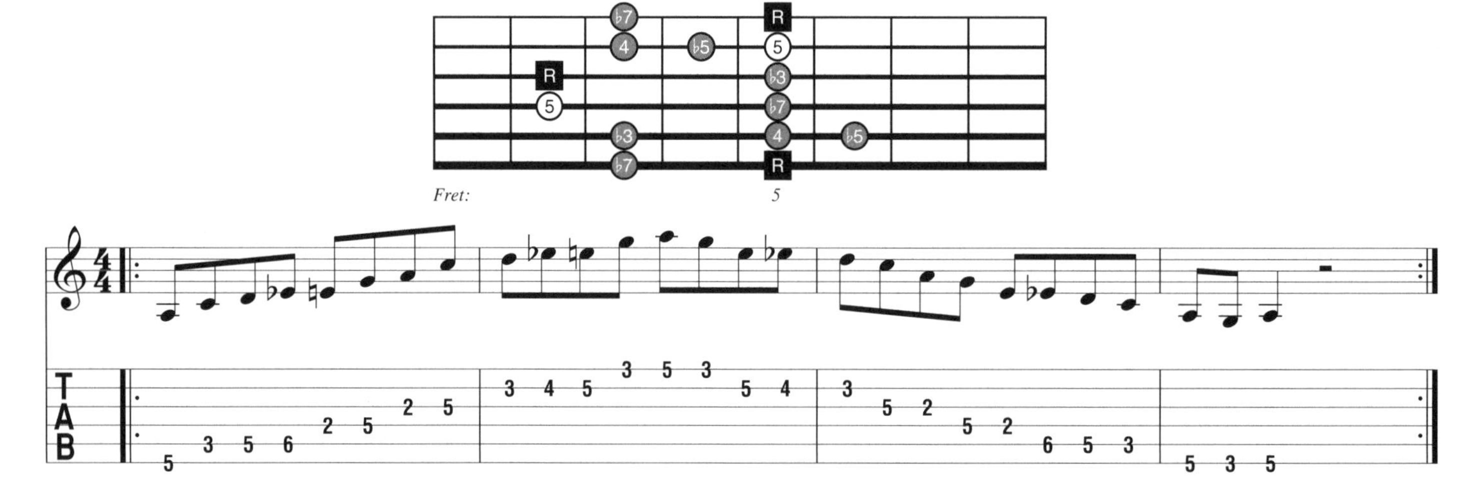

2nd Position:
A Major Pentatonic and A Blues Scales Combined

Fret: 5

FIG. 12.10. A Major and Minor Pentatonic and Blues Scales: Position 2

c. Mixing A Pentatonic and A Blues: Positions 6 and 7

The A major pentatonic scale fingering in figure 12.11 starts in the 6th position, then (optionally) shifts into the 7th position for notes along the 1st and 2nd strings. This same fingering was presented earlier, as 9th or 9th/10th position A minor (or C major) pentatonic fingerings on pages 126, 129, and 131. Notice that the high root (A) can be played on either the 1st string (5th fret) or on the 2nd string (10th fret). Most soloists prefer to shift up to play the A (root) and adjoining notes along the 2nd string because it connects well with higher A major and minor pentatonic and blues scale fingerings. Practice playing both scales with the audio, and eventually memorize the A pentatonic and blues scales in positions 6 and 7.

62

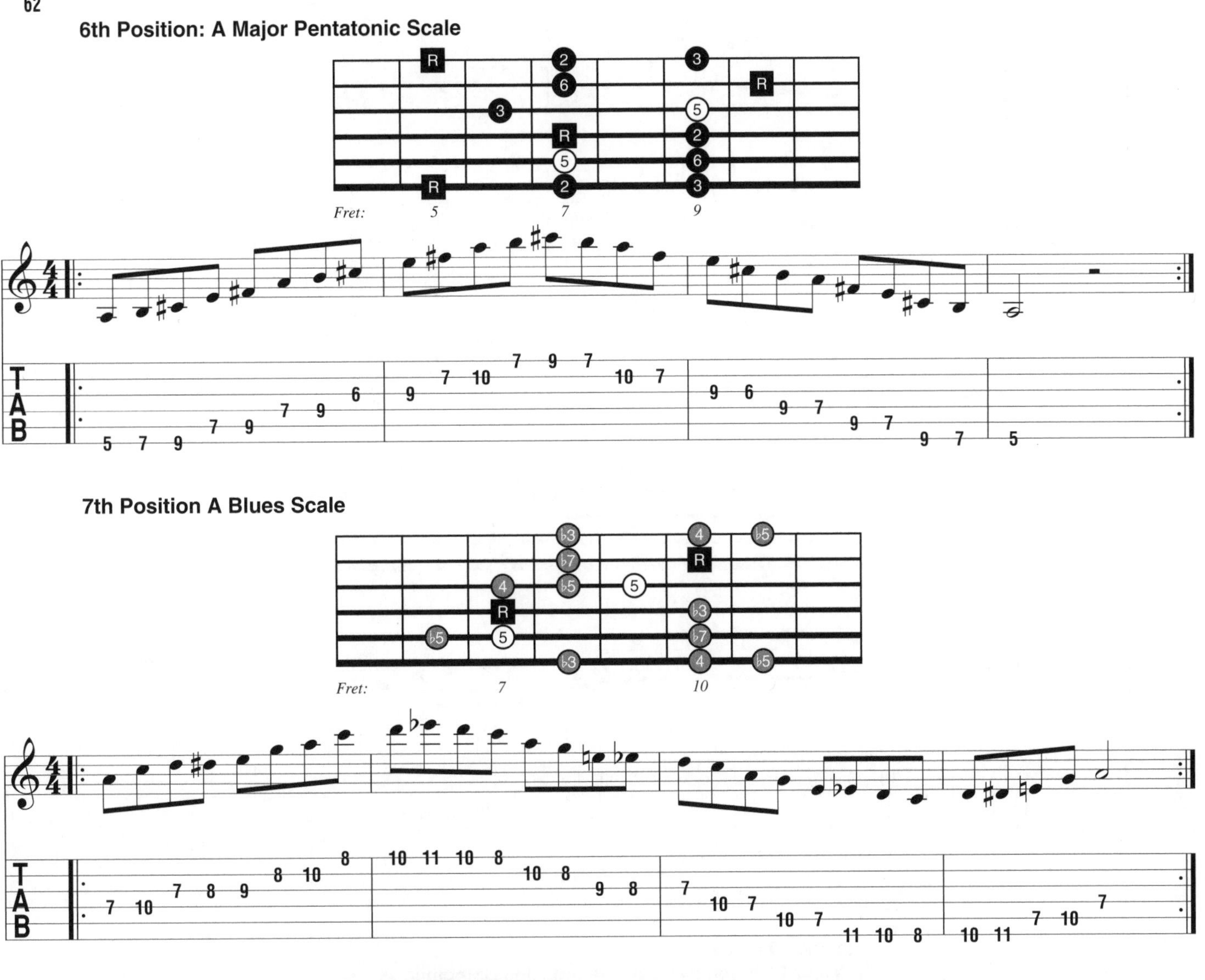

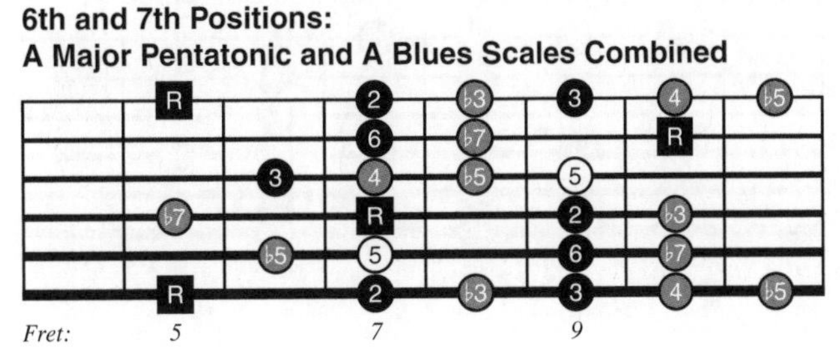

FIG. 12.11. A Major and and Blues Scales: Positions 6 and 7

d. Mixing A Pentatonic and A Blues: Positions 9 and 10

Practice (and memorize) the A pentatonic and blues scales in positions 9 and 10. Again, note the variation in this fingering for the A blues scale box. It can be played in position 9, or (optionally) can shift from position 9 to 10 on the 2nd and 1st strings. When you're ready, practice along with the audio.

63

9th Position: A Major Pentatonic Scale

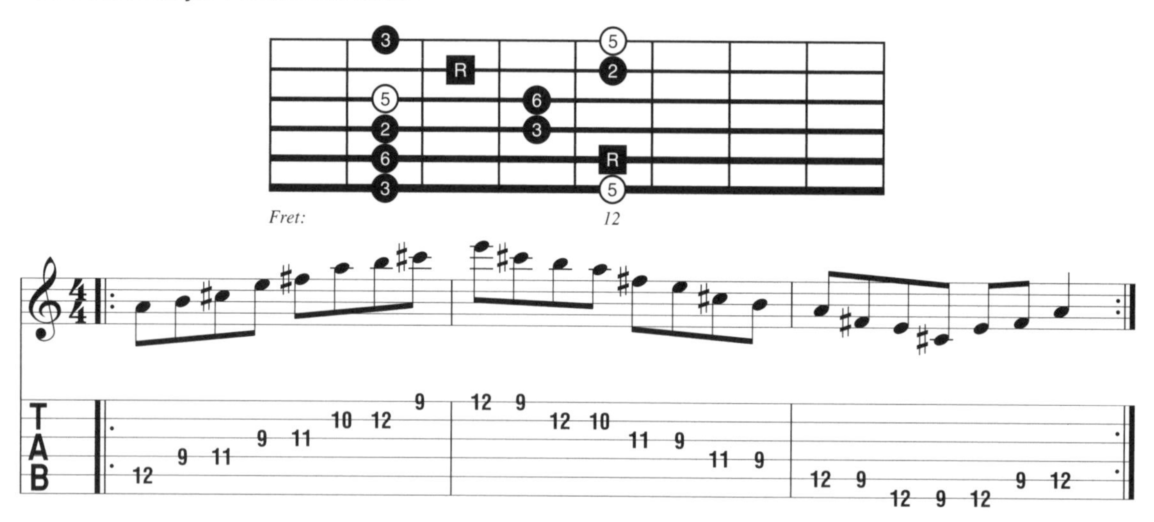

9th and 10th Positions: A Blues Scale

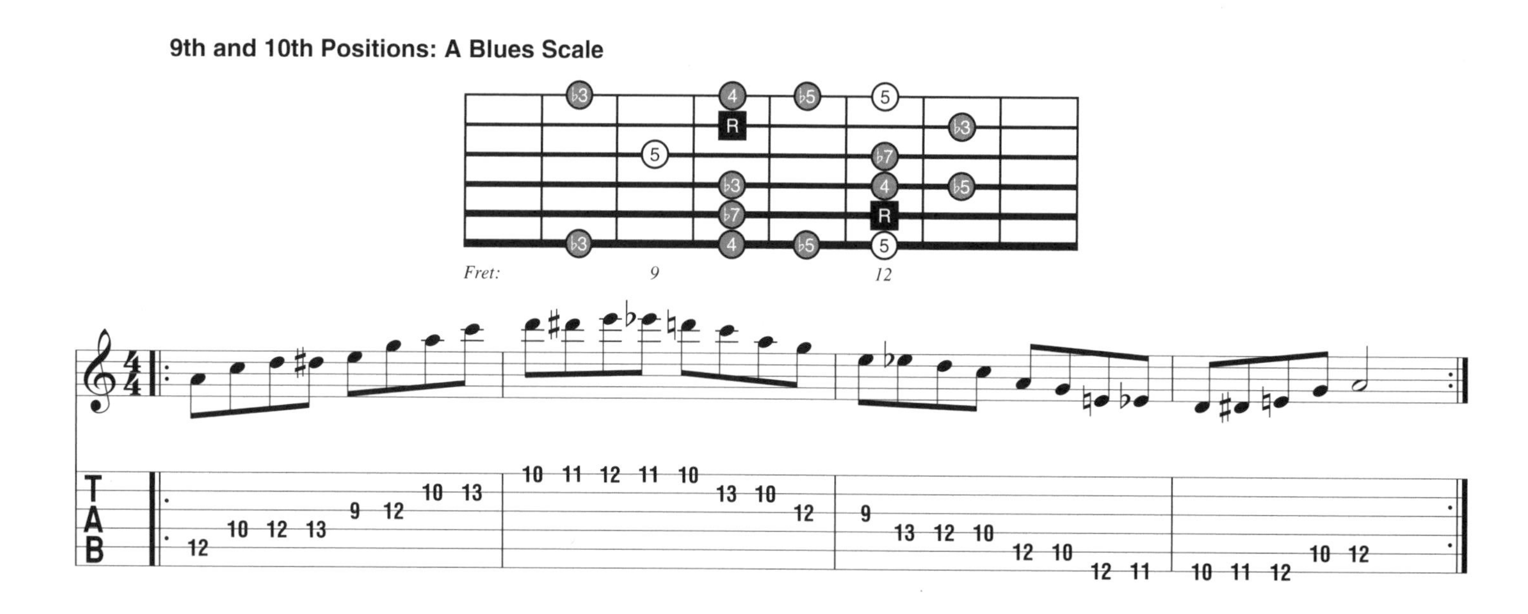

9th and 10th Positions:
A Major Pentatonic and A Blues Scales Combined

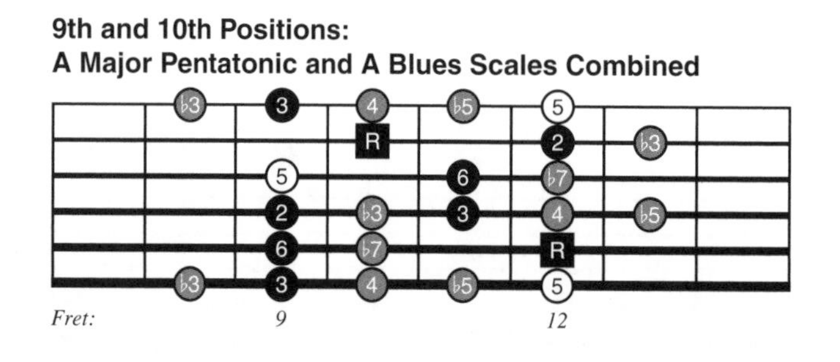

FIG. 12.12. A Major and Minor Pentatonic and Blues Scales, Positions 9 and 10

e. Mixing A Pentatonic and A Blues: Positions 11 and 12

For the key of A, the region shown in figure 12.13—the 12th position A minor pentatonic, along with the 11th position A major pentatonic scale—is perhaps the second most popular region for soloing. Again, I recommend that you memorize these (as well as the other) fingerings.

To illustrate why the 5th and 12th position minor-pentatonic scales are so predominantly played, play the A minor pentatonic scale in the 5th position again (figure 12.9). Notice that your left hand plays notes between the 5th and 8th frets. Next, play the 12th position A minor pentatonic scale. Again, watch your left hand; it spans notes between the 12th, 15th (or with a stretch), 16th frets. Between these two minor pentatonic fingerings, you've spanned a very huge amount of the fretboard: from the 5th to the 16th fret.

Both fingerings are very user friendly. Each works well as a "home base" region for soloing, and both are easy to move around, because they are built on A–7 barre chords. The 5th position A minor pentatonic is built on top of an (root 6) A–7 chord, and the 12th position A minor pentatonic lays on top of a (root 5) A–7 chord. Visualize the minor-seventh chord shapes inside those two pentatonic boxes as you solo. Use them. They outline chord sounds, and they're great notes to play!

5th and 12th Positions: A–7

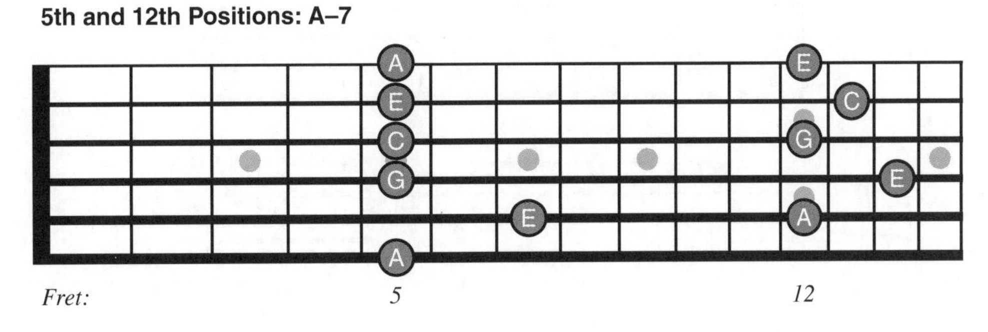

FIG. 12.13. A–7 in Positions 5 and 12

64

Practice (and memorize) the fingerings for the A pentatonic and blues scales in positions 11 and 12. When you're ready, practice along with the audio.

11th Position: A Major Pentatonic Scale

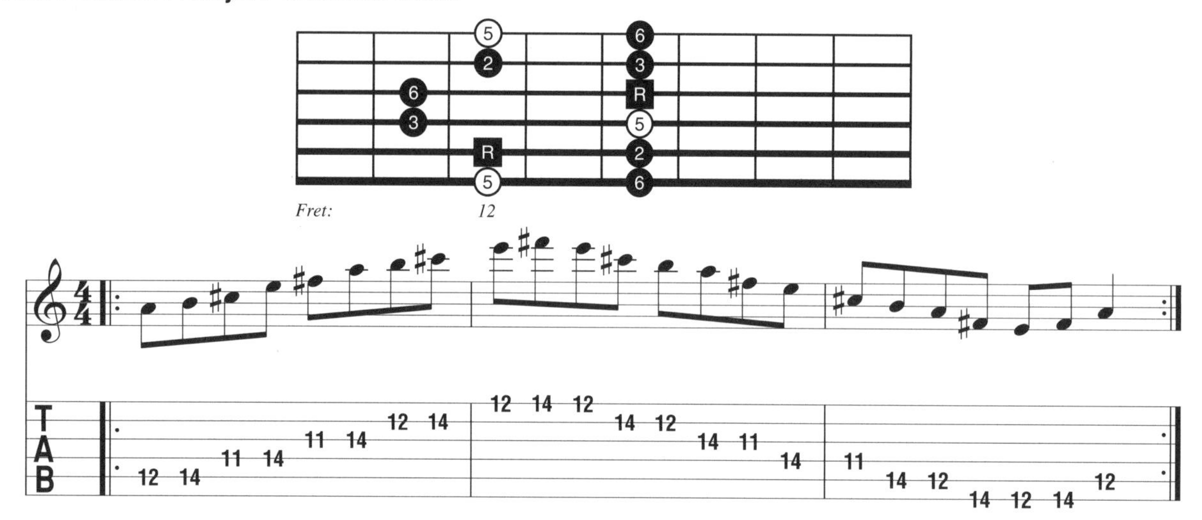

12th Position: A Blues Scale

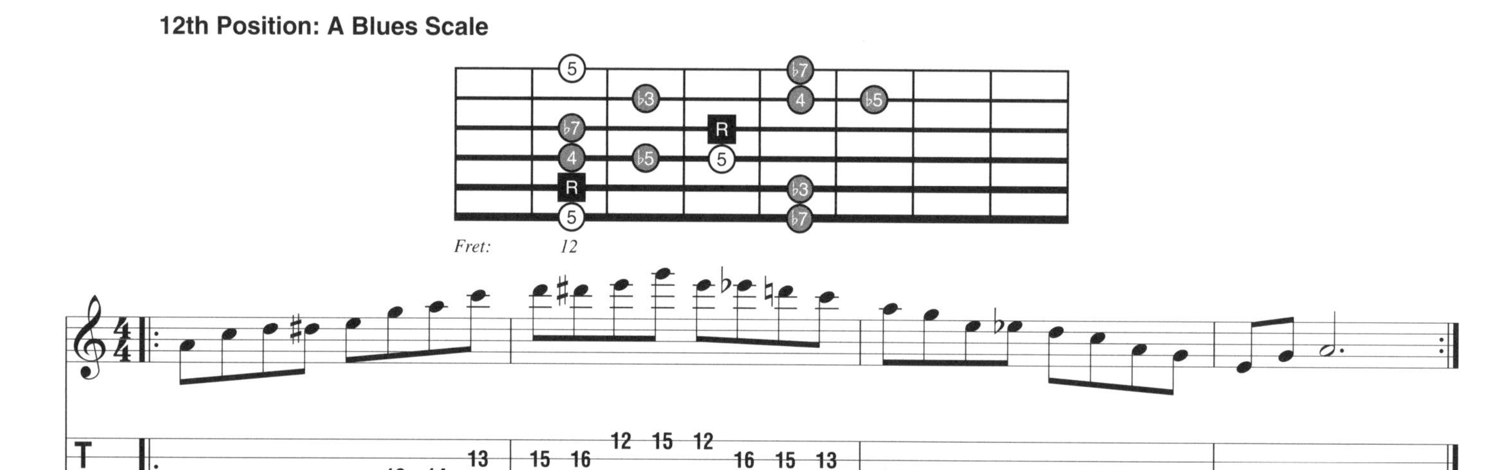

11th and 12th Positions:
A Major Pentatonic and A Blues Scales Combined

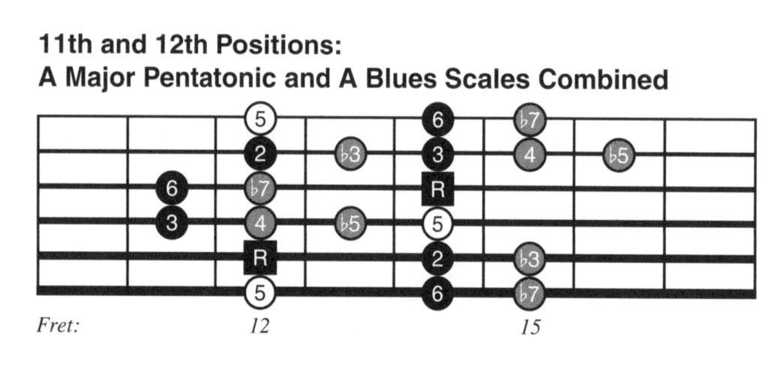

FIG. 12.14. A Major and Minor Pentatonic and Blues Scales: Positions 11 and 12

EXERCISE 7. PHRASES THAT MIX A PENTATONIC AND A BLUES, IN FIVE POSITIONS

Let's put some of the scales that you've been practicing to work. Listen to and practice the phrases below, then play along with the audio.

Figure 12.15 starts in the 4th position with a chromatic slide into notes (3 5 6 1 9 1) from the A major pentatonic scale. It slides/shifts up into 5th position, and ends with notes from A minor pentatonic. The three notes in the last bar (C A E) form an A minor triad arpeggio—and you may recognize B.B. King's fingerprints all over that.

65

4th and 5th Positions

FIG. 12.15. A Pentatonic and A Blues Phrases, Positions 4 and 5

Figure 12.16 starts in 5th position with A minor pentatonic, then moves to major pentatonic on beat 4 of bar 1, and then it slides up into the next higher A minor pentatonic box in the 7th position. B.B. King played slides like this in many of his solos, and so this phrase, like the previous one, was influenced by his approach to mixing the scales and sliding up and down the fingerboard.

66

5th and 7th Positions

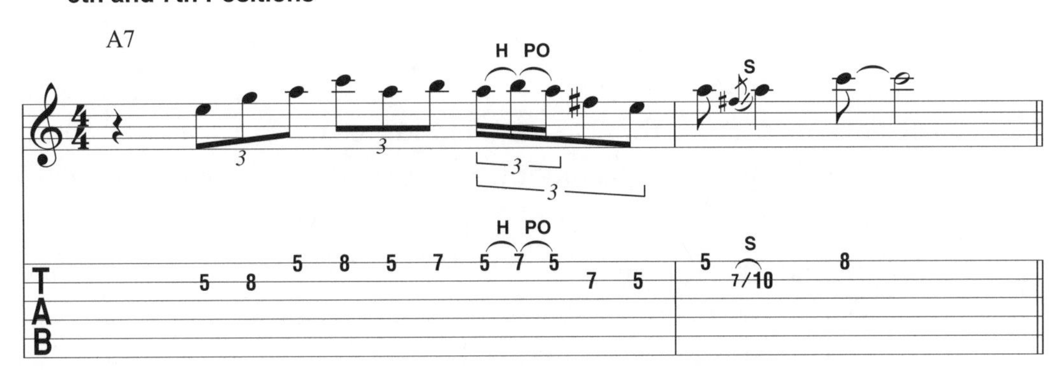

FIG. 12.16. A Pentatonic and A Blues Phrases, Positions 5 and 7

Figure 12.17 illustrates a mix of A major and minor pentatonic in the 2nd position, which is a great region on the fingerboard for killer string bends and soulful phrases. This lick was also influenced by B.B. King, since he sometimes plays string bends similar to the one in bar 1 on the "and" of beat 3 on the next page.

67

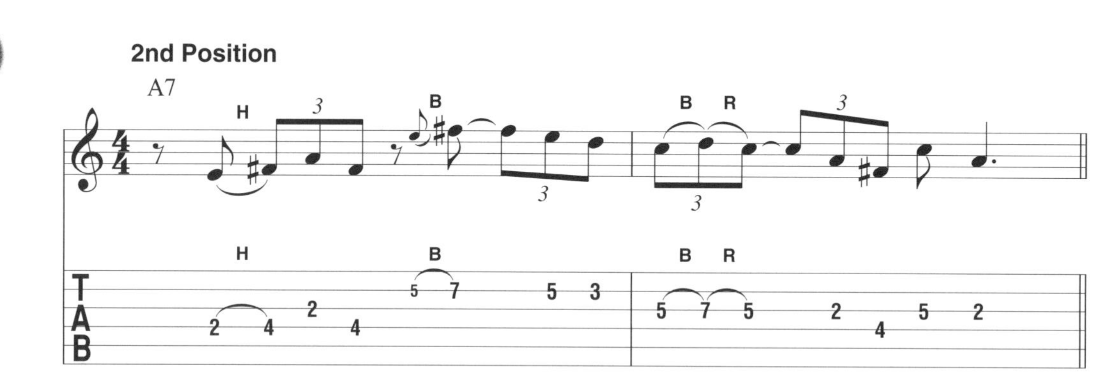

FIG. 12.17. A Pentatonic and A Blues Phrases, Position 2

Figure 12.18. is quite similar to the last phrase, only it's played twelve frets (one octave) higher (in position 14), and the bends are wider—minor-third instead of whole-step bends. Albert King got a great blues sound and feel in his solos by really "yanking on the strings," while playing wider bends, such as the minor third and major third bends below.

68

FIG. 12.18. A Pentatonic and A Blues Phrases, Position 14

Figure 12.19 is played in one of my favorite regions for soloing: the 11th and 12th positions, mixing A pentatonic with the A blues scale. This phrase starts with notes mostly from the blues scale in 12th position. Then it shifts down one fret to end on the 3 of the chord (the note C♯), which lies in the 11th position major pentatonic scale.

69

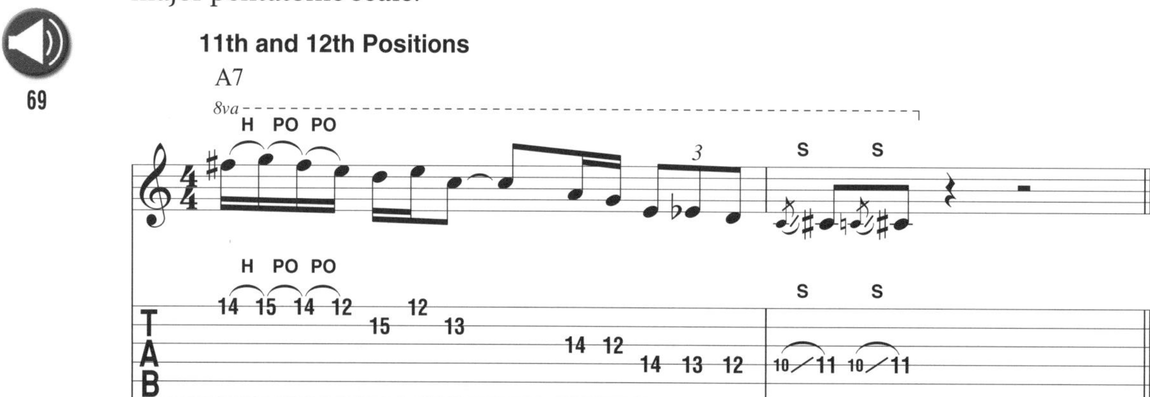

FIG. 12.19. A Pentatonic and A Blues Phrases: Positions 12 and 11

CLOSING

In closing, I'd like to offer a huge thanks to the "three Kings of the blues," Albert, B.B., and Freddy King, along with Albert Collins, Muddy Waters, Jimmy Rogers, Robert Lockwood, Jr., and too many other great electric and acoustic blues stylists to mention, for their inspiration, and for settin' the bar real high. And thanks to the current, and future generation of blues greats, also, for keepin' the fuel on the fire, and for moving the music forward!

Writing this book took me "back in school" once again, and researching rhythm parts and solos by T-Bone, B.B., and other greats has been rewarding and a real learning experience. My sincere hope is that you've also picked up a few new rhythm and soloing techniques, as you worked through these chapters!

—Mike Williams

APPENDIX

Blues Guitar Glossary and Articulation Key

Glossary

Blues Scale In its standard/textbook form: 1 ♭3 4 ♭5 5 ♭7 (a solo drawing notes from the D blues scale).

Chorus One time through a song's chord progression (a solo that lasts for two choruses).

Comp (or) Comping To accompany; to provide rhythmic and harmonic support (chords etc.) behind another instrument (guitar comps behind the vocal head and sax solo).

Fade Decrease in volume, until silent (repeat the riff and fade).

Fill Melodic phrase that embellishes a line, or is inserted where there would ordinarily be a rest (a guitar fill for two beats).

Groove The overall feel/style of a song, such as a slow blues, shuffle, or a calypso groove. Also describes a specific instrument's function/activity in the song. (The guitarist played a great groove on the reggae tune.)

Head The melody of the song (solo for two choruses, and then play the head).

Hook A defining and recognizable musical element, unique to a song, and often the song's title or the melody under the song's title (a melodic hook).

In Head Opening melody to the song (two choruses of in head before the solo).

Intro Song beginning, before the head begins; it could be an entire chorus or more in length (a guitar intro before the head).

Lick	Short melody or melodic phrase (a guitar lick).
Out Head	Closing melody to the song (after solos, play the out head).
Outro	Song ending. Could be a chorus, tag ending, or a new/different section (fade the outro).
Pentatonic Scales	5-note scales (solo drawing notes from the D minor-pentatonic scale). *Minor pentatonic* form: 1 ♭3 4 5 ♭7. *Major pentatonic* form: 1 2 3 5 6.
Relative Major	Major scale a minor third above the tonic minor scale. The scales share the same key signature (C major is the relative major of A minor).
Relative Minor	Natural minor scale a minor third below the tonic major scale. The scales share the same key signature (A minor is the relative minor of C major).
Riff	A melodic or chord figure that's repeated to form the melody, background, or section of a song ("C Jam Blues" and "Night Train" are classic riff-based heads). Also describes a repeated short melody (a riff-based solo).
Shout Chorus	A section of a song, or an interlude, that often features several instruments playing a (powerful) line or figure, that creates excitement (or a climax) in the arrangement (the horn section followed up with a big band–style shout chorus).
Solo	A melodic interpretation of a song's chord progression, generally improvised (the guitar's turn to solo).
Tag ending	Repeated chord pattern used to end a song, sometimes followed by a coda or a fade (for the outro, tag the main riff, then take the coda on cue).
Trading	Two or more instruments alternating (taking turns) while soloing over a song form, generally trading on the same number of measures (piano and guitar traded 8s and then 4s with drums).
Turnaround	Chord series, (or a melodic phrase) at the end of a progression, leading back to tonic chord (a II V turnaround).
Upper-Structure Triad	Triad containing a tension (G minor is an upper-structure triad of C7, including 5, ♭7, and 9).

Articulations

Accent (>) Play note louder.

Bend (B) Push/bend the string, raising the pitch. Often paired with R (release).

Hammer on (H) Quickly tap fretting-hand finger on fretboard/string to sound the note.

Marcato (^) Short and accented.

Pre-bend (PB) Pre-bend the note before picking/playing it.

Pull-off (PO) The opposite of a hammer on. Pull-off begins with the finger on the string; finger sounds the note as it slips off the string.

Release (R) Relax a bent string back to its original (unbent) pitch.

Slide (S) Glide finger on fretboard to new note while continuing to sound the string. *Legato slide*: pick the note, then slide, without picking again. *Pick slide*: pick the note, slide, and pick the note again at end of slide.

Staccato (.) Short and unaccented.

Tenuto (–) Full value, (long), and unaccented.

Trill (*tr*〰) Alternating notes, such as D and E. The first note is struck, then the rest are played as a series of hammer-ons and pull-offs in rapid succession.

ABOUT THE AUTHOR

Photo by Kenny Newell

Michael Williams has been active as a blues and jazz guitarist around New England since 1987. He has performed extensively throughout the United States and Canada as a member of Grammy-winner James Cotton's blues band, and with many other artists including David "Fathead" Newman, Mighty Sam McClain, the Bruce Katz Band, Sugar Ray Norcia, Darrell Nulisch, Toni Lynn Washington, Michelle Willson, Jerry Portnoy, Henry Butler, the Love Dogs, blues piano virtuoso David Maxwell, and as a leader with the Michael Williams Band.

Williams performed on James Cotton's CD, *35th Anniversary Jam*, which won a W.C. Handy Award, and received a Grammy nomination for the Best Traditional Blues Album in 2003. He performed on Bruce Katz's 2004 release entitled *A Deeper Blue*, and his playing, songwriting, and arranging are featured on Michelle Willson's CD *So Emotional*, which earned a four-star review in *Down Beat* magazine. Williams has a CD of his own entitled *Late Night Walk* (Blue Tempo Records), featuring ten original compositions with guest artists David "Fathead" Newman on tenor sax, Sugar Ray Norcia on vocals, and Bruce Katz on Hammond B3 organ and piano.

Williams is a professor at Berklee College of Music in Boston, where he has taught guitar since 1987. He specializes in teaching a mix of blues and jazz styles, and has traveled to Europe and South America on several occasions as a clinician and performer for the college. Williams authored and currently teaches an online course, *Blues Workshop*, for Berklee Online, the college's online extension school. He is the author of *Berklee Blues Guitar Songbook* (Berklee Press, 2010).

More Fine Publications from BERKLEE PRESS

GUITAR

BEBOP GUITAR SOLOS
by Michael Kaplan
00121703 Book $14.99

BERKLEE BLUES GUITAR SONGBOOK
by Mike Williams
50449593 Book/CD $24.99

BLUES GUITAR TECHNIQUE
by Mike Williams
50449623 Book/CD $24.99

BERKLEE GUITAR CHORD DICTIONARY
by Rick Peckham
50449546 Jazz $10.99
50449596 Rock $12.99

BERKLEE JAZZ STANDARDS FOR SOLO GUITAR
by John Stein
50449653 Book/CD $19.99

THE CHORD FACTORY
by Jon Damian
50449541 .... $24.95

CREATIVE CHORDAL HARMONY FOR GUITAR
by Mick Goodrick and Tim Miller
50449613 Book/CD $19.99

FUNK/R&B GUITAR
by Thaddeus Hogarth
50449569 Book/CD $19.95

GUITAR CHOP SHOP – BUILDING ROCK/METAL TECHNIQUE
by Joe Stump
50449601 Book/CD $19.99

JAZZ IMPROVISATION FOR GUITAR
by Garrison Fewell
A Harmonic Approach
50449594 Book/CD $24.99
A Melodic Approach
50449503 Book/CD Pack $24.99

A MODERN METHOD FOR GUITAR
by William Leavitt
Volume 1: Beginner
50449400 Book $14.95
50449404 Book/CD $22.95
50448065 Book/DVD-ROM $34.99
Volume 2: Intermediate
50449410 Book $14.95
Volume 3: Advanced
50449420 Book $16.95
1, 2, 3 Complete
50449468 Book $34.95
Jazz Songbook, Vol. 1
50449539 Book/CD $14.99
Rock Songbook
50449624 Book/CD $17.99

PLAYING THE CHANGES: GUITAR
by Mitch Seidman and Paul Del Nero
50449509 Book/CD $19.95

THE PRACTICAL JAZZ GUITARIST
by Mark White
50449618 Book/CD $19.99

THE PRIVATE GUITAR STUDIO HANDBOOK
by Michael McAdam
00121641 Book $14.99

BASS

BASS LINES
by Joe Santerre
50449542 Fingerstyle Funk: Book/CD $19.95
50449478 Rock: Book/CD $19.95

FUNK BASS FILLS
by Anthony Vitti
50449608 Book/CD $19.99

INSTANT BASS
by Danny Morris
50449502 Book/CD $14.95

READING CONTEMPORARY ELECTRIC BASS
by Rich Appleman
50449770 Book $19.95

DRUMS

BEGINNING DJEMBE
by Michael Markus & Joe Galeota
50449639 DVD $14.99

DOUBLE BASS DRUM INTEGRATION
by Henrique De Almeida
00120208 Book $19.99

DRUM SET WARM-UPS
by Rod Morgenstein
50449465 Book $12.99

DRUM STUDIES
by Dave Vose
50449617 Book $12.99

EIGHT ESSENTIALS OF DRUMMING
by Ron Savage
50448048 Book/CD $19.99

PHRASING: ADVANCED RUDIMENTS FOR CREATIVE DRUMMING
by Russ Gold
00120209 Book $19.99

WORLD JAZZ DRUMMING
by Mark Walker
50449568 Book/CD $22.99

KEYBOARD

BERKLEE JAZZ KEYBOARD HARMONY
by Suzanna Sifter
50449606 Book/CD $24.99

BERKLEE JAZZ PIANO
by Ray Santisi
50448047 Book/CD $19.99

CHORD-SCALE IMPROVISATION FOR KEYBOARD
by Ross Ramsay
50449597 Book/CD Pack $19.99

CONTEMPORARY PIANO TECHNIQUE
by Stephany Tiernan
50449545 Book/DVD $29.99

HAMMOND ORGAN COMPLETE
by Dave Limina
50449479 Book/CD $24.95

JAZZ PIANO COMPING
by Suzanne Davis
50449614 Book/CD $19.99

LATIN JAZZ PIANO IMPROVISATION
by Rebecca Cline
50449649 Book/CD $24.99

SOLO JAZZ PIANO – 2ND ED.
by Neil Olmstead
50449641 Book/CD $39.99

VOICE

THE CONTEMPORARY SINGER – 2ND ED.
by Anne Peckham
50449595 Book/CD $24.99

VOCAL TECHNIQUE
featuring Anne Peckham
50448038 DVD $19.95

VOCAL WORKOUTS FOR THE CONTEMPORARY SINGER
by Anne Peckham
50448044 Book/CD $24.95

TIPS FOR SINGERS
by Carolyn Wilkins
50449557 Book/CD $19.95

YOUR SINGING VOICE
by Jeannie Gagné
50449619 Book/CD $29.99

WOODWINDS

FAMOUS SAXOPHONE SOLOS
arr. Jeff Harrington
50449605 Book $14.99

IMPROVISATION
by Andy McGhee
50449810 Flute $14.99
50449860 Saxophone $14.99

THE SAXOPHONE HANDBOOK
by Douglas D. Skinner
50449658 Book $14.99

SAXOPHONE SOUND EFFECTS
by Ueli Dörig
50449628 Book/CD $14.99

Berklee Press Publications feature material developed at the Berklee College of Music.
To browse the complete Berklee Press Catalog, go to
www.berkleepress.com

ROOTS MUSIC

BEYOND BLUEGRASS

Beyond Bluegrass Banjo
by Dave Hollander and Matt Glaser
50449610 Book/CD $19.99

Beyond Bluegrass Mandolin
by John McGann and Matt Glaser
50449609 Book/CD $19.99

Bluegrass Fiddle and Beyond
by Matt Glaser
50449602 Book/CD $19.99

THE IRISH CELLO BOOK
by Liz Davis Maxfield
50449652 Book/CD $24.99

BERKLEE PRACTICE METHOD

GET YOUR BAND TOGETHER
With additional volumes for other instruments, plus a teacher's guide.

Bass
by Rich Appleman, John Repucci and the Berklee Faculty
50449427 Book/CD $14.95

Cello
by Matt Glaser and Mimi Rabson
00101384 Book/CD $14.99

Drum Set
by Ron Savage, Casey Scheuerell and the Berklee Faculty
50449429 Book/CD $14.95

Guitar
by Larry Baione and the Berklee Faculty
50449426 Book/CD $16.99

Keyboard
by Russell Hoffmann, Paul Schmeling and the Berklee Faculty
50449428 Book/CD $14.95

Viola
by Matt Glaser, Mimi Rabson and the Berklee Faculty
00101393 Book/CD $16.99

WELLNESS

MANAGE YOUR STRESS AND PAIN THROUGH MUSIC
by Dr. Suzanne B. Hanser and Dr. Susan E. Mandel
50449592 Book/CD $29.99

MUSICIAN'S YOGA
by Mia Olson
50449587 Book $14.99

THE NEW MUSIC THERAPIST'S HANDBOOK – SECOND ED.
by Dr. Suzanne B. Hanser
50449424 Book $29.95

EAR TRAINING, IMPROVISATION, MUSIC THEORY

BEGINNING EAR TRAINING
by Gilson Schachnik
50449548 Book/CD $14.99

THE BERKLEE BOOK OF JAZZ HARMONY
by Joe Mulholland & Tom Hojnacki
00113755 Book/CD $24.99

BERKLEE MUSIC THEORY – 2ND ED.
by Paul Schmeling
50449615 Rhythm, Scales Intervals: Book/CD $24.99
50449616 Harmony: Book/CD $22.99

BLUES IMPROVISATION COMPLETE
by Jeff Harrington
Book/CD Packs
50449486 B♭ Instruments $19.95
50449488 C Bass Instruments $19.95
50449425 C Treble Instruments $22.99
50449487 E♭ Instruments $19.95

A GUIDE TO JAZZ IMPROVISATION
by John LaPorta
Book/CD Packs
50449439 C Instruments $19.95
50449441 B♭ Instruments $19.99
50449442 E♭ Instruments $19.99
50449443 𝄢 Instruments $19.99

IMPROVISATION FOR CLASSICAL MUSICIANS
by Eugene Friesen with Wendy M. Friesen
50449637 Book/CD $24.99

REHARMONIZATION TECHNIQUES
by Randy Felts
50449496 Book $29.95

MUSIC BUSINESS

THE FUTURE OF MUSIC
by Dave Kusek and Gerd Leonhard
50448055 Book $16.95

MAKING MUSIC MAKE MONEY
by Eric Beall
50448009 Book $26.95

MUSIC INDUSTRY FORMS
by Jonathan Feist
00121814 Book $14.99

MUSIC MARKETING
by Mike King
50449588 Book $24.99

PROJECT MANAGEMENT FOR MUSICIANS
by Jonathan Feist
50449659 Book $27.99

THE SELF-PROMOTING MUSICIAN – 3RD EDITION
by Peter Spellman
00119607 Book $24.99

MUSIC PRODUCTION & ENGINEERING

AUDIO MASTERING
by Jonathan Wyner
50449581 Book/CD $29.99

AUDIO POST PRODUCTION
by Mark Cross
50449627 Book $19.99

MIX MASTERS
by Maureen Droney
50448023 Book $24.95

PRODUCING AND MIXING HIP-HOP/R&B
by Mike Hamilton
50449555 Book/DVD-ROM $19.99

PRODUCING DRUM BEATS
by Eric Hawkins
50449598 Book/CD-ROM Pack $22.99

RECORDING AND PRODUCING IN THE HOME STUDIO
by David Franz
50448045 Book $24.95

UNDERSTANDING AUDIO
by Daniel M. Thompson
50449456 Book $24.99

SONGWRITING, COMPOSING, ARRANGING

ARRANGING FOR LARGE JAZZ ENSEMBLE
by Dick Lowell and Ken Pullig
50449528 Book/CD $39.95

COMPLETE GUIDE TO FILM SCORING – 2ND ED.
by Richard Davis
50449607 .... $27.99

JAZZ COMPOSITION
by Ted Pease
50448000 Book/CD $39.99

MELODY IN SONGWRITING
by Jack Perricone
50449419 Book/CD $24.95

MODERN JAZZ VOICINGS
by Ted Pease and Ken Pullig
50449485 Book/CD $24.95

MUSIC COMPOSITION FOR FILM AND TELEVISION
by Lalo Schifrin
50449604 Book $34.99

MUSIC NOTATION
PREPARING SCORES AND PARTS
by Matthew Nicholl and Richard Grudzinski
50449540 Book $16.99

MUSIC NOTATION
THEORY AND TECHNIQUE FOR MUSIC NOTATION
by Mark McGrain
50449399 Book $24.95

POPULAR LYRIC WRITING
by Andrea Stolpe
50449553 Book $14.95

SONGWRITING: ESSENTIAL GUIDE
by Pat Pattison
50481582 Lyric and Form Structure: Book $16.99
00124366 Rhyming: Book – 2nd Ed. . $16.99

SONGWRITING STRATEGIES
by Mark Simos
50449621 Book/CD $22.99

THE SONGWRITER'S WORKSHOP
by Jimmy Kachulis
50449519 Harmony: Book/CD $29.95
50449518 Melody: Book/CD $24.95

AUTOBIOGRAPHY

LEARNING TO LISTEN: THE JAZZ JOURNEY OF GARY BURTON
by Gary Burton
00117798 Book $27.99

Prices subject to change without notice. Visit your local music dealer or bookstore, or go to **www.berkleepress.com**

0214

BEBOP GUITAR SOLOS
BERKLEE BLUES GUITAR
MICHAEL WILLIAMS
BLUES GUITAR TECHNIQUE
DICTIONARY
JAZZ STANDARDS FOR SOLO GUITAR
THE CHORD FACTORY
The Guitarist's Guide to Composing and Improvising
Jon Damian
Berklee
CHOP BUILDER FOR ROCK GUITAR

CREATIVE CHORDAL HARMONY FOR GUITAR
FUNK/R&B GUITAR
CREATIVE SOLOS GROOVES & SOUNDS
A MODERN METHOD FOR GUITAR
william leavitt
volume 1
playing the changes
GUITAR
A LINEAR APPROACH TO IMPROVISING
THE PRACTICAL JAZZ GUITARIST
THE PRIVATE GUITAR STUDIO HANDBOOK
MIKE MCADAM

berklee press

HAL•LEONARD®
CORPORATION
7777 W. BLUEMOUND RD. P.O. BOX 13819 MILWAUKEE, WI 53213